International Perspectives on Education Reform
Gita Steiner-Khamsi, Editor

Challenges to Japanese Education:
Economics, Reform, and Human Rights
*June A. Gordon, Hidenori Fujita,
Takehiko Kariya, and
Gerald LeTendre, Eds.*

South–South Cooperation in Education and Development
*Linda Chisholm and
Gita Steiner-Khamsi, Eds.*

Comparative and International Education:
Issues for Teachers
*Karen Mundy, Kathy Bickmore, Ruth Hayhoe,
Meggan Madden, and Katherine Madjidi, Eds.*

CHALLENGES TO Japanese Education

Economics, Reform, and Human Rights

EDITED BY
June A. Gordon, Hidenori Fujita,
Takehiko Kariya, and Gerald LeTendre

Teachers College
Columbia University
New York and London

Seori-shobo
Yokohama-shi, Japan
http://homepage3.nifty.com/seori/

Published simultaneously by Teachers College Press, 1234 Amsterdam Avenue, New York, NY 10027 and by Seori-shobo, 7-240-3F, Tobe-cho, Nishi-ku, Yokohama-shi, 〒220-0042, Japan

Copyright © 2010 by Teachers College, Columbia University

All rights reserved. No part of this publication may be reproduced or transmitted in any form or by any means, electronic or mechanical, including photocopy, or any information storage and retrieval system, without permission from the publisher.

Library of Congress Cataloging-in-Publication Data

Challenges to Japanese education : economics, reform, and human rights / June A. Gordon . . . [et al].
   p. cm. — (International perspectives on education reform)
Includes bibliographical references and index.
ISBN 978-0-8077-5053-7 (pbk. : alk. paper)
   1. Education—Japan. 2. Education—Aims and objectives—Japan.
3. Economics—Study and teaching (Secondary). 4. Human rights.
I. Gordon, June A., 1950–

LA1312.C43 2010
370.952—dc22
                                                                          2009031656

ISBN 978-0-8077-5053-7 (paper)

Printed on acid-free paper
Manufactured in the United States of America

17 16 15 14 13 12 11 10   8 7 6 5 4 3 2 1

Contents

Introduction   1
June A. Gordon and Gerald LeTendre

Views from the Japanese Side:
Challenges to Japanese Education   11
Takehiko Kariya

PART I
Policy, Finance, and National Reform

1 Whither Japanese Schooling?
Educational Reforms and Their Impact on
Ability Formation and Educational Opportunity   17
Hidenori Fujita

2 The End of Egalitarian Education in Japan?
The Effects of Policy Changes in Resource Distribution
on Compulsory Education   54
Takehiko Kariya

3 Educational Stratification:
Teacher Perspectives on School Culture and
the College Entrance Examination   67
Mamoru Tsukada

4 Educational Selection, Career Decisions, and School Support:
The Case of an Urban Commercial High School   87
Akira Sakai

PART II
Educational Inequalities and Marginalized Groups

5 Invisible Racism in Japan:
   Impact on Academic Achievement of Minority Children ... 109
   Yoshiro Nabeshima

6 Schooling of *Buraku* Women:
   Life Histories in Eastern Japan ... 131
   Haruhiko Kanegae

7 The Education of *Zainichi* Koreans and Their Identity ... 147
   Taeyoung Kim

8 The Education of Minorities in Japan:
   Voices of Amerasians in Okinawa ... 165
   Naomi Noiri

PART III
Reflections on Forces Affecting the Future of Japanese Education

9 Challenges to Japanese Education:
   Concluding Thoughts ... 181
   George A. DeVos

10 Societal and Cultural Context of Educational Issues ... 189
   Harumi Befu

11 A New Policy Context for Schooling in Japan ... 196
   June A. Gordon and Gerald LeTendre

About the Contributors ... 205

Index ... 208

JUNE A. GORDON AND GERALD LeTENDRE

Introduction

IN APRIL OF 2006, the Japanese Diet (parliament) submitted a plan to formally revise the Fundamental Law of Education, which had not been revised since the Allied Occupation in 1947. The proposals within the plan followed a wave of more specific educational reforms beginning in the early 1990s, in which the Japanese government had significantly altered teaching conditions in public schools. Ironically, these reforms were instituted after a decade in which Japanese educational practice had received worldwide praise but had been hotly contested within Japan. Indeed, some of the earlier reforms—such as the introduction of "relaxed education" (*yutori kyoiku*) and new math standards—had been blamed in the media for Japan's sinking rankings on international tests. The brief administrations of Prime Ministers Shinzo Abe (2006–2007) and Yasuo Fukuda (2007–2008) witnessed the reversal of several proposed reforms, including school vouchers, "league-tables" based on national testing, and school inspections. In 2008, new national curricula were yet again proposed and adopted. Due in part to the failure of the former national curricula, which had been created to realize education free of pressure, the new curricula revived some of the content that had been previously eliminated. Reform and counter-reform now seem to rule the day in Japanese educational politics.

Why, when Japan's test scores and educational reputation were remarkably high, did government officials engage in these multiple, and often contradictory, reforms? Despite the far-reaching nature of the curricular and financial reforms enacted in Japan, very little coverage has been given to these issues in the English literature. Much of the existing work suggests that Japan is experiencing many of the same educational concerns as other developed nations. And yet we are left with lingering questions about the particular nature of these reforms as played out in the Japanese context. Why, given the virtual adulation expressed by some Western observers of Japanese education, have the political pressures to reform Japanese education been so powerful, and why is the push occurring at this point in Japanese history?

It is imperative then, that we understand what issues face Japan, *as the Japanese see them*, if we are to understand how Japan will adapt and respond over the coming decades. Although Japan has had a significant impact on educational practice (at least in the English-speaking world), the effect has been largely mediated through Western scholarly organs and researchers (e.g., Stevenson & Stigler, 1992; Stigler & Hiebert, 1999). We have much more difficulty understanding how Japanese scholars perceive the impact of global forces on Japan, and how they respond to them. The emerging literature on national school systems indicates that nations at times may have very different responses to similar issues. The authors for this book offer an in-depth study of the of the issues facing Japan, how they are perceived or conceptualized, and what solutions or concerns arise from the Japanese perspective. We have created a mutually engaged perspective on how a nation can respond to the significant issues of global migration, economic competition, resource depletion, social stability, and minority group concerns.

GOALS OF THE BOOK

The idea for this book originated from an international symposium on the future of Japanese education held April 8, 2006, at the University of California, Berkeley, entitled, *Challenges to Japanese Education: Economics, Reform, and Human Rights*. The symposium was cosponsored by the Institute of East Asian Studies, the Center for Japanese Studies, the Institute for Area Studies, and the Graduate School of Education at UC Berkeley; the Center for East Asian Studies at Stanford University; and the College of Education at Pennsylvania State University. Fifty scholars were invited to attend and to participate in discussions following formal papers presented by eight Japanese scholars. Commentary on the papers was offered by three distinguished American scholars, each of whom has made major contributions to research on Japanese education and culture: Professors George DeVos, Harumi Befu, and Thomas Rohlen. After extensive revisions based on the symposium discussions and commentary from the invited audience of scholars, and in some cases the writing of completely new essays bringing us up to date on the latest policy issues, the papers were compiled and then received further editing over the last 2 years. The eight papers presented at the symposium fell into two main categories and hence for the purpose of guiding the reader's understanding of the complexity of issues now facing Japanese education we have divided these chapters into two parts. Part I is titled "Policy, Finance, and National Reform," and Part II is "Educational Inequalities and Marginalized Groups." In addition, we are honored to have the written commentary of Professors Takehiko Kariya, Harumi Befu, and George DeVos, who wrote pieces particularly for this book. An essay by Professor Kariya provides an introduction to the text.

The contributions by Professors DeVos and Befu, as well as a concluding chapter by Professors June A. Gordon and Gerald LeTendre, make up Part III, "Reflections on Forces Affecting the Future of Japanese Education." Biographical information for all contributors and an index complete the volume. June A. Gordon and Gerald LeTendre orchestrated preparation of the book.

The focus of the work is on K–16 schooling and the role that schools play in the broader social and cultural context of Japan's response to the continuing global movement of people, ideas, and organizational forms. The scholars were asked to address the specific question: *What role does education currently play in Japanese society and what does the future hold?* The book's analysis relies on multicultural and disciplinary perspectives of the major authors to better portray the complexity of Japan's situation with regard to immigration, education, and economics while setting an agenda for future educational research. At the same time, we have the goal of moving Japanese research concerns into the mainstream of Western-dominated educational and social science dialogues. Current hegemonic social and educational concepts—such as human rights, educational equity, gender parity, and minority rights—have been elaborated in a global culture that arises from core Euro-American cultural concerns (see Boli & Meyer, 1987; Ramirez & Boli, 1987). These concerns, and the research and interventions they have engendered, have resulted in a complex web of national, nongovernmental, and multilateral organizations that promote a plethora of educational reforms and ideas (see Chabbott, 2002; Resnick, 2006). Within the core of developed nations that provide the economic support and most of the people power for these organizations, Japan is the only non-Western nation of significant stature and influence.

We believe that we have a unique historical opportunity to understand the extent to which a globalized culture inhibits or constrains national educational policy and the reform of public schooling. Although the topic of educational "borrowing" has been addressed in global perspective (Popkewitz & Steiner-Khamsi, 2004), this book specifically focuses on Japanese perspectives of national and global trends. It also presents a contextualized analysis of current educational problems that include issues of human rights, migration, and economic integration (à la Douglass & Roberts, 2000), but asks what role education can play and how best to plan for change as seen by the Japanese educational research community.

Much has been made (and criticized) of the "uniqueness" of Japan and Japanese culture (especially the debates over *nihonjinron*, or discourses on the distinctiveness of the Japanese national character), yet Japan remains one of the few non-Western nations that face problems and share historical legacies (colonial expansion and exploitation) with Western developed countries. What Japan does, or will do, in education has ramifications for the rest of the world. Faced with this reality, we chose to try to foster a multinational dialogue with the explicit assumption that understanding how the Japanese perceive themselves—their problems and their role in the world—is critical information we need in order to understand how national educational agendas affect changes in the global culture of educational reform and intervention. To that end, this book is a collaboration between Japanese and non-Japanese scholars who have engaged in long-term research on educational and related issues. The authors assume that the educational system will play a key role in Japan's future. The major questions are to what end will the schools be asked to address or prevent social problems, and, ultimately, what will be the ramifications of Japan's actions for the world.

THE CREATION OF "GLOBAL" EDUCATIONAL KNOWLEDGE

We suggest that researchers need to pay attention to dual processes—national and transnational—that drive the creation of "scientific knowledge" in education. There is considerable risk of creating hegemonic systems of education that reinforce institutionalized patterns of knowledge and resource allocation (see Chabbott, 2007) while missing important, if often local, adaptations of core educational practices or rationales. Following Latour's (1987) assertion that all science is culturally situated, we need to understand how internal Japanese cultural changes regarding minority groups affect the scientific framing and study of the problem *and* how much this Japanese approach differs from global (largely Western and English) discourse. Because of their high degree of economic interpenetration and shared histories, nations such as the United States, Britain, and Australia—and, to a similar extent, Germany, Italy, France, and other current European Union members—followed similar national and international trajectories in the development of cultural attitudes and "scientific" thinking about minorities and education. This transnational culture was largely imposed on economically marginalized nations via transnational organizations such as the IMF (International Monetary Fund) and World Bank, but also through much more benign-appearing multilateral agencies such as UNESCO or UNICEF.

Not only is scientific knowledge culturally constructed, but scientific studies are also routinely used to advance specific political ends. For years, during Japan's economic surge, portrayals of Japanese schools were used to promote a sense of failure or crisis in U.S. schools (Berliner & Biddle, 1995; LeTendre, 1999). In the last decade, Japanese politicians have mirrored this strategy, co-opting the language of crisis and pointing to foreign education systems in an effort to legitimize sweeping education reforms (Takayama, 2007). Educational "borrowing" as a transnational phenomenon has become far more complex than a simple model of knowledge transfer can sustain. We need a model that takes into account the political viability of reforms as they cross borders and become established under the political volatility of educational regimes within nations. Yet, how do Japanese scholars and reformers see themselves? To what extent are the issues in Japan actually driven by forces that affect nations around the globe, and to what extent is Japan (academically) still an "island nation"? To a certain degree, Japan must now deal with issues (such as inequality) that it had previously hoped to hide. Discussions of social inequality have moved from the margins to a central place in social discourse (Okano & Tsuchiya, 1999), perhaps due in large part to growing awareness of the importance attached to this issue in the international community.

But are there real differences between Japan and other countries that should not be glossed over? Japan has not experienced the same kind of internal social demographic change and turmoil that other nations have experienced. The issues of minority status, integration, and the role of education were simply ignored or (in a more sinister view) deliberately targeted to be "forgotten." Japan never experienced the tumultuous postwar educational reforms that the United States did. There was no battle for integration, no banning of segregated schools, no multidecade process of court-imposed school desegregation. And, most importantly, there was no development of a detailed "scientific" study of the effects of marginalization, oppression, identity, and so forth, in schools like that which occurred in the United States.

Japanese researchers, then, face significant challenges in organizing a body of knowledge derived from the experience of Japanese groups that can stand in counterpoint to the continuously growing literature available in English. In the absence of such knowledge, will Japan be dragged along, unwillingly, on a path of continual educational reform? Some Japanese scholars have already foreshadowed such a scenario. For example, Hatakenaka (2005) argues that Japan's system lacked the administrative expertise (missing hybrids) needed to reorganize the tertiary system. Or, will key constituents with international cultural knowledge (such as the *kikushijyo,* or youth returnees from overseas, described by Goodman, 2003) provide the needed catalysts for change? How will immigration, once thought to be almost nonexistent, impact changes in schooling and society as the numbers of immigrants continue to grow? What role will schools play as the social stratification allotment function of education is increasingly challenged and the old assimilative function is no longer viable?

CHAPTERS AND ISSUES OF THE BOOK

The book begins with this introduction and an additional introductory comment from Professor Kariya. Part I deals with issues of policy, finance, and national reform. From 1986 to 1990, Japan experienced a "bubble economy" characterized by dramatic increases in real estate and stock prices. The collapse of the bubble spurred a wave of discussions about government funding and educational reform. The 1990s saw multiple, far-reaching attempts by the Ministry of Education to promote reform, and in 2001 the Ministry itself was reorganized to incorporate the Science and Technology Agency. As Hidenori Fujita elucidates in Chapter 1, "Whither Japanese Schooling? Educational Reforms and Their Impact on Ability Formation and Educational Opportunity," the imposition of reforms can be traced back to the start of the bubble economy with the creation of a special council in 1984 (under Prime Minister Yasuhiro Nakasone) to "review" the educational system. This was, Fujita argues, the actual beginning of a "third wave" of educational reforms—a politically motivated effort to reorganize Japanese education that had many parallels in ideology with the Reagan and Thatcher administrations and their respective educational reform agendas in the United States and Great Britain. Fujita identifies the competing ideological camps and the ensuing debates and argues that prior reforms, aimed at creating more "freedom" or "openness," in the curriculum have lost power. He identifies an underlying conflict between views of education as directed toward self-realization versus subject mastery and notes the many potential long-term consequences that educational reform may hold for Japanese society.

In a similar vein, Takehiko Kariya in Chapter 2, "The End of Egalitarian Education in Japan? The Effects of Policy Changes in Resource Distribution on Compulsory Education," critically analyzes the ways in which drives to reform (especially reforms based on decentralization) have undermined the quality of Japanese education and have increased income inequality. These changes, Kariya notes, have eroded the widespread beliefs of Japan as a middle-class society and have challenged the meritocratic nature of the educational system. He warns of the long-term negative consequences for Japanese education and society, including increased social stratification, if the current reform efforts remain unchanged.

In Chapter 3, "Educational Stratification: Teacher Perspectives on School Culture and the College Entrance Examination," Mamoru Tsukada analyzes the complex hierarchies that exist in Japanese secondary education. Tsukada highlights the elaborate high school cultures that have developed, identifying a new potential barrier to reform. Tsukada also identifies the key roles that teachers play, as well as the changing conflict in teachers' roles. His key finding—that teachers adjust themselves to the culture of the school in which they teach—is provocative. It suggests that teachers' ability to act as agents of social change or educational reform will be significantly limited, and that teachers may end up reproducing existing social relations and social inequalities in spite of their best intentions.

Akira Sakai in Chapter 4 follows a similar line of inquiry by providing us with a case study in "Educational Selection, Career Decisions, and School Support: The Case of an Urban Commercial High School." In the schools discussed, the focus is on student decision making, but it becomes readily apparent that teachers play a key role in shaping these decisions. Sakai depicts the dilemmas and choices several students face, and reveals how little accurate information many students possess in a system that some have argued is highly transparent. The student narratives reveal that while opportunities exist for young people to recover in society after high school, few of them actively attempt it. The chapter highlights the hierarchical nature of Japanese high schools and ways in which parents' expectations, an emerging sense of identity, and frank considerations of economic limitations all shape student decisions about continuing on in higher education. Sakai echoes Tsukada's finding that despite the flurry of policy reform, little appears to be changing in Japan's highly tracked high school system.

Part II of the book presents a startling picture of educational inequalities and marginalized groups in a society that has largely failed to move beyond questions of invisibility and legitimacy. To many non-Japanese readers, the issues raised in these four chapters may seem reminiscent of racial crises in the United States in the 1950s. However, the authors show that it is not appropriate to draw direct parallels between African Americans in the United States and the descendants of the *Burakumin* or *Zainichi* in Japan. Rather, the chapters by Nabeshima, Kanegae, Kim, and Noiri demonstrate the high degree to which educational and social change processes in Japan have been insulated from global trends and changes.

Yoshiro Nabeshima's Chapter 5, "Invisible Racism in Japan: Its Impact on Academic Achievement of Minority Children," focuses on the *Burakumin*—a people who historically presented diversity as a counterpoint to the myth of homogeneous Japan. The publication of *Japan's Invisible Race* in 1966 by DeVos and Wagatsuma was a monumental step in exploring the hidden aspects of Japanese culture and informing the world of the existence of the *Burakumin*. Unfortunately, the findings were not welcomed by the majority of Japanese. As Nabeshima has commented, the *Burakumin* were "an itch in the back" for Japanese nationalists who wished to portray their people as an undividable race. In his chapter, Nabeshima depicts the various struggles waged, largely at the local level, for improved education and culturally responsive schooling practices for the *Burakumin*. He details ways in which the legal and physical gains made in previous decades are in danger of being wiped out as national measures to ensure equal treatment have lapsed or been eliminated.

Haruhiko Kanegae, in Chapter 6, "Schooling of *Burakumin* Women: Life Histories in Eastern Japan," offers a longer term perspective on change. This chapter raises important questions, focusing on Japanese women of *Burakumin* descent. Kanegae asks to what extent discrimination against the *Burakumin* has been the same or different within the nation at different historical points in time. Along with invisibility, the homogenization of the "other" is a recurrent feature of discrimination against minority groups in many nations. Kanegae's study shows that the school experiences of *Burakumin* women in eastern Japan were significantly different from the experiences of those in western Japan, and he discusses the reasons for this divide. Education played a major role in terms of historical knowledge acquired, children's socialization, and degree of support for the radical antidiscrimination movements of the time. This chapter provides a bulwark against tendencies to depict Japan as a homogeneous society, showing the very real differences experienced by members of just one of Japan's several minority groups.

The reality of diversity is further elucidated in Taeyoung Kim's Chapter 7, "The Education of *Zainichi* Koreans and Their Identity." This paper follows a similar theoretical issue—problems of cultural oppression in a context of presumed and enforced invisibility and homogenization—but it deals with another "old" cultural minority in Japan, the Koreans. Kim discusses the colonial heritage that has impacted Koreans in Japan, creating variation in educational experiences and identities among those who have lived for an extended period of time in Japan—the *Zainichi*—and more recent arrivals. He also implicates the American Occupation administration for its role in refusing to recognize the legality of Korean schools in Japan, and discusses how both North and South Korean–oriented schools have struggled to survive. Kim poignantly relates the complex identity issues faced by young *Zainichi* as they navigate a world where individuals increasingly cross national borders with ease.

In Chapter 8, Naomi Noiri discusses a relatively new minority in "Education of Minorities in Japan: Voices of Amerasians in Okinawa." Noiri begins with a discussion of the "newcomers" to Japan—children of war-displaced orphans from China, as well as second- and third-generation Brazilians of Japanese descent—then focuses her attention on the education and identity of Amerasian children in Okinawa. From her years as a researcher in residence, she critically assesses the formal policies of treating all children equally in an era when the public school system is becoming more diverse. She chronicles the tremendous economic and identity issues faced by Amerasian children in Okinawa, and focuses on the ongoing marginalization of these children in mainstream schools.

The book concludes with Part III, "Reflections on Forces Affecting the Future of Japanese Education," in which George DeVos and Harumi Befu offer insights on the issues based upon their longstanding expertise and June A. Gordon and Gerald LeTendre offer a concluding discussion and look to the future.

THE LONG VIEW

The internationalization of Japan has brought with it only limited recognition of the problems posed by persistent social inequality and the role of educational systems in sustaining ethnic divisions. The chapters in this book provide a solid grounding in the issues that Japan will need to address if it is to make further progress in reducing long-term social divisions and inequality. The outlook for educational reform, however, is decidedly mixed, as years of political struggle for better education for groups such as the *Burakumin* and Korean Japanese have become overshadowed by economic concerns and political attempts to reform a system with a deeply ingrained culture of hierarchy and competition. One of the major questions facing Japan and addressed from a variety of perspectives in this book is the following: Will the educational gains made over the last 50 years reach a plateau as programs and policies are either eliminated or diluted to respond to the social needs of a wider, more diffuse range of individuals now included in Japan's unique way of defining human rights? This is a pivotal time to raise such a question. Not only is Japan's role in global politics undergoing a significant transformation—where domestic issues such as education are more likely to be influenced by international trends—but throughout the world there is considerable unrest and dissatisfaction with education and public schooling, as well as anxiety over global economic competition. Schooling is increasingly seen as much more than a "national project." As national systems of education expand enrollments at both ends of the spectrum—enrolling more and more of the population in prekindergarten programs at one end and in tertiary education at the other—national policymakers increasingly worry about how their system is performing in a global context. Through the action of multilateral agencies such as UNESCO (the United Nations Educational, Scientific and Cultural Organization) and numerous nongovernmental organizations (NGOs), national educational systems are now open to global scrutiny in the same way that nations monitor each other's compliance with global norms around free trade, human rights abuses, and environmental impacts.

Increasingly, national administrations in the G-8 (Group of Eight—Canada, France, Germany, Italy, Japan, Russia, the United Kingdom, and the United States) have linked their national economic performance to indicators of school effectiveness and have used comparative data to identify weak areas. OECD (Office of Economic Cooperation and Development) nations—which sponsor large, transnational testing programs such as TIMSS (Third International Math–Science Study)—have themselves become the objects of critique. For example, the report *How the World's Best-Performing School Systems Come Out on Top* (Barber & Mourshed, 2007) uses OECD international educational data to push a transnational agenda for teacher recruitment. All nations face considerable normative pressure to bring their educational systems into line with global norms. Thus, what Japan does in its schools has significant ramifications beyond the boundaries of Japan and is, in some sense, no longer completely under the control of the Japanese.

REFERENCES

Barber, M., & Mourshed, M. (2007). *How the world's best-performing school systems come out on top.* New York: McKinsey Foundation.

Berliner, D., & Biddle, B. (1995). *The manufactured crisis.* New York: Addison-Wesley.

Boli, J., & Meyer, J. (1987). The ideology of childhood and the state: Rules distinguishing children in national constitutions, 1870–1970. In G. M. Thomas, J. W. Meyer, F. O. Ramirez, & J. Boli (Eds.), *Institutional structure: Constituting state, society and the individual* (pp. 217–241). Beverly Hills, CA: Sage.

Chabbott, C. (2002). *Constructing education for development: International organizations and education for all.* London: RoutledgeFalmer.

Chabbott, C. (2007). Carrot soup, magic bullets, and scientific research for education and development. *Comparative Education Review 51*(1), 71–94.

DeVos, G., & Wagatsuma, H. (Eds.). (1966). *Japan's invisible race: Caste in culture and personality.* Berkeley: University of California Press.

Douglass, M., & Roberts, G. (Eds.). (2000). *Japan and global migration: Foreign workers and the advent of a multi-cultural society.* New York: Routledge.

Goodman, R. (2003). The changing perception and status of Japan's returnee children (*kikokushijo*). In R. Goodman, C. Peach, A. Takenaka, & P. White (Eds.), *Global Japan: The experience of Japan's new immigrant and overseas communities* (pp. 177–194). London & New York: RoutledgeCurzon.

Hatakenaka, S. (2005). The incorporation of national universities: The role of missing hybrids. In J. S. Eades, R. Goodman, and Y. Hada (Eds.), *The 'big bang' in Japanese higher education: The 2004 reforms and the dynamics of change* (pp. 52–75). Victoria, Australia: Trans Pacific Press.

Latour, B. (1987). *Science in action.* Cambridge, MA: Harvard University Press.

LeTendre, G. (Ed.). (1999). *Competitor or ally: Japan's role in American educational debates.* New York: Falmer.

Okano, K., & Tsuchiya, M. (1999). *Education in contemporary Japan: Inequality and diversity.* New York: Cambridge University Press.

Popkewitz, T., & Steiner-Khamsi, G. (Eds.). (2004). *The global politics of educational borrowing and lending.* New York: Teachers College Press.

Ramirez, F. O., & Boli, J. (1987). The political construction of mass schooling: European origins and worldwide institutionalization. *Sociology of Education 60*(1), 2–17.

Resnick, J. (2006). International organizations, the "education-economic growth" black box, and the development of world education culture. *Comparative Education Review 50*(2), 173–195.

Stevenson, H. W., & Stigler, J. W. (1992). *The learning gap.* New York: Summit Books.

Stigler, J., & Hiebert, J. (1999). *The teaching gap: Best ideas from the world's teachers for improving education in the classroom.* New York: Free Press.

Takayama, K. (2007). *A Nation at Risk* crosses the Pacific: Transnational borrowing of the U.S. crisis discourse in the debate on education reform in Japan. *Comparative Education Review 51*(4), 423–446.

TAKEHIKO KARIYA

Views from the Japanese Side
Challenges to Japanese Education

THERE ARE SEVERAL FORCES behind the transformation of Japanese education reform, some of which are similar to, and others that are different from, forces in other countries. Here I will add a few points to the discussion presented in the Introduction, employing a comparative perspective.

SIMILARITIES

Along with the changes in "welfare states" in advanced countries, education and vocational training have been targeted as a major social policy area. In many countries, enhancing "employability" is used as a means to reconcile between the choices of cutting the budget for social welfare (without increasing socioeconomic inequality) and strengthening national economies (for entering "mega competitions" under the knowledge-based economy). Under these circumstances, neoliberal reforms offer policies such as school choice, deregulation, decentralization, and devolution to local boards of education and schools, as well as national testing and school evaluation. Regarding curricula and pedagogy, "21st-century skills" or "new competencies" and "high skills" are targeted as the goal of achievement. Problem-solving skills, communication skills, and skills for applying knowledge to daily life and jobs are all required.

Japanese society, like other advanced societies, is taking a step toward being more sensitive to human rights, alongside global trends in multiculturalism and postcolonialism. Gender and ethnic discrimination also have become more often officially criticized, and this is true in education as well. In these aspects, Japan is in the same circle as many other nations, with ideas for educational reform being borrowed from abroad, particularly from the United States and the United Kingdom.

DIFFERENCES: ADMIRATION FOR WESTERN "INDIVIDUALISM"

However, there are differences as well. For a long time, especially after World War II, Japanese intellectuals and media thought of Japanese society and Japanese people as not yet being as "individualized" as Western societies. "Collectivism" is a key word used to describe both the strength and weakness of Japanese society. But the term collectivism, which contrasts with individualism, implies that the Japanese do not have enough individuality. Creating *"jiritsu-shita-kojin* (independent individuals)" has long been a goal of education, especially among liberals.

From this view, the Japanese educational system has been regarded as an overly centralized system with strict standardization. The state's control over education is often criticized as depriving local schools and teachers of freedom. Standardization (such as standardized national curricula, class size, school buildings, and other facilities) on the one hand contributes to equalizing quality and quantity of education, but on the other hand is regarded as failing to educate individuals with individuality and creativity. It is believed that people who are educated through such a standardized system tend to lack a sense and ability for self-assertion, self-expression, self-responsibility, and critical thinking. For liberal and progressive thinkers and social critics, Japanese education should be reformed toward a more individualistic system.

Individualization (*koseika-kojinka*) is a key word. It conveys three senses: one referring to Western individualism in the Enlightenment sense; the second representing "self" in a sociopsychological sense, which should be praised and fulfilled; and the third signifying an individual decision maker in an economic sense, someone who should make clever choices in the market or quasi-market. Such triple-layered admiration for individualization is the backdrop of education reform in Japan and characterizes the features of the reforms and their discourses. The target for reform is the centralized, exam-driven, uniform education, which is supposed to deprive individuals of choice and individuality. Both liberal and neoliberal reformers work together to destroy or deconstruct the old regime. Classical liberals (who seek independent individuals in the Enlightenment sense), neoliberals (who seek rational choice makers in the educational marketplace), and progressive educationalists (who seek admiration for self and child-centered education) all criticize the centralized and exam-driven education system in Japan. Shared among them are solutions such as decentralization of education administration and budget, introduction of new curricula for 21st-century skills, alleviation of entrance exam pressure, and weakening of the standardization of education. Although they have different political interests, they share these ideas for education reform. This alliance of different reform groups strengthens the pressure toward education reform.

It is a bit curious why the Japanese borrow the ideals of education reform from Western societies such as the United Kingdom and the United States, even though these education systems do not seem to produce good results. One answer to this question is that the Japanese still admire Western individualism and the role that education plays in developing individuality. However, one pitfall unintentionally produced by this alliance of reformers has been inequality in education. The reform agenda of weakening standardization and centralization of education was so broadly advocated that few noticed that the change might increase inequality in education. In addition, unlike the situation in other countries, the education budget has not been increased for Japanese education reform. With limited resources, an education system reformed for individualization faces difficulty in responding to each individual student, especially when class sizes in Japanese schools are significantly larger than in other OECD (Office of Economic Cooperation and Development) countries. In such classroom situations, disadvantaged students tend to suffer by being deprived of good learning due to changes in pedagogy for individualized learning.

RECENT CHANGES

After the administration of Prime Minister Shinzo Abe stepped down, the power of the Educational Reform Committee (*kyouiku saisei kaigi*) also decreased. Although the council proposed school vouchers, "league-tables" based on national testing, and school inspections, most of which were ideas borrowed from the United Kingdom, all of those reforms stopped under the administration of Prime Minister Yasuo Fukuda. In 2008, new national curricula were decided upon and publicized. Reflecting the failure of the former national curricula, which had been created to realize *yutori kyoiku* (education free of pressure), the new curricula revived some of the content that had been eliminated and reduced the number of classes used for *sogo tekina gakushuu no jikan* (comprehensive learning time).

Under the new 5-day (rather than 6-day) school system, the contents of curricula have remained the same. Some critics worry that there is now too much content packed into a limited number of school days. The MEXT (Ministry of Education) understood this concern and attempted to increase the number of teachers to reduce the teachers' load. However, the Ministry of Finance stopped the plan and restricted the increase to only a limited number of part-time teachers. It is not certain how the new curricula will work in the schools. Two national tests were also implemented, and results of the testing have already been released. One interesting finding is that the average test score in each prefecture correlates with the percentage of schools with more disadvantaged students in the prefecture.

PART I

Policy, Finance, and National Reform

HIDENORI FUJITA

Whither Japanese Schooling?

Educational Reforms and Their Impact on Ability Formation and Educational Opportunity

EDUCATIONAL REFORM for excellence—the restructuring of education—has been a global concern since the 1980s. Japan is no exception to this trend. In 1984, the Japanese government established its ad hoc National Council on Educational Reform, which spent 3 years reviewing the nation's education system, generating four reports to the Prime Minister that have been the basis for more than two decades of fundamental change. Why does Japan need to urge radical reforms? The idea may sound strange to foreign observers, because various international comparative surveys and studies have suggested that Japanese schools have been relatively successful compared with schools in Western developed countries such as the United States and United Kingdom (as indicated by results of IEA/TIMSS and OECD/PISA standardized testing; Finkelstein, 1991; Foljanty-Jost, 2003; Shields, 1989; Shimahara & Sakai, 1995).

To answer the basic question of why radical educational reform is needed in Japan, this chapter examines the current reforms and their impact on schooling and teaching, to determine where Japanese education is going, focusing on educational opportunity, ability formation, and the public nature of school education (i.e., the nature of school education as public goods and social capital). As part of the reform effort, the system of Japanese schooling has been reexamined in all these aspects and reorganized toward an unequally differentiated system that emphasizes the diversification of public schools, freedom of choice, ability grouping, curriculum differentiation even at the compulsory education level, and quality assurance by market competition and external school evaluation. In addition, tighter control over public schools and their teachers has been achieved by such measures as outcome-based school evaluation, performance-based teacher evaluation, a partially merit-based pay scheme for teachers, hierarchical reorganization of teachers, and a teaching certificate renewal system. In examining the nature, background, and impact of these reforms and to reconsider how our schooling can be improved appropriately for the 21st century, the discussion follows this outline:

1. The age of educational reform
   a. The third wave of educational reform and restructuring of schooling
   b. Features of Japanese schooling, its success, and current reforms
2. Developing the academic ability necessary for the 21st century
   a. Implications of PISA and TIMSS results
   b. Effective teaching: Which approach is more appropriate?
   c. Educational reforms: Consequences for student performance
3. Whither Japanese education and society?
   a. Differentiated society: A widening gap between rich and poor
   b. Rich flight to private and privileged public schools
   c. Skewed policymaking and the moral shift toward privatization
   d. Social exclusion through educational exclusion
4. A vision for 21st-century education and society
   a. *Kyosei* as an organizing principle for education, society, and human life
   b. Four forms of symbiosis, social capital, and *kyosei*
   c. How to design education, life space, and society
5. Education as an unfinished project

THE AGE OF EDUCATIONAL REFORM

The Third Wave of Educational Reform and Restructuring of Schooling

The first wave of educational reform emerged at the time of modern nation building, when each nation state established its modern educational framework and gradually developed a system of compulsory education in line with the idea of "the one best system" (Tyack, 1974). In Japan, this took place during the Meiji Restoration period, which began about 130 years ago (the Government Order of Education was promulgated in 1872). The second wave emerged in the mid-20th century, as the system was reorganized according to such guiding ideas as equal opportunity, comprehensive secondary education, and universal access to higher education. In Japan, this second reform took place after the end of World War II (Fujita, 1993, 1997, 2000b, 2000c).

The third wave emerged in the 1980s and still continues, with the restructuring or reorganization of all aspects of school education: opportunity structure, curriculum, teaching practices, educational governance, educational administration, and school management. This third wave is operating under such guiding ideas or ideologies as excellence, efficiency, and accountability; neoconservatism, neoliberalism, and market fundamentalism; postmodernism and post-Fordism; consumerism, privatization, and marketization (choice and competition); deregulation, devolution, and new public management (NPM);

testism, inspectionism, and performance-based evaluation or outcome-based education (OBE).

In the United States, the third wave of educational reform began under the Ronald Reagan administration with the publication of *A Nation at Risk* (National Commission on Excellence in Education, 1983) and has continued with the enactment of Goals 2000: Educate America Act and No Child Left Behind in 2002. In Britain, it started under the Margaret Thatcher administration with the 1988 Education Act and the introduction of a new pattern of school inspection by the Office for Standards in Education (OFSTED) in 1992 (Ball, 1993, 1994; Brown & Lauder, 1992; Chubb & Moe, 1990; Clune & Witte, 1990; Cookson, 1994; Department for Education, UK, 1992; Flude & Hammer, 1990; Fuller & Elmore, 1996; Tyack, 1990; Whitty, Power, & Halpin, 1988).

In Japan, similar radical reform has been under way since the 1980s, though its original orientation was opposite to those of American and British reform trends (Fujita, 1993, 1997, 2000a, 2000b, 2000c, 2005b, 2006a). The Japanese Ministry of Education, Culture, Sports, Science and Technology (hereafter MEXT or Ministry of Education) launched the so-called *Yutori-Kyoiku* reform in 1980, by revising the National Curriculum to cut down lesson hours and content in order to give schools, teachers, and students more freedom and autonomy and thereby make schooling and learning less rigid or stressful and more enjoyable (that is, more *Yutori*). The administration of Prime Minister Yasuhiro Nakasone then established the ad hoc National Council on Educational Reform (*Rinji-Kyoiku-Shingikai*, hereafter NCER) in 1984, the reports of which initiated the succeeding neoliberal and market-oriented reforms. These reforms changed the organizing principle of the school system from equal opportunity to individual choice, gradually restructuring the system to expand differentiation of the learning process and educational opportunity according to students' ability and their family backgrounds both within school (ability grouping) and among schools (school ranking and selectivity based on school choice). This differentiation has been accelerated by expanding school choice plans and establishing selective 6-year secondary schools, along with the introduction of many other programs, such as school evaluation (since 2002), national assessment tests of students' academic performance for sixth- and ninth-graders (since 2007), performance-based teacher evaluation (first introduced at Tokyo Metropolis in 2000 and gradually spreading to some other localities), and a renewal system for teacher certification (every 10 years; established in 2007). The impact of these changes—how schooling, teaching, and learning would be damaged—will be discussed in the sections that follow. But some policy changes are now expected. In the September 2009 general election (House of Representatives), the Democratic Party swept the board, and the new administration of Prime Minister Yukio Hatoyama has proposed revising the national test into a sample test and abolishing the teacher certification renewal system. It is not clear, however, whether the parental school choice scheme and other neoliberal and market-oriented policies will be changed or not.

Features of Japanese Schooling, Its Success, and Current Reforms

Japan's educational system is now at a crossroads. Proponents of radical reform are inclined to throw out the good elements of the established system, the framework of which is the result of reforms implemented soon after World War II. The post-war reform brought a program of compulsory education through 6 years of elementary school and 3 years of junior high school. Anyone who graduated from junior high school would be eligible for senior high school; passing an entrance examination was necessary to gain admission to a student's school of choice, but everyone could get into a senior high school if they were willing to attend one that might not be their first choice. Senior high school graduates could, in turn, go on to college or university by passing entrance examinations (in contrast to the situation today, where about half of the higher education institutions have open admission). Thus, a total of 16 years of formal schooling—6 years (elementary), 3 years (junior high), 3 years (high school), and 4 years (college), with the first 9 years compulsory—became the norm. This is an egalitarian, meritocratic, single-track system that emphasizes academic achievement for entering the senior high school and university of a student's choice. However, more than 98% of elementary students and about 93% of junior high school students attend public schools near their homes, based on the decisions of local boards of education.

The Ministry of Education prescribes the national curriculum (course of study) and screens the content and the level of textbooks (authorized textbooks) for elementary and secondary education. Prefectural boards of education (similar to the U.S. state boards of education) and ordinance-designated city boards of education (those of large cities with populations of more than 500,000) hire public school teachers and reassign them to schools within the same prefecture or city about every 7 or 8 years, according to the teacher allocation scheme for each locality. All of these factors have contributed to ensuring a standard quality of teaching and learning across the nation and within each locality (Fujita, 2007a, 2009).

Some other features of Japanese schooling and teaching include the following:

1. A range of school rituals, events, and extracurricular activities that provide students rich chances to participate in collaborative activities and develop their concerns and merits, as well as feeling a sense of belonging to the school

2. A holistic approach to teaching, learning, and caring that contributes to developing a learning and caring community
3. Traditional homeroom-based lessons and participatory learning that promote mutual learning among students of various ability levels (OECD Examiners, 1971; Stevenson & Stigler, 1992)
4. A collaborative culture of teaching and distributed leadership in the school that contribute to development of a professional learning community (Fujita, 1999c, 2000a, 2000b, 2000c, 2003a, 2005a, 2005b, 2006a, 2009; Sato, 1995, 1997, 1999)
5. Extensive teacher training programs provided by both MEXT and each local board of education, a "School-Based Research and Development Program" designated and funded by MEXT or by each local board of education, and voluntary study associations of teachers, including lesson study groups, all of which contribute to developing teachers' professional competence and their sense of mission and dedication, and thereby enhance the quality of teaching and learning (Akita & Lewis, 2008; Fujita, 1991a, 1991b, 1991c, 1993, 1996, 1997, 2000c, 2005b, 2009; Lewis, 2002; Shimahara & Sakai, 1995)

Under this system, Japan has achieved one of the highest levels of quality of schooling, as illustrated by such measures as enrollment ratios, retention or graduation rates, daily attendance rates, academic performance, and levels of school disorder problems and juvenile crimes. As of April 2008, about 98% of those who graduated from junior high school entered senior high school and about 68% of senior high school graduates went on to higher levels of education, including 4-year universities, 2-year colleges, or 3-year special training (vocational and technical) colleges. The daily attendance rates for elementary and secondary schools are above 95%, and the retention or graduation rate for senior high school is about 97%, with only about 3% dropouts since the 1960s.

The high quality of teaching and learning has been demonstrated by several international comparative studies on student performance conducted by the International Association for the Evaluation of Educational Achievement (IEA; the Trends in International Mathematics and Science Study, or TIMSS) in 1964–1970, 1978, 1994–1995/1999 (supplement), 2003, and 2007 and by the Organisation for Economic Co-operation and Development (OECD; through the Programme for International Student Assessment, or PISA) in 2000, 2003, and 2006. Each time, the average scores of Japanese students were among the top five countries, except for reading literacy scores on PISA, which were among the second group of countries. The results of these comparative studies and Japan's post-war economic success have combined to draw the attention of other countries to Japanese schooling, making Japanese education a model for educational reform since the 1980s (e.g., as promulgated in *A Nation at Risk* in the United States).

School disorder problems such as school violence, vandalism, and bullying are less serious in Japan than in other developed and urbanized countries (Department of Education and Science, UK, 1983; Fujita, 1997, 2001b; Kiyonaga, 2000; Lawrence, 1998; Morita, 1998), as shown in Figure 1.1. It is safe to say that these relatively low levels of school disorder problems and juvenile crimes have been maintained by the well-organized programs and the collaborative culture of Japanese schools and local communities, which try to care for, guard, and support all children. While it is assumed, and partially verified by research, that these successes are associated with positive features of schooling and teaching, the latest educational reforms have undermined the foundations of these positive features and would do further serious damage.

Ironically, Japan launched its latest wave of radical educational reform just when many other countries were paying attention to and trying to learn from Japanese schooling (Fujita & Wong, 1998/1999). Since the late 1980s, based on the recommendations of NCER outlined earlier, various reform measures and policies have been introduced and implemented at all levels of education from elementary to higher education. If Japanese education has been relatively successful and functioning well, why does Japan need to carry out new and radical reforms, changes that model the systems of the United States and Britain, and what would be the consequences of those reforms?

Two major reasons for change that proponents of radical reform have repeatedly cited are the following:

1. The upheaval arising from so-called "school disorder" phenomena such as school violence, vandalism, bullying, truancy due to "school-phobia," and various psychic disorder problems since the late 1970s, as well as the "aggravation of atrocious juvenile crimes" (*Shonen-hanzai no Kyoakuka* in Japanese)
2. The rising concern with the need to improve educational standards for coping with such social changes as innovation in information communication technologies, globalization, and a knowledge-driven economy (Fujita, 1991c, 1993, 1997, 1999c, 2000b, 2000c, 2000d, 2001b, 2005b)

In relation to the first reason, the mass media took an active role in sensationalizing reports of serious juvenile crimes, school violence, and bullying. Many critics and various reform committees soon elevated them into major policy issues to be coped with by radical educational reform, saying that these phenomena indicate "the system fatigue of Japanese schooling" and accordingly a need for radical reform of schooling (Fujita, 2001b, 2003b). This argument is still used by many politicians, critics, and policy documents for claiming the necessity of further radical reform, even though the assertion has not been proven and many studies have shown that such disorder problems are

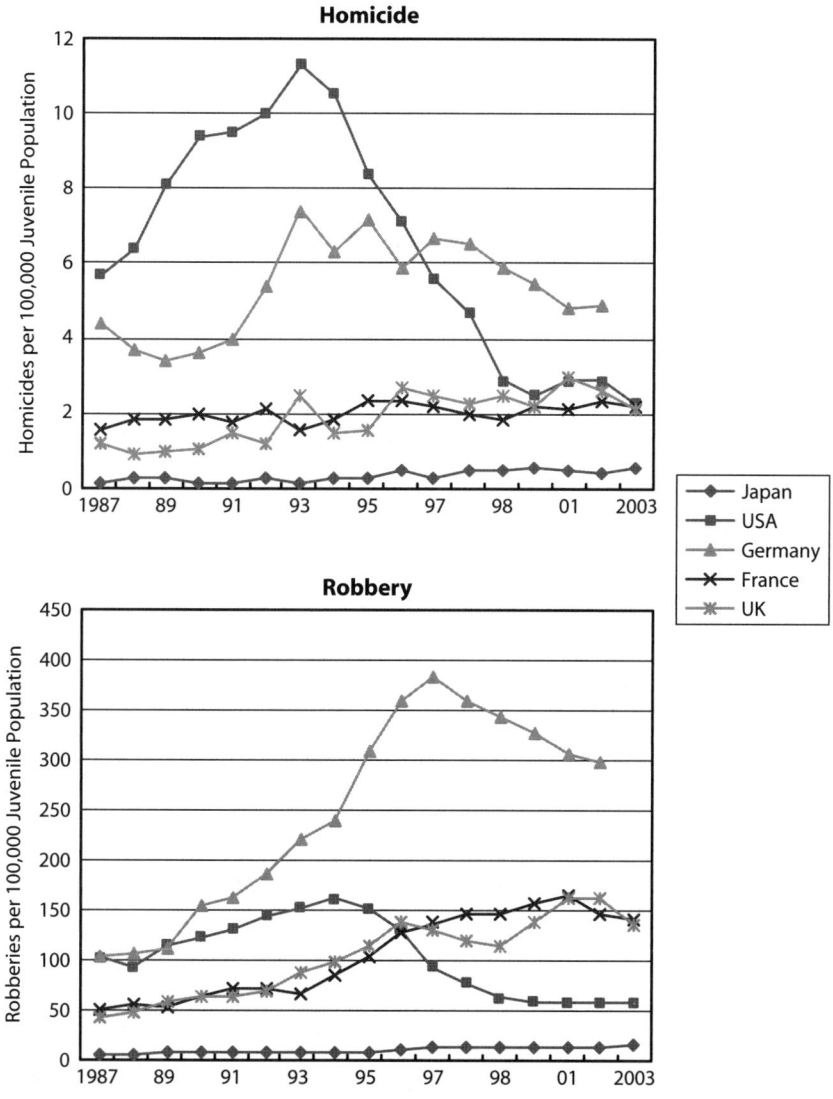

FIGURE 1.1 Changes in Juvenile Homicide and Robbery Rates

Source. Criminal White Paper, 1998 and 2005, Ministry of Justice, Japan. In addition, original data were extracted from the following statistical documents for each country: USA: *Crime in the United States,* data from the U.S. Department of Commerce office of economic statistics; UK: *Criminal statistics, England and Wales,* data from the British Central Statistical Office; Germany: *Polizeliche Kriminalstatistik,* data from the German Statistics Bureau; France: *Aspects de la criminalité et de la délinquance constatées en France, La Situation Démographique*; Japan: Statistics of the Police Department, population data from the Statistics Bureau of the Management and Coordination Agency.

even more common in many developed and urbanized societies (Fujita, 1997, 1999a, 2000c, 2001b). For example, juvenile homicide and robbery rates have been extremely low in Japan, as indicated in Figure 1.1, and the number of juvenile homicides has been stable (between 100 and 110) for the last four decades (Research and Training Institute, Ministry of Justice, 2006). Current reforms, such as school choice and ability grouping, tend to damage the collaborative and caring culture of schools and undermine the critical foundations that have contributed to maintaining the relatively less serious level of disorder problems in Japan. This damage is discussed later as a problem of social capital and *kyosei*.

As for the second reason, there has been a global concern claiming the urgent necessity of radical educational reform, which I discuss in the sections that follow.

HOW CAN WE DEVELOP THE ACADEMIC ABILITY NECESSARY FOR THE 21ST CENTURY?

Implications of PISA and TIMSS Results

Globalization has taken place not only in the economy but also in knowledge, skills, and qualifications. There has been a push for global standardization (i.e., the rise and imposition of a global standard) emerging as a result of the information technology revolution and economic globalization. This is an underlying reason that international comparative studies of students' scholastic performance such as OECD/PISA and IEA/TIMSS have drawn the attention of many researchers, policy makers, and media people across nations.

Expressions like "TIMSS impact" and "PISA shock" were often used when the results of TIMSS 1995/1999 and PISA 2000 testing were released. Since the results of PISA 2000 came out, the media have paid more attention to PISA, and not TIMSS, in Japan. Why? What kinds of influence does this biased attention have on educational policies, teaching, and learning? How should we read the results of PISA and TIMSS, and what kinds of implications should we draw from these two test findings?

It is generally assumed that TIMSS assesses subject-based knowledge or academic achievement, whereas PISA assesses comprehensive scholastic ability, generic skill, literacy in a broad sense, or generative ability. Table 1.1 presents some results (average score rankings of the top 11 countries) from TIMSS 2007 for eighth-graders and PISA 2006 for 15-year-old students. Four nations—all Asian—ranked among the top 11 in all four tests reported in Table 1.1 (see boldface entries in the table). According to my field observations, there are some commonalities in terms of culture and styles of schooling, teaching, and learning among these East Asian countries (to be discussed later).

TABLE 1.1 Top-Scoring Nations on International Achievement Tests: PISA 2006 (15-year-olds) and TIMSS 2007 (eighth-graders)

Rank	PISA/Math	PISA/Science	TIMSS/Math	TIMSS/Science
1	**Taiwan**	*Finland*	**Taiwan**	*Singapore*
2	*Finland*	**Hong Kong**	**Korea**	**Taiwan**
3	**Hong Kong**	*Canada*	*Singapore*	**Japan**
4	**Korea**	**Taiwan**	**Hong Kong**	**Korea**
5	*Netherlands*	*Estonia*	**Japan**	England
6	*Switzerland*	**Japan**	Hungary	Hungary
7	*Canada*	*New Zealand*	England	Czech Republic
8	*Macao*	*Australia*	Russia	Slovenia
9	*Lichtenstein*	*Netherlands*	United States	**Hong Kong**
10	**Japan**	*Lichtenstein*	Lithuania	Russia
11	*New Zealand*	**Korea**	Czech Republic	United States

Note. Countries in **boldface** ranked among the top 11 in all four tests (both PISA and TIMSS); *italicized* countries did not participate in either PISA or TIMSS. Some of the PISA top-scoring nations that did not participate in TIMSS 2007 did, however, participate in TIMSS 2003. In TIMSS 2003/Math, Netherlands ranked 7th, Estonia ranked 8th, and New Zealand ranked 20th among the 45 participating countries/regions. In TIMSS 2003/Science, Estonia ranked 5th, Netherlands ranked 8th, and New Zealand ranked 13th.

Some questions arise:

1. Why are most of the top countries the same in both PISA and TIMSS?
2. Is it true to say that PISA and TIMSS measure different academic abilities?
3. Why do East Asian students tend to outperform students of many Western countries?

My quick answers to these questions are as follows: First, both PISA and TIMSS are measuring basically the same ability, not different ones. Second, any ability would not be developed without spending sufficient time and effort—along with enthusiasm or positive attitude toward learning—and training by appropriate approaches and methods. Finally, the level of student effort, including study hours outside school, is generally higher in East Asian countries than in many Western developed countries.

These questions are important, in part because several countries have recently implemented national or regional standardized testing in addition to ordinary testing such as mid-term and end-of-term exams at school, all with the goal of improving test scores. The questions are important also because many countries have begun to shift their educational systems to stress one or the other of the supposed two types of knowledge being tested: subject-based knowledge versus broad literacy or generative ability. Some of the high-scoring

East Asian countries, such as Singapore and South Korea, have recently started to emphasize the importance of PISA-type comprehensive literacy with a constructivist approach to teaching and learning. In contrast, since the late 1990s, some Western developed countries with relatively low levels of performance on PISA and TIMSS, such as the United States and Britain, have begun emphasizing the importance of basic knowledge accumulation, with some elements of a classical approach to teaching and learning that includes testing and mastery learning, even if it is limited in teaching practices.

The Japanese experience is interesting in this respect. As mentioned earlier, the *Yutori* education reform emphasized the importance of a constructivist approach and introduced special "lesson hours of comprehensive learning" in which schools and teachers organize content and select relevant materials for exploratory learning or project learning. Since the early 2000s, however, there has been a movement back toward a classical approach to learning that places an emphasis on basic knowledge accumulation and testing, although MEXT and proponents of *Yutori* education reform continue to say that the basic policy has not been or should not be changed.

However, the Ministry of Education has decided that the revised national curriculum will be enforced beginning in 2010, with a 10% increase in total lesson hours, especially for math, science, English, and gymnastics. The increase in gymnastics is partially due to the ideological concerns of certain influential political leaders and partially due to the declining trend in physical strength and locomotive power of Japanese youth. Another reactive strategy was the introduction of national assessment tests of students' academic performance for all sixth-graders and ninth-graders throughout the nation starting in 2007, which was enacted despite strong opposition and criticism. While each local board of education for public schools and each private and national school could decide if they would participate or not, all national schools and all local boards of education, except one, have participated, whereas only about half of private schools have participated.

Under the impact of PISA, this national test is divided into two parts (two types of problems) for both math and Japanese literacy. The Type A test is an achievement test for assessing accumulated knowledge, while the Type B test, designed along the lines of PISA, is a comprehension test for assessing the ability to solve problems by utilizing what students have learned. As shown in Table 1.2, the correlations between Type A and Type B are relatively high and are strikingly similar between the results for 2007 and 2008, except for the Japanese test for the sixth-graders. This exceptional, relatively lower coefficient for the 2007 test (underlined in the table) is probably due to the fact that its marking criteria were not consistent (the criteria were uncertain and wavered at the early stage of marking, and then became less rigid).

These high and stable correlations suggest that both tests, Type A and Type B, measure basically the same academic ability, even though some dif-

TABLE 1.2 Correlation Between Scores on Type A and Type B Tests (Ministry of Education National Test)

	Subject			
	Japanese		Mathematics	
	2007	2008	2007	2008
Sixth-graders (elementary)	<u>0.670</u>	0.741	0.715	0.717
Ninth-graders (junior high)	0.709	0.706	0.827	0.830

Note. The relatively low value of the underlined correlation may be the result of inconsistent marking criteria used early in the scoring process.

Source. Ministry of Education and National Institute for Educational Policy Research, Reports (2007 and 2008) on National Assessment Test of Students Academic Ability and Learning.

ferent aspects are covered. It is also quite possible that the same could be said for PISA and TIMSS as well. If this is indeed the case, then two critical questions to be examined would be as follows: What is the nature of the knowledge that is being tested by the two types of questions? What kinds of functions or effects do the two types of testing and their associated teaching approaches have in learning and schooling?

Effective Teaching: Which Approach Is More Appropriate?

In Japan, especially since the 1990s, proponents of radical educational reform have repeatedly emphasized the importance and urgent necessity of developing "new" academic ability and adopting new learning methods instead of the classical ones. Table 1.3 is a summary comparison between the classical approach and the new approach to teaching and learning.

This summary certainly is oversimplified, and all abilities listed under the umbrella of the new approach are not necessarily neglected or undervalued in the classical approach. In fact, child-centered participatory learning has

TABLE 1.3 Comparison Between Classical and New Approaches to Teaching and Learning

Classical approach (objectivism)	New approach (constructivism)
Functional literacy	Generative ability
Discipline-based knowledge	Generic skills and competence
Subject-based knowledge	Critical thinking ability
Knowledge accumulation	Creative thinking ability
Mastery learning	Exploratory learning
Transmission and accumulation	Child-centered participatory learning
Repetition and memorization	Interdisciplinary learning

gradually spread in Japan, especially since the 1980s, and many schools and teachers have modified and enhanced their classroom management and teaching along the lines of its precepts. For example, Stevenson and Stigler wrote on lessons in Japan as follows:

> Lessons are oriented toward problem-solving rather than rote mastery of facts and procedures, and make use of many different types of representational materials. The role assumed by the teacher is that of knowledgeable guide, rather than that of prime dispenser of information and arbiter of what is correct. There is frequent verbal interaction in the classroom as the teacher attempts to stimulate students to produce, explain, and evaluate solutions to problems. (1992, p. 177)

Given the evidence, it is important to take the following into account when we think about the effectiveness of teaching and learning:

1. It is generally assumed that various kinds of abilities, including those listed in Table 1.3, are important, and either one of the two approaches does not necessarily deny the importance of the abilities attributed to the other approach.
2. Actual lessons are mostly a mixture of the two approaches, and the importance lies not in assuming the superiority of one over the other but in enhancing the quality of teaching and learning.
3. There are always significant gaps between theory and practice and between objectives and results or functions, and there is no sure evidence that either of the approaches guarantees effectiveness in terms of developing the particular abilities attributed theoretically to its approach. The effectiveness of the approach varies to a great extent, depending on various contextual factors such as competence or preference of each individual teacher and student, features of students as a study group, classroom climate, particular lesson task, subject, and grade level.
4. Even if the above-mentioned point 3 is generally the case, it is safe to say that the compatibility of the two approaches tends to vary among students, especially as related to their levels of competence and to cultural correlates (students' family background and cultural experiences), as discussed by Bernstein (1973a, 1973b, 1977a, 1977b, 1977c, 1990, 1996) and Bourdieu (1979; Bourdieu & Passeron, 1970).

Table 1.4 presents a comparison of the new and classical approaches to teaching and learning, based on the work of Bernstein (1973a, 1973b, 1977a, 1977b, 1977c), with some additions by the present author. In Bernstein's terminology, "classification" refers to how strongly (clearly) or weakly knowledge, people, status, roles, objects, and activities are classified in the world,

TABLE 1.4 Features of Classical and New Approaches to Teaching and Learning

	Classical approach	New approach
Instructional philosophy	Objectivism Visible pedagogy	Constructivism Invisible pedagogy
Curriculum type	Collection Strong classification	Integration Weak classification
Learning style	Mastery learning Strong framing	Exploratory learning Weak framing
Evaluation criteria	Concrete/objective One-dimensional	Meta-level Multidimensional
Selectivity of schooling	Old middle class and working class	New middle class

Note. This listing of features of the two approaches is based on the work of Bernstein (1973a, 1973b, 1977b), with additions by the present author.

including schools, classrooms, lessons, families, and other settings. "Framing" refers to how strongly (orderly in terms of sequence, timing, pacing, attitude, and behavioral pattern) or weakly activities and interactions are framed or controlled by the authorities, rules and norms, or other forces. For example, the classical timetable of lessons and teacher-dominated instruction are examples of strong framing, whereas weak framing is common in project learning or individualized learning, and in open schools.

According to Bernstein's arguments, the new approach—"invisible pedagogy" in his terms—emphasizes integrated curriculum and exploratory learning, in which the goals of learning and the criteria for evaluation are not clear to some students and their parents, especially those who do not have rich cultural or linguistic experiences of metaphysical, symbolic, or sophisticated thinking and discourse in daily life. Because the curriculum is integrated and complicated or sophisticated, and because the learning goals and evaluation criteria are not clear to some students, it is difficult for some students to identify what kinds of effort they should make in order to master the learning materials and to attain high grades for performance. In contrast, the classical approach—"visible pedagogy" in Bernstein's terminology—emphasizes mastery learning and a collection type of curriculum that classifies a variety of knowledge into subject areas and arranges the areas systematically. Accordingly, in visible pedagogy, the goals of learning and the criteria for evaluation are generally clear to most students, and it is easy for them to understand how to study and what kinds of effort are necessary to master the learning materials and enhance their performance. This may be one of the reasons why the Kumon method of learning and its form of private tutoring have gradually spread in some Western countries, including the United States.

Bernstein's theory seems to hold some relevance to the current issues of effective learning and the performance gap between the top-level East Asian countries and the middle-level Western countries in PISA and TIMSS. Invisible pedagogy or exploratory learning has been significantly emphasized and widely adopted in some advanced Western countries, such as Britain and the United States, whereas visible pedagogy or mastery learning has been emphasized and widely adopted in many East Asian countries, such as Japan, Hong Kong, Korea, Singapore, and Taiwan, all of which are among the top-scoring group on TIMSS and/or PISA. Of course, this is not the sole cause or background for the performance gap; behind it there are many additional factors, such as ethnic/cultural/linguistic diversity, class differences, organization of schooling, and the culture of teaching and learning.

As discussed earlier, the *Yutori* education reform in Japan emphasized the importance of the new approach, or invisible pedagogy, and reorganized the national curriculum and MEXT direction for lessons along these lines, cutting down the lesson hours and content of major subjects, including math, science, social studies, and Japanese language, especially since full-scale implementation of the 5-day school week and the revised national curriculum in 2002. Since then, for example, the total number of annual lesson hours is much smaller in Japan than in many Western countries, including Britain, France, and Germany. For the 2003–2004 school year, for 9th–11th-graders the totals were 869 hours in the UK, 830 hours in France, 780 hours in Germany, 709 hours in Japan, 703 hours in Korea, and 654 hours in Finland; for 12th–14th-graders the totals were 940 hours in France, 870 hours in Germany, 870 hours in the UK, 867 hours in Korea, 817 hours in Japan, and 796 hours in Finland (OECD, 2005). In addition, ability grouping has become widely introduced in both elementary and junior high schools (in about 70% of the public schools), especially in math, Japanese, and English.

Educational Reforms: Consequences for Student Performance

Now the question that must be examined is whether these changes have contributed to enhancing the quality of teaching and learning or the performance of students. The following PISA results highlight some ironic consequences. As shown in Table 1.5:

1. The percentages of students scoring at the highest level are significantly larger in Finland than in Japan, with the exception of math in 2003.
2. The percentages of students scoring at Level 1 or below are much smaller in Finland than in Japan.
3. The percentages of students scoring both at the highest level and at Level 1 or below in Finland are fairly constant across the three testing

TABLE 1.5 Comparison of PISA Results for Japan and Finland: Percentages of Students Scoring at the Highest and Lowest Proficiency Levels

	2000		2003		2006	
	Highest level	Lowest level	Highest level	Lowest level	Highest level	Lowest level
Science						
Japan					2.6	12.1
Finland					3.9	4.1
Math						
Japan			8.2	13.3	4.8	13.0
Finland			6.7	6.8	6.3	5.9
Reading						
Japan	9.9	10.0	9.7	19.0	9.4	18.4
Finland	18.5	6.9	14.7	5.7	16.7	4.8

Note. The highest level for Math and Science is Level 6, and for Reading it is Level 5; the lowest level for all subject areas is the sum of Level 1 and results below Level 1. The proficiency levels for Science in 2000 and 2003 and for Math in 2000 were not calculated because the numbers of test questions were insufficient.

Source. Reports of OECD/PISA, http://www.mext.go.jp/a_menu/shotou/gakuryoku-chousa/sonota/07032813.htm.

years, while in Japan the percentage of students scoring at the highest level went down significantly in math from 2003 to 2006 (from 8.2 to 4.8) and the percentage at Level 1 or below went up dramatically in reading from 2000 to 2003 and 2006 (from 10.0 to 19.0 and 18.4).

These results suggest the following for Japanese education and educational policies:

1. The percentage of the highest performing students has declined, even though the teaching practice of ability grouping has spread to a majority of schools and has become almost the norm.
2. There is a strong possibility that the increase of low achievers, as well as the overall downward trend of Japanese students' performance, has been caused by the full-scale implementation of the 5-day school week, with its associated cuts in lesson hours and content, as well as the expansion of the new approach (invisible pedagogy) in the course of *Yutori* education reform. It is quite important to examine whether these observations have some validity or not, but unfortunately no research has been conducted nor any consideration paid in the policy discourse. My speculation is as follows: Most of the low achievers are those who do not or cannot study outside of school (or at home) for various reasons or who live under poor home conditions and accordingly do not

have sufficient opportunities to study and be cared for unless those opportunities are given at school. The results shown in Table 1.5, especially the increase in low achievers, suggest that the current reforms have decreased the teaching and caring functions of schools, especially for those children living under poor conditions at home and in their neighborhoods.
3. Whatever the causes of the performance decline, it is safe to say that making all students, and especially those at the bottom levels, happy in learning and school life is decisively important for schools to be successful.

WHITHER JAPANESE EDUCATION AND SOCIETY?

Differentiated Society: A Widening Gap Between Rich and Poor

Since the late 1990s, the expression "differentiated society" (*Kakusa-shakai*) has become popular in both the mass media and social science discussions in Japan. Related phenomena have been widely reported, discussed, and studied by the media, social critics, and social scientists—economists, sociologists, and education scholars in particular (Fujita, 2007b; Hara & Seiyama, 1999; Kariya, 2001; Sato, 2000; Shirahase, 2006; Tachibanaki, 1998, 2006). Since 2005 the problems of a differentiated society have become especially politicized and have been taken up as policy issues in the Diet. The core problems include a dramatic increase in households below the poverty line, as well as increases in the numbers of low-wage, unstable workers operating under limited-term contracts and of unemployed or quasi-unemployed people. For example, the relative poverty rate was 15.3% as of 2000, which is very high relative to the United States and Ireland among developed OECD countries (Föster & d'Ercole, 2005). Furthermore, significantly, these problems are assumed to have been caused not only by the bursting of the economic bubble, succeeding financial crisis, and sluggish economy, but also by unfairly biased, relentless policies dominated by the neoliberal and market-fundamentalist ideologies. Such ideologies, along with neoconservative ideologies, have dominated recent educational reforms. All of these reforms were pushed forward by the ruling political powers, despite the critical voices of many education scholars, the great majority of teachers, and almost all individuals and organizations concerned with education. Under these circumstances, Japan, which was once called an "all one hundred million, middle-class society" (*Ichioku Sou-churyu Shakai*) in the 1960s and 1970s, has been moving quickly toward becoming a differentiated society. Figure 1.2 shows this widening gap between rich and poor in education. The percentages of students aided for schooling due to poverty have increased rapidly since 2000.

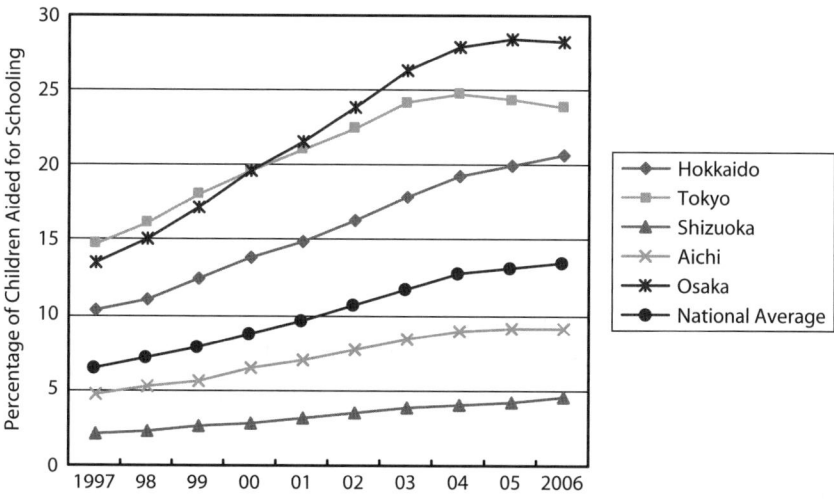

FIGURE 1.2 Increase of Children Aided for Schooling

Source. "The information material submitted to the Committee on Financial Affairs, the House of Representatives," February 2008, Ministry of Education, Japan. Quoted from Gan (2000).

Figure 1.3 shows the correlation between aid for schooling and academic performance in the 23 wards of Tokyo as of 2004. In this figure, two graphs are shown: one for elementary school students and the other for junior high school students. The vertical axis represents mean performance on tests in major subject areas (four subjects for elementary level and five subjects for junior high level), while the horizontal axis represents percentage of aided students. Clearly there is a high correlation between the poverty level of wards and their students' academic performance (correlation values are about 0.8 for both elementary and junior high levels). Similar correlation between family background and student academic performance or educational attainment at an individual level was found also in earlier studies, and the basic correlative pattern has not changed over decades of educational reform (Fujita, 1978, 1980, 1982, 1989).

Rich Flight to Private and Privileged Public Schools

The newly emerging problem in Japan is not an issue of simple educational inequality due to family background at an individual level, but the inequality mediated by the institutional differentiation of localities and schools that has been produced by policies dominated by neoliberal and market-fundamentalist ideologies. It is because this differentiation leads to the problems of social exclusion and institutionalization that a differentiated society is linked with

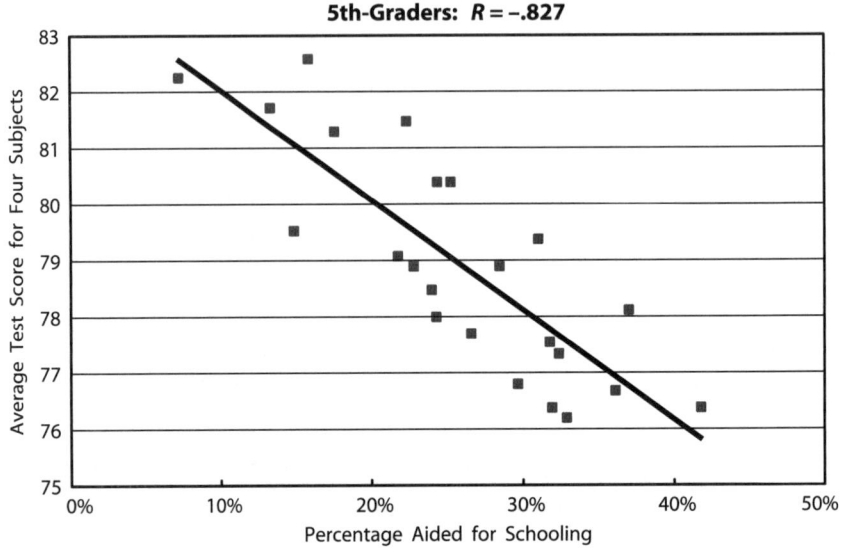

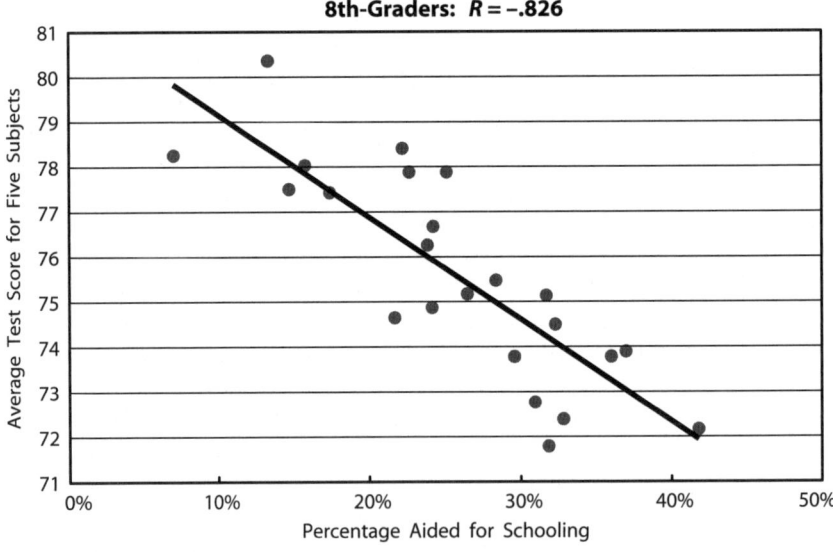

FIGURE 1.3 Correlation Between Aid for Schooling and Academic Performance: Tokyo, 23 Wards, 2004.

Source. Academic performance: Tokyo Metropolitan Government Board of Education. Aid for schooling: Most data retrieved from the home page of each ward; the remainder obtained by telephone research with each ward.

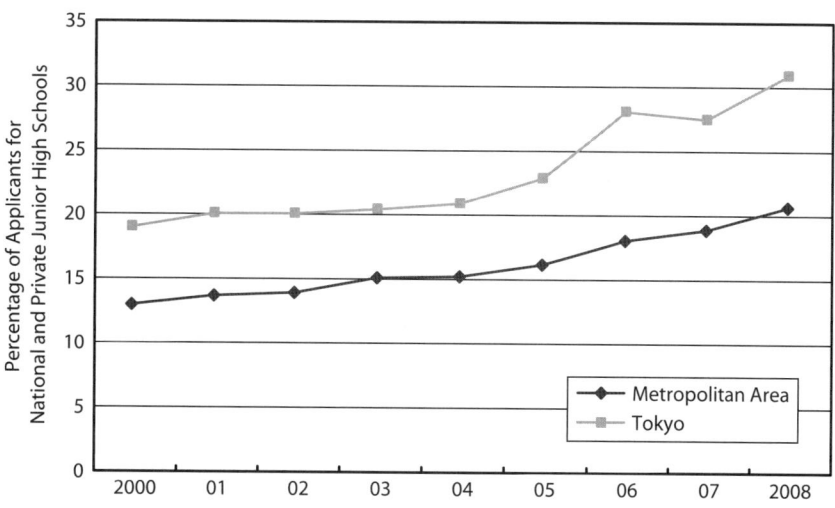

FIGURE 1.4 Increase in Applicants for Private and National Junior High Schools in Tokyo and Its Metropolitan Area, 2000–2008

Source. Nichinoken Co. Retrieved April 20, 2009, from http://www.nichinoken.co.jp/free.html

differentiated education. Figure 1.4 shows a recent increase in applicants for national and private junior high schools in Tokyo and the Tokyo metropolitan area (most of which are selective and competitive schools). The graph shows a clear tendency of "rich flight" to national and private schools or "rich exit" from public schools. The expression "rich flight" references the "white flight" that has taken place in the United States since the 1930s (Fujita, 2006a), as well as similar phenomena found recently in many big cities throughout the world.

One unique facet of the Japanese case is the tendency for this flight to take place on the basis of educational concern among middle- and upper-class families (hereafter, "rich families"). Brown (1990) observed what appears to be a similar trend in the United Kingdom; he named it "parentocracy." He says: "We are entering a time in which we face "the rise of the educational "'parentocracy,' where a child's education is increasingly dependent upon the *wealth* and *wishes* of parents" (p. 65).

In Tokyo and the surrounding metropolitan area, many "rich family" parents are very much concerned about their children's education and are now trying to send their children either to private schools, to schools affiliated to national universities, to public 6-year secondary schools, or to more popular public schools under the school choice plan. Including all these schools of choice, the school choice plan is gradually increasing in big cities. However, two localities in Tokyo and Gunma Prefecture recently decided to suspend or abolish the school choice plan for reasons that it damages community cohesion as well as collaborative culture and vigor among residents and parents both in local communities and in schools.

In this respect, Japanese society and education are now at a critical juncture: Which direction will our society and education take? The choice is an unequally differentiated, exclusive system or an equality-oriented, inclusive system (Fujita, 1997, 2003c, 2005a, 2006a, 2007c). The political power balance is complicated and the outcome uncertain, but there are two trends that will push Japan toward further differentiation. One is the dominant reform ideologies and the change of power relations in the policymaking process, that is, the power shift from the education circle, including the Ministry of Education and its advisory body, to political authorities such as the cabinet and advisory bodies to the Prime Minister. The other trend is the growing concern in the mass media and the general public with regard to educational privatization among "rich families" and its associated moral changes.

Skewed Policymaking and the Moral Shift Toward Privatization

The advisory bodies that have exercised overwhelming influence in determining the basic direction of recent educational reforms in Japan are the Council on Economic and Fiscal Policy (CEFP), which is a consultative organ placed within the Cabinet Office and headed by the Prime Minister, and such advisory bodies to the Prime Minister as the Council for the Promotion of Regulatory Reform, the National Commission on Educational Reform, and the Council for Education Rebuilding (succeeded by and reorganized as the Meeting on Education Rebuilding since 2007). The dominant ideologies or ideas commonly shared by these bodies are neoliberalism, market fundamentalism, market and managerial efficiency, new public management (NPM), outcome-based education (OBE), and so forth, and the policy platform is commonly expressed by such catchphrases as "Structural reform without exceptions" and "Do not stop the reform." Almost all members of these bodies do not represent voices from the education circle but are spokespersons for the government party and business interests. Furthermore, all of these bodies are under the direct control of the Prime Minister and the cabinet, and not the control of the Education Minister, the Ministry of Education, or its advisory body, the Central Council of Education (CCE), which have initiated major educational reforms and policies for the last five decades, since the 1950s.

The revision of the Fundamental Law of Education (FLE) was initiated by the National Commission on Educational Reform in 2000, which proposed 17 major directions for reform, including the FLE revision and 56 concrete reform measures (Fujita 2001a). I was one of 26 Commission members and the only one who clearly expressed a negative opinion about the revision of FLE. I was labeled as "an outspoken opponent of all reforms" by some cabinet members and conservative media people, despite the fact that I was against only 7 of the 56 reform measures. Following this proposal, the CCE went through deliberations on the revisions and made a proposal to move forward with the changes. Since the release of the CCE report, many dissenting voices have been raised from various circles. All opinion surveys by newspaper companies and others showed that the great majority of respondents were negative about the revision. For example, in one survey, those who answered "the approval at this Diet should not be strained" was 55% (53% among supporters of the then-ruling Liberal Democratic Party, LDP), while those who answered "the approval at this Diet is necessary" were only 19% (25% among LDP supporters) (*Nihon Keizai Shinbun*, 2006). To a survey question "Do you think education will become better by the revision of Fundamental Law of Education," 28% answered "become worse," 46% responded "unchanged," and only 4% replied "become better" (*Asahi Shimbun*, 2006). Nevertheless, the bill revising the FLE was steamrolled by the government parties and approved in December 2006. Then, in June 2007, three education-related bills, including revision of the Teacher Certificate Law, were also approved under pressure applied by the administration of Prime Minister Shinzo Abe.

Some comments from politicians illustrate how biased and irrational the background concerns driving this revision were. At various gatherings, several leading politicians of the LDP expressed their concerns about the FLE, expressing unexplainable prejudice and antagonism against the teachers' union, saying "The FLE should be revised in order to crash teachers' unions." In fact, Nakayama Nariaki, then Minister of Land, Infrastructure, Transport and Tourism (also former Education Minister in the administration of Prime Minister Junichiro Koizumi) was forced to resign in September 2008 due to his unreasonable statements, such as "Japan Teachers Union is the cancer of Japanese Education" and "We should demolish it" (*Asahi Shimbun*, 2008).

In 2002, the CCE decided against proposing introduction of a teaching certificate renewal system. Under pressure of the Koizumi administration's policy platform for "Structural reform without exceptions," the Education Minister in 2004 submitted the Reform Program of Compulsory Education to the CEFP. Part of that program was a teaching certificate renewal system. The CCE was consulted again, despite its earlier rejection of the idea, and finally in 2006 proposed introduction of a teaching certificate renewal system.

The central government provides a subsidy for teacher salaries to maintain the basic quality of schooling throughout the country, irrespective of the financial standing of each locality. In 2005, after 8 months of intensive deliberation, the CCE proposed that it was absolutely necessary to maintain at least the current level of subsidy (one half) and requested an increase. But this proposal was not seriously considered, and the cabinet instead cut the subsidy to one third. This decision was made through discussions of the CEFP, the Ministry of Finance, and the Ministry of Internal Affairs and Communications, in spite of the previous agreement in the cabinet that the final decision should be made on the basis of the CCE proposal. In fact, the Japanese government's expenditure for elementary and secondary education as a percentage of GDP (gross domestic product) is only 3.5%, which is much lower than the average of 5% among the OECD countries (OECD, 2007).

Revised laws have also strengthened the administrative/managerial control over teachers and expanded the possibility of restricting and oppressing the freedom and autonomy of teachers. Because political and administrative authorities establish the laws and regulations that govern education and exercise control according to those laws and regulations, they are excluded from those who may exercise "unjust control" (the term used in the Fundamental Law of Education). In addition, new status positions for teachers have been introduced, such as acting principal, head teacher, and master teacher (School Education Law), effectively creating a hierarchical organization of teaching staff: principal, acting principal, vice-principal, head teacher, master teachers, and ordinary teachers.

Such examples illustrate how skewed recent educational policymaking in Japan has become. It does not consider the real needs and conditions for improving school education, but has been influenced by noneducational considerations such as financial concerns to cope with budgetary deficits and by some twisted ideological concerns or prejudices. Behind these policy trends and political moves, there is a significant moral crisis that can be observed in the following illustrative phenomena.

For the last couple of years, there has been a marked increase in popular weekly magazine features on the following types of themes: maps of railways and subways in the Tokyo metropolitan and Kansai areas in relation to school rankings in terms of the entrance examination difficulty for private junior high schools, popularity rankings of public elementary and junior high schools of choice in Tokyo, university rankings based on various quality measures, nationwide rankings of senior high schools in terms of the numbers of successful applicants who passed entrance examinations for famous universities, success stories of the students (and their family supports) who passed the entrance examinations for Tokyo University and Kyoto University (the two most prestigious universities in Japan), stories about how academic ability can be developed and what kinds of activities help children's academic performance, and guidelines for what should be considered in choosing a good *juku* (private tutoring and cram school). There has also been a dramatic increase in *juku* advertisements in railway stations and in rail and subway cars. Furthermore, it has become almost the norm that real estate agents use school-related information for selling or improving a property, noting that the property is located in the district of a particular "good" public school.

Japan is an education-conscious and degree-conscious society. Since the 1970s, it has been widely known that Japanese education is overwhelmingly influenced and distorted by severe entrance examinations for senior high schools and universities. For example, the system was described as "examination hell" by OECD Examiners (1971). Because of such perceptions, since the late 1960s reforms have been made in the entrance examination system under such slogans as "Do not make the spring of fifteen-year-old children cry!" (*Juhgo no Haru o nakasuna*), and then in 1980 the *Yutori* education reform was pushed forward. Now, however, the reform trend has been reversed and, even worse, the essential ideals of equal opportunity, providing rich learning space for all children, and caring and supporting them until their graduation have been disregarded by reformers, their proponents, and many in the media. Yet there are still many different movements that hold high regard for those ideal features and seek to revitalize schools and local communities with those ideals. I support such efforts.

Social Exclusion Through Educational Exclusion

In the context of the educational restructuring described herein, as well as labor policies and socioeconomic changes since the 1990s, social inequality has entered a new phase in Japan. The problems of social exclusion have become a major social concern and a central policy issue. The form and function of schooling, or differentiated and privatized schooling, should be reexamined as possible mechanisms for causing or exacerbating the problems of social exclusion. Of course, in Japan there were problems of social discrimination and exclusion long before the current educational reforms began. Two typical and partially overlapping examples are *Dowa Mondai* (or *Buraku Mondai*) and the discrimination against the *Zainichi*. *Dowa Mondai* is the engrained discrimination against people of some lineages (the *Burakumin*) and from some residential areas, which originated from the system of social stratification under the Tokugawa Regime from 1603 to 1867 (Edo Period). The problem persists despite social integration policies, including "Education for Social Integration," that have been attempted since the 1940s. Another group experiencing discrimination is the *Zainichi* (Koreans living in Japan), many of whom are descendants of Koreans who came to Japan during the period of Japanese colonial rule over the Korean Peninsula. It would be safe to say that these problems have been improving gradually, as Japan has experienced rapid economic growth and its associated urbanization since the 1960s and especially with the internationalization and sociocultural diversification that have been occurring since the 1980s. However, there are still many difficulties and obstacles for those facing discrimination that should be removed. In any case, these problems have not been rooted in educational discrimination and segregation but in social and historical causes. In contrast, it is educational inequality and exclusion that have become some of the major contributors to the newer problems of social exclusion. In other words, social exclusion through educational exclusion has emerged along with the expansion of school education and now threatens to become a serious social problem, arising out of recent education and labor policies and the economic crisis.

One aspect of this socioeducational exclusion is illustrated in Figure 1.5. The plots show clearly that junior high school graduates and senior high school dropouts outnumber individuals from all other education categories as a percentage of the new inmate population of detention homes for both homicide and robbery. This overrepresentation suggests that youngsters in these two categories are faced with serious difficulties in their lives, being stigmatized, discriminated against, and treated unfairly, hence being socially excluded and more likely to turn to crime, or that their criminal acts tend to be treated unfairly and severely. This suggests further that not only junior high graduates and senior high dropouts, but also low educational achievers in general, tend to be at risk.

It is common knowledge that the labor market and employment conditions including wages, insurance, and other fringe benefits are poorer for those with lower educational credentials. Furthermore, the situation has become worse during the last two decades, partly due to the lengthy economic stagnation since the collapse of the bubble economy and partly due to the labor policies that have put the needs and concerns of management before those of the workers. According to labor statistics, "non-regular employment" among all employees has dramatically increased, from 16.4% in 1985 to 33.7% in 2007 (Ministry of Health, Labor and Welfare, 2008). This increase is remarkable, especially among the younger generation: from about 20% in 1982 to 72% in 2007 for ages 15–19, and from about 12% to 43% for ages 20–24 (Cabinet Office, Government of Japan, 2008). The "non-regular employment" category includes day laborers, part-time workers, short-term contract-based workers (monthly or yearly contracts), and workers for temporary employment agencies. As of June 2007, the average monthly salary for regular male workers was 347,500 yen (243,300 yen for females), while it was only 224,300 yen for non-regular male workers (168,800 yen for females). In addition, the job turnover rate has been quite high for the last two decades and even higher among those with lower educational credentials. As of May 2005, the rate for those experiencing a job change within 3 years after employment was 66.7% for junior high school graduates, 47.9% for senior high school graduates, and 35.9% for university graduates (Cabinet Office, Government of Japan, 2008).

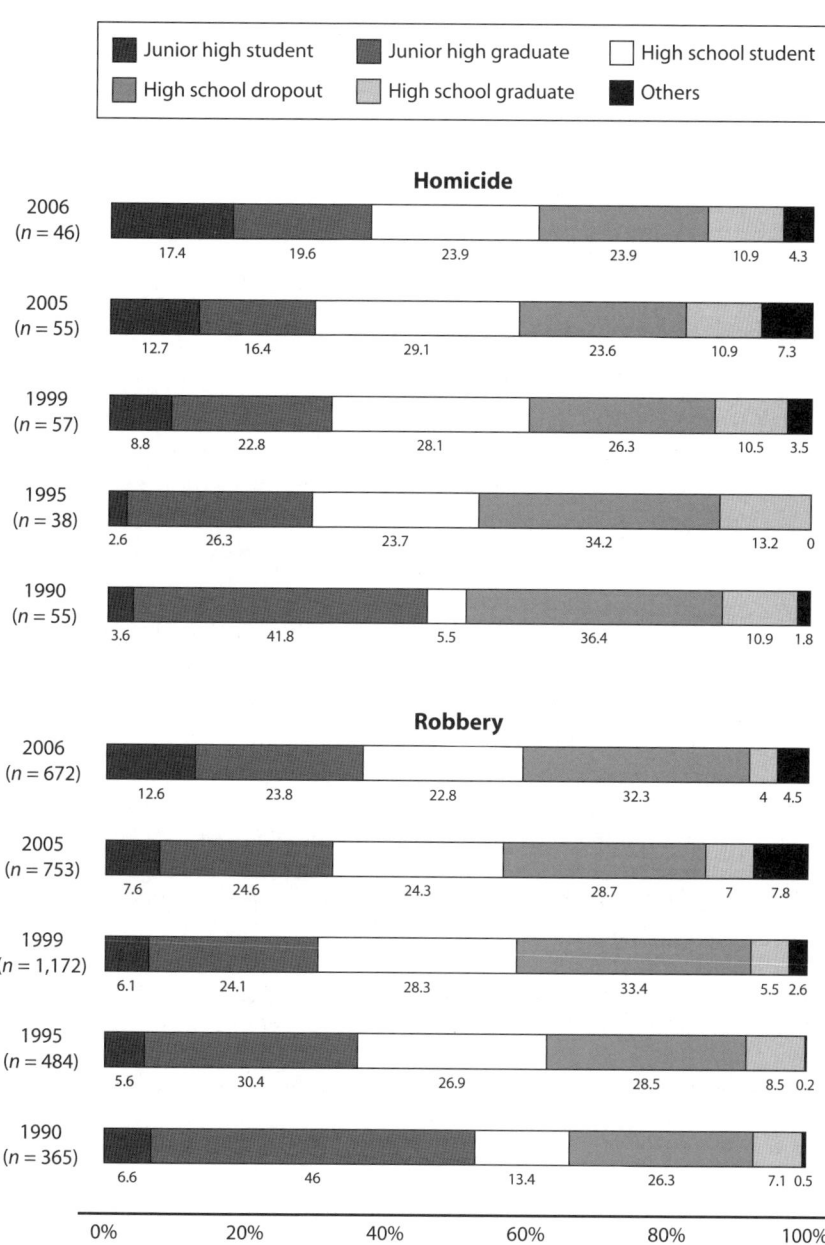

FIGURE 1.5 Educational Composition of New Inmates in Detention Homes: Homicide and Robbery

Source. Annual Report of the Correction Statistics, Ministry of Justice, Japan.

All of these statistics suggest the following:

1. Life-long employment, a seniority-based wage system, and collectivism, which were once praised as strong features of the Japanese style of business management, have now crumbled to a significant extent.
2. The labor market and job conditions have become severe, especially for youth.
3. Those with lower educational accomplishments tend to be significantly at risk both in the labor market and in social life.

Thus, the problem of non-regular employment has become a major policy issue, partly because the tough situation for youth and non-regular workers has become impossible to ignore and partly because of the increase of young homeless people and subsequent increased occurrence of robbery-murder and random killings by non-regular workers. Unfortunately, however, not much attention is paid to the relationships between the problems of educational differentiation, exclusion, and privatization on the one hand and those of social exclusion and unsafe, insecure social conditions on the other.

A VISION FOR 21ST-CENTURY EDUCATION AND SOCIETY

Japan has been considered one of the safest, most secure, and most orderly countries to have also realized economic prosperity (Vogel, 1979) and one whose educational excellence has contributed to its socioeconomic success (e.g., National Commission on Excellence in Education, 1983). As described in the foregoing, however, current educational reforms have been reorganizing the system of schooling and undermining the foundations of what is best in Japanese education. Therefore, the following pages are devoted to discussing what is critical for successful education and what kind of vision is more plausible for successful education.

Kyosei *as an Organizing Principle for Education, Society, and Human Life*

Daniel Bell (1976) identified the following three organizing principles or value orientations for modernization and socioeconomic development: efficiency in the economic dimension (economic rationality), equality (or equal opportunity) in the political dimension, and self-realization in the cultural dimension. He then argued that a modern capitalist society like America faces difficulties caused by the contradictions among those three organizing principles, especially between efficiency and self-realization. This theoretical framework and arguments are insightful and important. In addition to these three values, however, there is one more value that is critically important as an organizing principle for modern society and education: peaceful symbiosis/co-existence/

co-living, or *kyosei* in Japanese (Fujita, 1997, 1999a, 1999b, 1999c, 2000c, 2005a, 2005b, 2006a).

Kyosei is a basic value for social and human security, peaceful social order and daily life activities, and social solidarity, as well as for a sustainable economy and society. It is the value that tends to be considered a natural given and not necessarily recognized as important when and where it is maintained and enjoyed by most of the people. In these days, however, especially since the 1980s, many people have started to recognize the breakdown of *kyosei* and appreciate the importance of its rebuilding or revitalization. Internationally, the problem has been accelerated by a wide range of phenomena and concerns about them: environmental pollution and destruction (Carson, 1962; Meadows, Meadows, Randers, & Behrens, 1972) and so-called new threats, such as proliferation of weapons of mass destruction, international terrorism, wars within states, state failure, and trans-border diseases (e.g., SARS or new strains of influenza), as well as the long-standing problems of famine, hunger, and poverty. All of these threaten our lives, human security, and the ecology of the globe.

In Japan, the term *kyosei* has been widely used to refer to all the issues associated with these phenomena and problems and has become the most popular keyword for organizing and reorganizing various social projects and activities, including ecology movements and businesses promoting various ecologically friendly goods. In Japanese, *kyo* stands for "co-," "sym-," or "together," and *sei* represents "life," "live," "living," or "vivid." Thus, *kyosei* literally means "co-living," "living together," or "symbiosis," which presupposes the coexistence of more than two units such as persons, groups of people (including races, ethnic groups, and classes), organizations, nations, and even various species, as well as material goods and natural environments. The concept also presupposes or expects some kind of relation, interaction, or interdependence among these various units. Furthermore, the term has been used with a positive connotation, such as "mutually supportive and respectful, peaceful and sustainable, and to be pursued, realized and maintained" (Fujita, 2005a).

There are several terms that overlap more or less with *kyosei*, such as peace, conviviality, and symbiosis (Fujita, 2005a; Murakami, Kawashima, & Chiba, 2005). But as far as issues of a societal dimension are concerned, *peace* is generally used to mean the situation in which there is no war, armed conflict, or coercive force between countries or within a country. *Conviviality* usually refers to an interpersonal relationship, interaction, or communication that is friendly and pleasantly cheerful. Ivan Illich (1971, 1973) proposed "convivial society" as a vision of ideal society and "conviviality" as an organizing principle for human relations and social networks, in contrast with what is often seen in modern industrialized and schooled society, where people's actions, attitudes, and relations to others and to their environments are exploitative and alienated. In contrast, *kyosei* is much broader than conviviality or peace. It is not limited only to the relationships among human beings but refers also to the relationships between human beings and various nonhuman species, materials, industrial products, and environments, as well as relationships between various species. It is not limited only to war-related situations but is used also to refer to the forms, conditions, and situations of our daily life—interpersonal and social interaction, social projects, and activities, including business.

Four Forms of Symbiosis, Social Capital, and Kyosei

Symbiosis also refers to the relationship between two or more different living things and organizations, not only people but also various species. The term has been used in biology since the 19th century, and was introduced into sociology in the 1920s by the Chicago School as one of the key terms of human and social ecology (Park, 1952; Park, Burgess, & McKenzie, 1925). But this term does not assume positive connotations like *kyosei*. Symbiosis includes not only mutuality but also commensalism, amensalism, antagonism, competition, and neutrality (sharing the same space without any interaction or interdependence). Considering these differences, I have used symbiosis as an analytical concept and *kyosei* as a normative as well as analytical concept, and have proposed four ideal types of social symbiosis: embracive symbiosis, segmented/segregated symbiosis, market-oriented symbiosis, and civic and inclusive symbiosis (Fujita, 1999b, 2000c, 2005a). Table 1.6 summarizes the features of these four types.

Kyosei as an idealistic or normative concept is congruent with the fourth type of symbiosis, that is, civic and inclusive symbiosis (see Table 1.6). In other words, it is defined as a fourth type of social symbiosis and is characterized by such value orientations as acceptance of differences and multiplicity, open and equality-oriented systems and social organization, equality as a citizen and social inclusion, common basic knowledge and responsibility as a citizen in school curriculum and teaching, and seeking to develop participatory learning and learning/caring community in school, the local community, and society.

Why is *kyosei* critically important for successful schooling and learning? It is because students learn not only through formal curriculum and schooling but also through hidden curriculum and day-to-day experiences both within schools and outside schools. Those experiences are more or less framed and regulated by institutional and organizational arrangements and cultural norms as well as the socioeconomic structure and its associated conditions for daily life and learning. If students are socially excluded or unequally and unfairly treated by those arrangements and norms, it would be difficult for them to be positively disposed toward learning.

In this respect, there is some similarity between *kyosei* and the new concept of social capital that was reinvented intellectually by James Coleman

TABLE 1.6 Four Types of Social Symbiosis

Embracive symbiosis	Segmented/segregated symbiosis	Market-oriented symbiosis	Civic and inclusive symbiosis (*kyosei*)
MAJOR FEATURES			
Undifferentiated social status and knowledge Shared common value Learning embedded in the daily life and work place	Hierarchically differentiated and specialized social status and knowledge Segregated life space and segmented work place Curriculum and ability tracking Individual appropriation of knowledge	The same structural features of segmented/segregated symbiosis. In addition, more emphasis on: • Indifference in common values and others • Individualized learning and freedom of choice • Partially segmented learning space based on partially multi-tracked system	Basic structure may not be much different from that of segmented/segregated symbiosis. More emphasis on: • Acceptance of differences and multiplicity • Open and equality-oriented systems and social organization • Equality as a citizen and social inclusion • Common basic knowledge and responsibility as a citizen • Participatory learning and learning/caring community
HISTORICAL STAGE WITH SOME CONSISTENCY			
Premodern, pre-industrial society	Modern, industrial society	Postmodern, neoliberal, market-fundamentalist society	Society that values the idea of *kyosei* as an organizing principle of society and education and as a guiding principle of daily life

(1988) and expanded by Robert D. Putnam (1995, 2000, 2001). This (new) social capital may be called "soft social capital," in contrast to traditional social capital or "hard social capital" such as roads, railways, harbors, and the systems of electricity, water supply, and communication. According to Putnam (2000, 2001), the three major components of social capital are social networks, the associated norms of reciprocity, and trust, the last one of which depends on the first two. In this terminology, a social network is developed on the basis of institutional and organizational arrangements, while the norms of reciprocity are part of the cultural norms. There are three important distinctions made by Putnam that need to be considered when thinking about social capital and *kyosei*:

1. Bridging (or inclusive) social capital versus bonding (or exclusive) social capital
2. Place-based social capital versus function-based social capital
3. Generalized reciprocity versus specific reciprocity

For the first distinction, Putnam proposes the importance of bridging (or inclusive) social capital to maximize "the positive consequences of social capital—mutual support, cooperation, trust, institutional effectiveness" and to minimize "the negative manifestations—sectarianism, ethnocentrism, corruption" (Putnam, 2000, p. 22). It is because bonding forms of social capital are "by choice or necessity, inward looking and tend to reinforce exclusive identities and homogeneous groups," that "by creating strong in-group loyalty, [they] may also create strong out-group antagonism," but bridging forms of social capital or "networks are outward looking and encompass people across diverse social cleavages" and "can generate broader identities and reciprocity" (pp. 22–23). Regarding Putnam's second distinction, he says that "Place-based social capital is being supplanted by function-based social capital. We are withdrawing from those networks of reciprocity that once constituted our communities" (p. 184). Finally, in cases of specific reciprocity, "I'll do this for you if you do [something] for me. Even more valuable, however, is a norm of generalized reciprocity: I'll do this for you without expecting anything specific back from you, in the confident expectation that someone else will do something for me down the road. The Golden Rule is one formulation of generalized reciprocity" (pp. 20–21).

Based on these distinctions, *kyosei* can be redefined as an organizing principle for developing the place-based, bridging (or inclusive) social capital that promotes generalized reciprocity, or as a guiding principle for us in organizing social and educational systems and institutions that are open (or inclusive), supportive, and trustworthy for all people and that value justice, equality, fairness, and caring for all of the people in the school, the local community, the nation state, and even the globe.

How to Design and Organize Education, Life Space, and Society

Considering *kyosei* as it has been described, a framework for the organizing principles of society and education can be proposed as depicted in Figure 1.6 (Fujita, 1997). Two major points of this framework that differ from Bell's framework (with its three values: efficiency, equality, and self-realization) are

Whither Japanese Schooling?

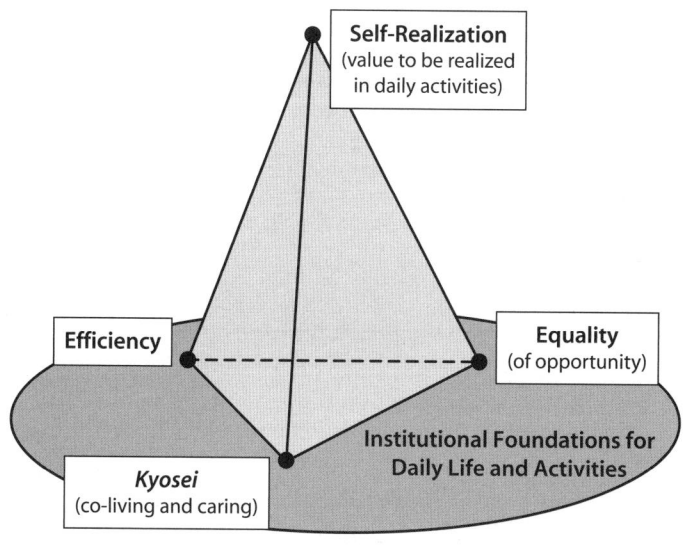

FIGURE 1.6 Organizing Principles of Life Space and Education
Source. Fujita (1997).

the addition of *kyosei* as a fourth value and the drawing of a distinction between self-realization and the other three values. Self-realization is a value to be realized through daily activities and sought in a cultural dimension, whereas the other three values—efficiency, equality, and *kyosei*—are the kinds of values that must be institutionally secured and assured in various systems and organizational arrangements.

Of course, this distinction is not absolute. Efficiency is improved by a better or cheaper way of doing something, and equality of opportunity often depends on treatment or people's attitudes and actions, even when the institutional and organizational arrangements (rules and systems) are essentially equality-oriented. In this respect, *kyosei* is more problematic, because it includes both institutional/organizational and attitudinal/behavioral dimensions. The model shown in Figure 1.6 portrays the following:

1. Social systems, including the educational system, as institutional foundations for daily life and various activities including teaching and learning, should be organized by the core values of efficiency, equality of opportunity, and *kyosei*, as well as other relevant values.
2. Social systems, as well as environments (both natural and artificial), are the stage for daily life, including teaching and learning, and the value of self-realization is pursued and realized through daily activities and practices.

As discussed earlier, however, in educational reforms in Japan (especially since the late 1990s), the value of self-realization has been emphasized and adopted as a major principle for reorganizing the schooling system. These reforms have introduced or expanded such schemes and practices as ability grouping, parental choice of public schools, and creation of 6-year secondary schools, employing such slogans as "Individualization of schooling," "To provide a variety of alternatives and to give freedom of choice," and "To give sufficient chances for smart students to develop their ability." As a result, as of May 2003, ability grouping was practiced in about 87% of public elementary and junior high schools; as of May 2006, parental choice of public schools had been introduced in about 4.4% of districts (74 out of 1,696 districts) at the elementary school level and 7% of districts (93/1,329) at the junior high school level (mostly in the inner wards of Tokyo and in relatively large cities of other prefectures); and as of May 2008, 6-year secondary schools comprised 5.7% of the total (301/5,243 senior high schools). All of these actions differentiate educational opportunity from an early stage of elementary or lower secondary schooling based on a child's ability as evidenced at that point in time—ability that at such an early age tends to be influenced significantly by the economic and cultural capital of the child's family. As discussed earlier, this differentiation of schooling tends to stimulate and increase private concerns with public schooling, and thus not only undermines the basis for equal opportunity but also undermines the basis for *kyosei* or friendly relationships and collaborative activities in the local community, thereby causing a decline in community cohesion and caring. This decline is one of the major reasons for the proliferation of projects for rebuilding local communities since the 1990s.

EDUCATION AS AN UNFINISHED PROJECT

Education is an unfinished project. Of course, its functioning and success depend on the schooling system, formal curriculum, school facilities, and styles of educational administration, school management, and teaching. But these are not sufficient conditions. Education (or teaching and caring) is essentially a labor-intensive project. Its proper functioning and success depend on the continuous, sincere, and appropriate daily practices and efforts of teachers, other school staff, parents, community, local education board staff, and others who care about children's daily life and learning and who collaborate to improve it. It is critically important that all concerned feel they are a part of the network to maintain and improve this unfinished project and are willing to participate in it. For this, the system and institutional and organizational arrangement need to be not exclusive but inclusive, not unfair but fair and trustworthy. Regrettably, educational reforms in Japan, especially since the 1990s, have oriented toward the opposite direction (Fujita, 2006b, 2007c).

In conclusion, one last point must be noted. Both reformers and critics have repeatedly emphasized that dream and dignity are very important and must be cherished among students. As pointed out in this discussion, however, educational reforms in Japan, especially since the 1990s, have differentiated the chances of cherishing dream and dignity between smart students and those of "rich families" versus those who are not smart or who come from poor family backgrounds. Furthermore, public schools and their teachers have been under relentless attack, and the foundations for their autonomy, dream, and dignity have been damaged. It is certain, however, that trust, dignity, dream, and happiness are all critically important for successful schooling, not only for students but also for teachers. These values are the backbone for the continuous, sincere efforts and dedication of all parties.

REFERENCES

Akita, K., & Lewis, C. (2008). *Learning from lessons: Teacher inquiry and lesson study* [*Jugyo no kenkyu, kyoshi no gakushu: Lesson study eno izanai*]. Tokyo: Akashi-shoten.

Asahi Shimbun [*Asahi Shimbun* newspaper]. (2006, November 25). Kyoiku kihonho: "Yokunaru" wazuka 4% [Fundamental Law of Education: Only 4% answered "Becoming better by the revision"]. Morning paper, Tokyo edition, p. b7.

Asahi Shimbun [*Asahi Shimbun* newspaper]. (2008, September 26). Nakayama kokkoso ga mondai hatsugen: Narita «Gonedoku», Nihon wa tan itsu-minzoku, Nikkyoso tsuyoito . . . [Minister of Land, Infrastructure and Transport Nakayama's problematic remark: Narita's gaining advantage by complaining; Japan is a homogeneous state; Strong Japanese teachers union has made . . .]. Morning paper, Tokyo edition, p. 39.

Ball, S. (1993). Education, markets, choice and social class: The market as a class strategy in the UK and the USA. *British Journal of Sociology of Education, 14,* 3–19.

Ball, S. (1994). *Education reform: A critical and post-structural approach.* London: Routledge.

Bell, D. (1976). *The cultural contradictions of capitalism.* New York: Basic Books.

Bernstein, B. (1973a). *Class, codes and control: Vol. 1. Theoretical studies towards a sociology of language.* London: Routledge & Kegan Paul.

Bernstein, B. (1973b). *Class, codes and control: Vol. 2. Applied studies towards a sociology of language.* London: Routledge & Kegan Paul.

Bernstein, B. (1977a). Class and pedagogies: Visible and invisible. In J. Karabel & A. H. Halsey (Eds.), *Power and ideology in education* (pp. 511–534). New York: Oxford University Press.

Bernstein, B. (1977b). *Class, codes and control: Vol. 3. Towards a theory of educational transmissions.* London: Routledge & Kegan Paul.

Bernstein, B. (1977c). Social class, language and socialisation. In J. Karabel & A. H. Halsey (Eds.), *Power and ideology in education* (pp. 473–486). New York: Oxford University Press.

Bernstein, B. (1990). *Class, codes and control: Vol. 4. The structuring of pedagogic discourse.* London: Routledge.

Bernstein, B. (1996). *Pedagogy, symbolic control and identity: Theory, research, critique.* London: Taylor & Francis.

Bourdieu, P. (1979). *La distinction: Critique sociale du jugement.* Paris: Editions de Minuit.

Bourdieu, P., & Passeron, J.-C. (1970). *Reproduction in education, society and culture.* London: Sage. (English version published 1977. R. Nice, Trans.)

Brown, P. (1990). The 'third wave': Education and the ideology of parentology. *British Journal of Sociology of Education, 11,* 65–85.

Brown, P., & Lauder, H. (1992). *Education for economic survival: From Fordism to Post-Fordism?* London: Routledge.
Carson, R. (1962). *Silent spring.* Boston: Houghton Mifflin.
Chubb, J. E., & Moe, T. M. (1990). *Politics, markets, and America's schools.* Washington, DC: The Brookings Institution.
Clune, W. H., & Witte, J. F. (Eds.). (1990). *Choice and control in American education. Vol. 1: Theory of choice and control in American education. Vol. 2: The practice of choice, decentralization and school restructuring.* London: Falmer Press.
Cabinet Office, Government of Japan. (2008). *Seishonen-Hakusho 2008 [White paper on youth, 2008].* Tokyo: Cabinet Office, Government of Japan.
Coleman, J. S. (1988). Social capital in the creation of human capital. *American Journal of Sociology, 94*(Suppl.), S95–S120.
Cookson, P. W. (1994). *School choice: The struggle for the soul of American education.* New Haven, CT: Yale University Press.
Department for Education, UK. (1992). *Choice and diversity: A new framework for schools.* London: HMSO.
Department of Education and Science, UK. (1983). *Police liaison with the Education Service.* London: HMSO.
Finkelstein, B. (Eds.). (1991). *Transcending stereotypes: Discovering Japanese culture and education.* New York: Intercultural Press.
Flude, M., & Hammer, M. (Eds.). (1990). *The Education Reform Act, 1988: Its origins and implications.* London: Falmer Press.
Foljanty-Jost, G. (2003). *Juvenile delinquency in Japan: Reconsidering the "crisis."* Leiden: Kominklijke Brill NV.
Föster, M., & d'Ercole, M. M. (2005). Income distribution and poverty in OECD countries in the second half of the 1990s. *OECD Social Employment and Migration Working Papers, No. 22.*
Fujita, H. (1978). *Education and status attainment in modern Japan.* Doctoral dissertation, Stanford University, Stanford, CA.
Fujita, H. (1980). Shinro-sentaku no mekanism [Mechanism of career choice]. In T. Yamamura & I. Amano (Eds.), *Seinenki no shinro sentaku [Career choice at the stage of adolescence]* (pp. 105–128). Tokyo: Yuhikaku.
Fujita, H. (1982). Kyoiku no kikai [Opportunity for schooling]. In Y. Tomoda (Ed.), *Kyoiku-shakaigaku [Sociology of education]* (pp. 160–182). Tokyo: Yushindo.
Fujita, H. (1989). A crisis of legitimacy in Japanese education: Meritocracy and cohesiveness. In J. J. Shields, Jr. (Ed.), *Japanese schooling: Patterns of socialization, equality, and political control* (pp. 124–138). University Park: Pennsylvania State University Press.
Fujita, H. (1991a). Educational policy dilemmas as historic constructions. In B. Finkelstein, A. E. Imamura, & J. J. Tobin (Eds.), *Transcending stereotypes: Discovering Japanese culture and education.* Yarmouth, ME: Intercultural Press.
Fujita, H. (1991b). *Kodomo, gakko, shakai [Child, school and society: In the irony of the affluence].* Tokyo: The University of Tokyo Press.
Fujita, H. (1991c). Gakkoka/johoka to ningen-keisei-kukan no henyo [The irony and contradictions of the highly schooled and high information society as educational environment]. *Gendaishakaigaku Kenkyu [Contemporary Sociological Studies]: Vol. 4* (pp. 1–33). Sapporo, Japan: Hokkaido Sociological Association.
Fujita, H. (1993). Kyoiku no koukyosei to kyodosei [The publicness and communality/collaboration of education]. In H. Morita, H. Fujita, I. Kurosaki, Y. Katagiri, & M. Sato (Eds.), *Kyoikugaku Nenpo 2 Gakko: Kihan to Bunka [Annals of Education: Vol. 2. The school: Norms and culture]* (pp. 3–33). Tokyo: Seori-shobo.
Fujita, H. (1996). Kyoiku no shijosei/hi-shijosei [The compatibility with marketization of education]. In H. Morita, H. Fujita, I. Kurosaki, Y. Katagiri, & M. Sato (Eds.), *Kyoikugaku*

Nenpo 5 Kyoiku to Shijo [Annals of Education: Vol. 5. Education and market] (pp. 55–95). Tokyo: Seori-shobo.

Fujita, H. (1997). Kyoiku-kaikaku: Kyosei-jidai no gakko-dukuri [Education reform: Schooling in an age of kyosei]. Tokyo: Iwanami-shoten. (Chinese version published in Beijing: Chinese Educational Publishing Co., 2000)

Fujita, H. (1999a). Today's juvenile problem and educational reform in Japan: Its reappraisal and future implications. http://www.childresearch.net/RESOURCE/RESEARCH/1999-1998/FRIEND/DATA3.HTM

Fujita, H. (1999b). 'Shimin-teki kyosei' to kyoiku-kaikaku no kdai ['Civic kyosei' and the tasks of education reform]. In H. Fujita, I. Kurosaki, Y. Katagiri, & M. Sato (Eds.), Kyoikugaku Nenpo 7: Gender to Kyoiku [Annals of Education: Vol. 7. Gender and education] (pp. 375–394). Tokyo: Seori-shobo.

Fujita, H. (1999c). Towareru kyoiku no koukyosei to kyoshi no yakuwari [The publicness of education reexamined and roles of teachers]. In S. Yufu (Ed.), Kyoshi no Genzai, Kyoshoku no Mirai [The present of teachers and the future of teaching profession] (pp. 180–204). Tokyo: Kyoiku-shuppan.

Fujita, H. (2000a). Choice, quality and democracy in education: A comparison of current educational reforms in the United States, the United Kingdom and Japan. http://www.childresearch.net/RESOURCE/RESEARCH/2000/FUJITA/DATA3.HTM

Fujita, H. (2000b). Education reform and education politics in Japan. The American Sociologist, 31(3), 42–57.

Fujita, H. (2000c). Shimin-shakai to kyoiku [Civic society and education]. Tokyo: Seori-shobo.

Fujita, H. (2000d). Crossroads in Japanese education. Japan Quarterly, 47(1), 49–55.

Fujita, H. (2001a). ShinJidai no kyoiku o doukousousuruka [How to design schooling in a new age?]. Tokyo: Iwanami-shoten.

Fujita, H. (2001b). Sengo Nihon niokeru seishonen-moondai/kyoiku-mondai: Sono tenkai to genzai no kadai [Problems of youngsters and education in post-war Japan: Its change and current issues]. In H. Fujita, I. Kurosaki, Y. Katagiri, & M. Sato (Eds.), Kyoikugaku Nenpo 8: Kodomo-mondai [Annals of Education: Vol. 8. Problems of children] (pp. 73–114). Tokyo: Seori-shobo.

Fujita, H. (2003a). Education reform and Japanese education at risk. Gakko-Kyoiku Kenkyu [Bulletin of Japanese Association of School Education], 18, 8–23.

Fujita, H. (2003b). The reform of the Japanese education system as an answer to delinquency. In G. Foljanty-Jost (Ed.), Juvenile delinquency in Japan: Reconsidering the "crisis" (pp. 143–172). Leiden: Brill.

Fujita, H. (2003c). Giji-shijo-teki na kyoiku-seido-kousou no tokucho to mondaiten [Quasi-market models of educational system: Their features and problems]. Kyoiku-shakaigaku Kenkyu [The Journal of Educational Sociology], 72(May), 73–94.

Fujita, H. (2005a). Kyosei: A vision for education and society in the 21st century. In Y. Murakami, N. Kawashima, & S. Chiba (Eds.), Toward a peaceful future: Redefining peace, security, and kyosei from a multidisciplinary perspective. (pp. 53–65). Pullman: Washington State University Press/The Foley Institute.

Fujita, H. (2005b). Gimukyoiku o toinaosu [Compulsory education reexamined]. Tokyo: Chikuma-shobo.

Fujita, H. (2006a). Kyoiku-kaikaku no yukue: Kakusa-shakai ka kyosei-shakai ka [Whither education reform: Differentiated society or kyosei society?]. Tokyo: Iwanami-shoten.

Fujita, H. (2006b). BCQ: Change or reform? Journal of Educational Change, 7, 101–102.

Fujita, H. (2007a). The qualifications of the teaching force in Japan. In R. Ingersoll (Ed.), A comparative study of teacher preparation and qualifications in six nations (pp. 41–54). Madison, WI: CPRE, Consortium for Policy Research in Education.

Fujita, H. (2007b). Kakusa-shakai no kouzou to saiseisan mekanizumu [The structure of a differentiated society and its reproduction mechanism]. In A. Naoi & H. Fujita (Eds.), *Kouza Shakaigaku 13 Kaiso [Sociology Series 13: Stratification]* (pp. 157–200). Tokyo: University of Tokyo Press.

Fujita, H. (Ed.). (2007c). *Dareno tameno 'Kyoiku-saisei' ka [For whom is 'education rebuilding'?]* Tokyo: Iwanami-shoten.

Fujita, H. (2009). How craft knowledge is generated and disseminated in Japan. In J. D. Bransford, D. J. Stipek, N. J. Vye, L. M. Gomez, & D. Lam (Eds.), *The role of research in educational improvement* (pp. 189–207). Cambridge, MA: Harvard Education Press.

Fujita, H., & Wong, S.-Y. (1998/1999). Postmodern restructuring of the knowledge base in Japanese mass education: Crisis of public culture and identity formation. *Education Journal, 26*(2)/27(1), 37–53.

Fuller, B., & Elmore, R. F. (Eds.). (1996). *Who chooses? Who loses? Culture, institutions and the unequal effects of school choice*. New York: Teachers College Press.

Gan, S. (2000). Poverty of children and the system of aid for schooling. *Prism of Economy, 65*, 28–49.

Hara, J., & Seiyama, K. (1999). *Shakai-kaisou: Yutakasa no nakano fubyodou [Social stratification: Inequality in a wealth society]*. Tokyo: University of Tokyo Press.

Illich, I. (1971). *Deschooling society*. New York: Harper & Row.

Illich, I. (1973). *Tools for conviviality*. New York: Harper & Row.

Kariya, T. (2001). *Kaisouka-Nihon to kyoiku-kiki [Stratified Japan and the crisis of education]*. Tokyo: Yushindo.

Kiyonaga, K. (Ed.). (2000). *Sekai no ijime [Bullying in the world]*. Tokyo: Shinzansha.

Lawrence, R. (1998). *School crime and juvenile justice*. New York: Oxford University Press.

Lewis, C. (2002). Does lesson study have a future in the United States? *Nagoya Journal of Education and Human Development, 1*, 1–23.

Meadows, D. H., Meadows, D. L., Randers, J., & Behrens, W. W., III. (1972). *The limits to growth: A report for the Club of Rome's project on the predicament of mankind*. New York: Universe Books.

Ministry of Health, Labor and Welfare. (2008). *Roudoukeizai-hakusho 2008 nendo-ban [White paper on the labor economy, 2008]*. Ministry of Health, Labor and Welfare, Japan.

Morita, Y. (Ed.). (1998). *Sekai no ijime [Bullying in the world]*. Tokyo: Kaneko-shobo.

Murakami, Y., Kawashima, N., & Chiba, S. (Eds.). (2005). *Toward a peaceful future: Redefining peace, security, and kyosei from a multidisciplinary perspective*. Pullman, WA: Washington State University Press/The Foley Institute.

National Commission on Excellence in Education. (1983). *A nation at risk: The imperative for educational reform*. Washington, DC: U.S. Government Printing Office.

Nihon Keizai Shinbun [The *Nikkei* newspaper]. (2006, November 28). Kyoiku-Kihonho-an "Kon-Kokkai de" 19%; Jimin-Shijiso mo 25% Domari [Bill of revising Fundamental Law of Education: Only 19% answered "To be voted in this Diet" and 25% even among the supporters of Liberal Democratic Party]. Morning paper, Tokyo edition, p. 2.

OECD (Organisation for Economic Co-operation and Development). (2005). Education at a glance, 2005: OECD indicators. Retrieved September 1, 2009, from www.oecd.org/dataoecd/44/26/35333415.pdf

OECD (Organisation for Economic Co-operation and Development). (2007). Education at a glance, 2007: OECD indicators. Retrieved September 1, 2009, from www.minocw.nl/documenten/39313286[1].pdf

OECD Examiners. (1971). *Nihon no kyoiku-seisaku [Educational policy, Japan]* (J. Fukashiro, Trans.). Tokyo: Asahi Shinbun.

Park, R. E. (1952). *Human communities: The city and human ecology*. Glencoe, IL: Free Press.

Park, R. E., Burgess, E. W., & McKenzie, R. D. (1925). *The city.* Chicago: The University of Chicago Press.

Putnam, R. (1995). Bowling alone: America's declining social capital. *Journal of Democracy, 6*(1), 65–78.

Putnam, R. D. (2000). *Bowling alone: The collapse and revival of American community.* New York: Simon & Schuster.

Putnam, R. D. (2001). Community-based social capital and educational performance. In D. Ravitch & J. P. Viteritti (Eds.), *Making good citizens: Education and civil society.* New Haven, CT: Yale University Press.

Research and Training Institute, Ministry of Justice. (2006). *Hanzai-hakusho 2006 nendo-ban* [White paper on crime, 2006]. Tokyo: Research and Training Institute, Ministry of Justice, Japan.

Sato, M. (1995). *Learning: Its death and resuscitation* [Manabi: Sono shi to saisei]. Tokyo: TaroJiro-sha.

Sato, M. (1997). *Aporia of being teacher* [Kyoshi toiu aporia]. Tokyo: Seori-shobo.

Sato, M. (1999). *Pleasure of learning* [Manabi no kairaku]. Tokyo: Seori-shobo.

Sato, T. (2000). *Fubyodo-shakai Nihon* [Unequal society Japan]. Tokyo: ChuoKouron-sha.

Shields, J. J., Jr. (Ed.). (1989). *Japanese schooling: Patterns of socialization, equality, and political control.* University Park: Pennsylvania State University Press.

Shimahara, N. K., & Sakai, A. (1995). *Learning to teach in two cultures: Japan and the United States.* New York: Garland.

Shirahase, S. (Ed.). (2006). *Henkasuru shakai no fubyodo* [Changing social inequality]. Tokyo: University of Tokyo Press.

Stevenson, H. W., & Stigler, J. W. (1992). *The learning gap: Why our schools are failing and what we can learn from Japanese and Chinese education.* New York: Simon & Schuster.

Tachibanaki, T. (1998). *Nihon no keizai-kakusa* [Economic differentials in Japan]. Tokyo: Iwanami Shoten.

Tachibanaki, T. (2006). *Kakusa-shakai* [Differentiated society]. Tokyo: Iwanami Shoten.

Tyack, D. B. (1974). *The one best system: A history of American urban education.* Cambridge, MA: Harvard University Press.

Tyack, D. B. (1990). 'Restructuring' in historical perspective, tinkering toward utopia. *Teachers College Record, 92*(2), 170–191.

Vogel, E. F. (1979). *Japan as number one: Lessons for America.* Cambridge, MA: Harvard University Press.

Whitty, G., Power, S., & Halpin, D. (1988). *Devolution and choice in education: The school, the state and the market.* Buckingham, UK: Open University Press.

TAKEHIKO KARIYA

The End of Egalitarian Education in Japan?

The Effects of Policy Changes in Resource Distribution on Compulsory Education

ADVANCED SOCIETIES have faced difficulties in maintaining "welfare states." One solution—investment in human capital—has been given special attention and accorded special status in global policy discussions (Esping-Andersen, Gallie, Hemerijk, & Myers, 2002; Giddens, 1998). Educational reforms have been regarded as part of this solution because of their capacity to enhance human capital, thereby providing "full employability" to everyone. But unlike direct redistribution of socioeconomic resources (e.g., unemployment benefits, provision of public jobs, or other kinds of welfare payments), the policies aimed at improving employability through education and training reforms are really a matter of providing *opportunities* rather than guaranteed compensations. In this sense, equality of educational opportunity becomes a more important issue than ever before.

On the other hand, advanced societies also encounter severe global competition. "Knowledge-based economies" or "high-skills societies" require new types of skills or competencies of workers, such as problem solving, communication, teamwork, and so forth, in addition to high cognitive skills. Corresponding to these changing demands, educational reforms in many advanced societies have targeted the development of students' new skills or competencies, including such "soft skills" as problem solving, communication, and self-learning. This trend is seen not only in education but also in the workplace, where on-the-job training emphasizes more and more of these new skills. Without these skills, or the opportunity to learn them, one is placed in a less advantaged employment position. Here again, equality of education and training to facilitate learning of these skills has become more important as a social equity issue than in the past.

These two mega-trends go together under the long-term process that is globalization. These trends also necessitate recruitment and training of more highly skilled/qualified teachers, better pedagogical methods and materials, and better organized learning environments. In other words, more investment in education, more efficient mechanisms of educational resource allocation, and more appropriate measures of "accountability" are all needed to achieve high levels of human capital development and equity of access to education and training. This makes the twin issues of limited resources and funding for education especially salient. In this chapter, I focus on recent policy changes in educational resource allocation at the compulsory education level. In particular, I pay attention to the policy changes in the financing of the teaching professions (under the name of "decentralization of tax" reforms). These policy changes raise new questions about equality of educational opportunity and the roles of the central government regarding provision of compulsory (i.e., mass) education.

In the United States, many studies have been done on the effectiveness of public education expenditures. Some studies, including the famous Coleman Report (Coleman et al., 1966), deny strong independent effects of school expenditures on students' academic achievement after controlling for their socioeconomic background, whereas others show positive and significant net effects of public expenditures on schooling (see comprehensive review articles by Hanushek, 1986, 1989). Thus, in the United States, research findings on the net effect of expenditures on school education are mixed. It is also true that there are enormous disparities in per-student expenditures among different school districts, although the net effect is unclear.

It may be surprising for foreign observers to find that, in contrast to the United States, there are few such studies in Japan. There are good reasons why Japan has almost no studies on the issue. First, unlike the United States, the central government in Japan has played a large role in subsidizing school expenditures, including teachers' salaries, to equalize the quality of education. As discussed in detail later, the Japanese way of subsidizing compulsory education differs greatly from that in the United States and other countries. Thanks to Japan's centralized system, expenditures for compulsory education, particularly for teachers' allowances, are progressively allocated. The poorer regions are paid more by the government than are the wealthier regions. Because of this "progressive redistribution" of educational finances, both researchers and policymakers in Japan have not had to pay much attention to the issue of inequality of expenditures as a cause of inequality in education in general.

Second, differences in academic achievement among students were generally much smaller in Japan than in the United States. International comparative studies, such as the Trends in International Mathematics and Science Study (TIMSS) and the Programme for International Student Assessment (PISA), confirm that distributions of Japanese students' test scores are narrower than in other countries, including the United States. Western observers, such as Cummings (1980), have characterized Japanese education as highly egalitarian, which, some of them even said, contributed to greater social equality as well. Although most recent international studies indicate that score distributions of Japanese students are no longer as narrow as those of some other countries, the belief that Japanese education is egalitarian is still strong among many Japanese and foreign observers. Because of this, few studies have examined the allocation of educational expenditures.

Third, Japanese society and education evince a sort of taboo about discussing inequality in school. Under the "mass education society" regime, almost everyone has experienced education selection meritocratically through the high school entrance examination system (Kariya, 1995), with enrollment for secondary education over 90% and that for higher education more than 30% since the mid-1950s. As a result, there was a strong consensus among educators and the population in general that sorting children into differently ranked schools was a form of "discrimination" based on ability. Curiously, in Japan, selection according to individual ability is viewed as a form of meritocracy, but any sorting-out practice that could have given students a feeling of inferiority is regarded as "discriminatory education" (*sabetsu kyoiku*). Thus, there has been a long-term desire in Japan to avoid seeing relationships between students' achievement or ability and their socioeconomic status. Until recently, Japanese schools did not allow researchers to ask about students' socioeconomic background, even in international surveys like TIMSS or PISA. Due to this strong aversion to seeing differences, educators and education administrators avoided possible connections between inequality and socioeconomic backgrounds.

The analyses presented in this chapter break this taboo by sociologically examining what the financial structures and practices for compulsory education in Japan mean and considering the possible impact of current policy reform proposals on the future of Japanese education. I will first briefly explain how national subsidies (the national funds for public schools) are distributed over compulsory education to cover personnel costs (i.e., teacher salaries) and what the system means with regard to equality of educational opportunity. Then, I will present budget estimates of teachers' salaries and allowances in different prefectures over the next 14 years and discuss what damage the proposed policy reforms would inflict if implemented in their current state. Finally, I discuss the societal impact of these proposed changes for the future of Japanese education and society in terms of social and educational inequality.

HOW ARE RESOURCES FOR COMPULSORY EDUCATION DISTRIBUTED IN JAPAN?

Equality of educational opportunity is globally recognized as an important value in modern society because it is expected to make possible a "fair" society. In fact, economic and social resources are quite often distributed unequally.

Therefore, to gain differentiated resources and life chances, a basic rule of society is the creation of fair competitions, and education plays a major role in this. Despite the universally accepted importance of the value of equal educational opportunity, the various ways to realize it differ greatly among different societies. In some countries, "free education," which waives any fees for enrollment in schools and universities, is regarded as the main instrument of attaining equality of educational opportunity. In others, "open admission" to people regardless of their wealth, ethnicity, or gender (though "merits" may be seriously considered) governs eligibility for entering secondary or higher education institutions.

Even in compulsory education, there are various ways in which different countries guarantee equal opportunity. Focusing only on ways of distributing resources for compulsory education, we can distinguish three types. The first type is provision of minimum free schooling for a certain number of years. In this type, every child should be given a chance to have a certain length of schooling, even though the curricula, teacher quality, school budget, and school physical and cultural conditions might be dissimilar. Countries like the United States, with a decentralized education system, tend to be in this category. Because often the poorer districts can pay less for compulsory education per student than the wealthier districts, this type of equal opportunity for compulsory education has difficulty increasing equality in education. In a sense, we can call this a "regressive distribution" of compulsory education resources.

The second type is more centralized financially: Budget and other physical and personnel resources are distributed equally, giving each school or school district some discretion in conducting their own affairs. In this type, the cost of education is usually calculated based on a per capita formula. Sometimes, as in the United Kingdom, additional funding is given to the disadvantaged, but basically this approach distributes education expenditures equally to each student. So, we can call this type an "even distribution" of compulsory education expenditures.

The third type is similar to the present Japanese practice, and we call it a "progressive distribution" of compulsory education resources. In this type, the cost for education is usually calculated based on "needs" in order to equalize quality of education in *each school* rather than on a per capita basis. To do this, poorer districts and schools are usually paid more per student than wealthier districts. Under this system, national tax revenue is redistributed in a progressive way to equalize not just length of education but quality of education.

Despite such great differences among nations, compulsory education is (with small differences in concerns) believed to be the infrastructure of equality of educational opportunity. Because every household with school-age children is obliged to send their children to school under compulsory education, the means of providing compulsory education is key to understanding how each society successfully or unsuccessfully creates myths of equality of educational opportunity.

The foregoing explanations are based on more or less ideal types. I will next explain briefly how the current Japanese system works and consider what it means sociologically with regard to egalitarianism in Japanese education. From 1952, with the enactment of the State Subsidies Law for Compulsory Education, until 2005, the central government was legally required to pay half of teachers' salaries and other allowances. Another law, the Class Size and School Staff Standards Act, mandated that each prefecture calculate the number of staff needed. The maximum size of each classroom is set at 40 students, and using the numbers of students and schools, with some consideration of the geographical allocations of schools and special needs, the number of staff needed is calculated. Then, applying a nationally standardized pay scale as reference (though each prefecture is not required to use this scale for actual payment), necessary expenditures for personnel for compulsory education are calculated. In the end, the central government paid about half of this amount for each prefecture and the prefecture paid the other half.

In practice, under this procedure, per capita costs for compulsory education among prefectures differ greatly. In 2004, in the most expensive prefecture, Kochi, each school child cost 865,000 yen (about $8,000) per year just for teaching staff salaries and other allowances, while in the least expensive prefecture, Saitama, the amount was about 470,000 yen (roughly $4,300)—about 1.8 times more for Kochi than Saitama. Kochi is one of the poorest prefectures in terms of its local government budget and average household resources. It also has to maintain many small schools in mountainous areas. In contrast, Saitama is located near Tokyo and is a relatively wealthy prefecture. Thus, to equalize conditions of education, the central government pays almost two times more in expenditures to educate Kochi children (in terms of personnel cost for compulsory education than to educate children in Saitama. This cost far exceeds expectations for a simple per capita calculation under an ideal "even" distribution (the second type discussed above) and goes beyond that indicated for the first type, a "regressive" distribution of education resources.

In this sense, Japan's first nine years of education are some of the most egalitarian among advanced countries in terms of expenditures. The provision of such egalitarian compulsory education successfully provides a strong basis for a social consciousness that the "starting line" is set equally for every child until the end of the middle school years, even though many would consider this a myth or an illusion of "mass education society." Empirical research has shown that Japan, in fact, is not an equal society (Ishida, 1993; Sato, 2000). My previous work described Japan as an unequal mass society created, in part, by mass education (Kariya, 1995). In an objective sense, revealed by empirical sociological analysis of available data, Japanese society has never been an egalitarian society and its education system has never been truly egalitarian. However, the State succeeded in projecting a strong image that there was equal opportunity in compulsory education. The progressive distribution of educational finances for compulsory education was used, in part, as a symbol for policies and practices the State deliberately allowed in order to lend credence to the belief in equal educational opportunity. Whether or not access to quality education is evenly distributed is still an empirical question but, as discussed earlier, the Japanese government has so far successfully mitigated people's suspicions about unequal conditions of education. Consequently, Japanese society is more supportive of educational policy, and is far less driven by such disputes, than is the populace of the United States.

RECENT POLICY CHANGES AND THE POTENTIAL CRISIS IN EGALITARIAN EDUCATION

Centralized education systems can successfully distribute resources and budget allocations equally to different regions. In addition, several other national mechanisms contribute to equalizing educational quality, and thus educational opportunity, in Japan. These include a national curriculum, nationally inspected school textbooks, a nationally controlled teacher training and certification system, and nationally regulated physical school conditions and environment. By providing similar socialization experiences within and among school environments, as well as imposing similar cognitive demands on students, these mechanisms and systems of equalization tend to hide the influence of family background on a child's socialization. Although there are obvious and substantial family-related environmental differences for children when they enter the compulsory education system, the egalitarian subsidy policies conceal starting-line disparities between culturally advantaged and disadvantaged families.

On the other hand, such an intensely centralized system has been criticized because it deprives local school districts and schools of self-governance. Too-strong control from the central government, called "the domination of Ministry of Education" (*monkashoshihai*), is thought of as an evil in Japanese education, particularly by liberal researchers on education and by school teachers. Not only educators, but liberal political scientists and economists as well, severely criticize the dominance and control by the Ministry of Education (MEXT) over local schools. Supported by long-time antagonism against MEXT dominance, the decentralization of central government power, particularly fiscal decentralization, has been on the discussion table for policy changes since Prime Minister Junichiro Koizumi's structural reform planning began in the early 2000s.

In 2004, the government decided on a plan to transfer tax-collecting authority worth 3 trillion yen to local governments and cut the same amount in subsidies to offset the revenue loss. Out of the 3 trillion yen, about 0.85 trillion yen in subsidies for teachers' salaries from MEXT was targeted for transfer. Finally, in December 2005, the government decided to shift this amount of responsibility to local governments by reducing the federal support rate for teachers' salaries from 50% to 33%. The government is still discussing whether or not all of the national subsidy system will be abolished in the future in order to transfer more of the tax-collecting authority from the central government to the local governments. In addition, abolition of the Class Size and School Staff Standards Act was proposed, and introduction of a per capita base calculation for financing personnel expenditures for school education was suggested. Behind this is a serious problem of national and local government debt and the necessity for severe budget cutting to balance the national budget. The current egalitarian subsidy system for compulsory education is about to disappear.

WHAT WILL HAPPEN IF THE GOVERNMENT ABOLISHES THE SUBSIDY SYSTEM?

Groups of local politicians, mayors, and governors were active in trying to abolish the centralized subsidy system. They thought transferring about 0.85 trillion yen worth of tax-collecting authority to local governments could increase their autonomy and discretion over their local budgets. They seemed to expect that because the number of school-age children is declining, they could cut down the total cost for compulsory education, and therefore their control over local budgets would increase if the tax-collecting authority is transferred to them. However, they are wrong. My prediction, based on calculations of future teachers' salaries and other allowances, such as retirement benefits, pension fees, and so on, shows that the total cost for compulsory education will not decrease but will increase, even though the number of students will decrease. As shown in Figure 2.1, the age distribution of teachers in public elementary and middle schools is strongly skewed toward those who are in their middle 40s and 50s. About 70% of elementary school teachers and approximately two thirds of middle school teachers are older than 40. In the next 10–15 years, this mass of middle-aged teachers will retire, after having received yearly salary increases. In the Japanese public employment system, it is hard to dismiss these "expensive" teachers, due to life-long employment customs. Thus, retirement benefits (which are paid through yearly local budgets), plus salaries that increase yearly for the active teachers, will produce incremental increases in personnel expenditures for compulsory education, despite the declining number of school children.

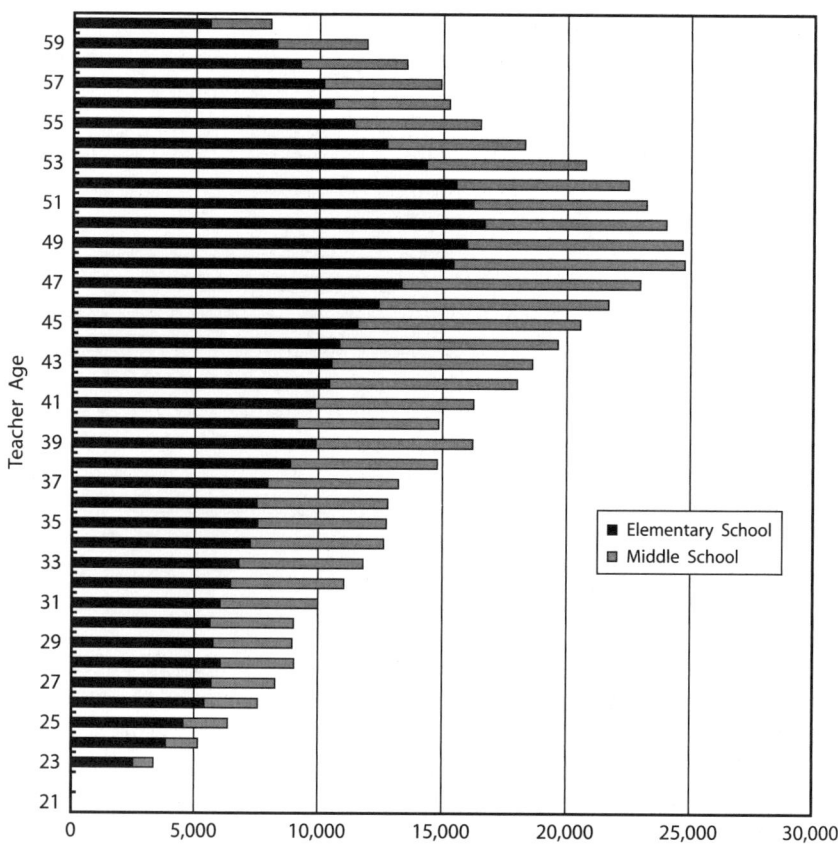

FIGURE 2.1 The Age Distribution of Teachers in Public Elementary and Middle Schools

More importantly, the amount of incremental cost per student will increase among different prefectures at different rates. Different age distributions and student populations in the 47 prefectures will cause these results. Such differences will give rise to unequal pressures on local budgets in different prefectures at different times. Taking age distributions and predicted future student numbers for each prefecture into consideration, I calculated future personnel expenditures for compulsory education in 47 prefectures until 2018.

Before examining the details, a look at the total change in expenditures will provide a quick orientation. As shown in Table 2.1, compared with the total cost in 2004, beginning in 2007, every year about 30–40 billion yen more than the 2004 expenditure will have to be paid for all forms of teachers'

TABLE 2.1 Predicted Total Personnel Cost for Compulsory Education Relative to Cost in 2004

Year	Total cost (100 million yen)	Difference from year 2004
2004	589	0
2005	594	5
2006	608	19
2007	619	30
2008	623	34
2009	625	36
2010	624	35
2011	626	37
2012	629	40
2013	631	42
2014	632	43
2015	630	41
2016	627	38
2017	624	35
2018	620	31

allowances across all of Japan, and this level of expenditure will continue for more than 10 years. I also computed the average personnel cost among the 47 prefectures, standard deviations, and ratios between the means and standard deviations, from 2004 to 2018. The ratio between the means and standard deviations is called the coefficient of variation, providing a normalized measure of dispersion of a probability distribution. The ratio increased from 0.126 in 2004 to 0.142 in 2018, indicating that the degree of difference among the 47 prefectures is expanding. That is, the gap of per capita cost for compulsory education is expanding at different rates among different prefectures. Calculation of the difference between the most and least expensive prefectures per capita also shows that the gap between the maximum and minimum cost is increasing. In sum, as long as the government tries to maintain equal quality of education in its present form, more expenditures must be made.

Figure 2.2 shows the changes in correlation coefficients between the year 2001 indicators of financial power (i.e., an index of the ratio between local tax revenues and expenditures needed in each prefecture; the smaller the index, the weaker the financial power) and the rates of increase for future expenditures for compulsory education (2004 is the base year). Correlations are positive until 2010, after which negative correlations appear and the absolute value of these increases over time. This result indicates that for the next several years, financially more powerful prefectures will face greater increases in personnel cost for compulsory education than financially weak prefectures. However, from 2011 on, this tendency will be reversed; then, poorer prefec-

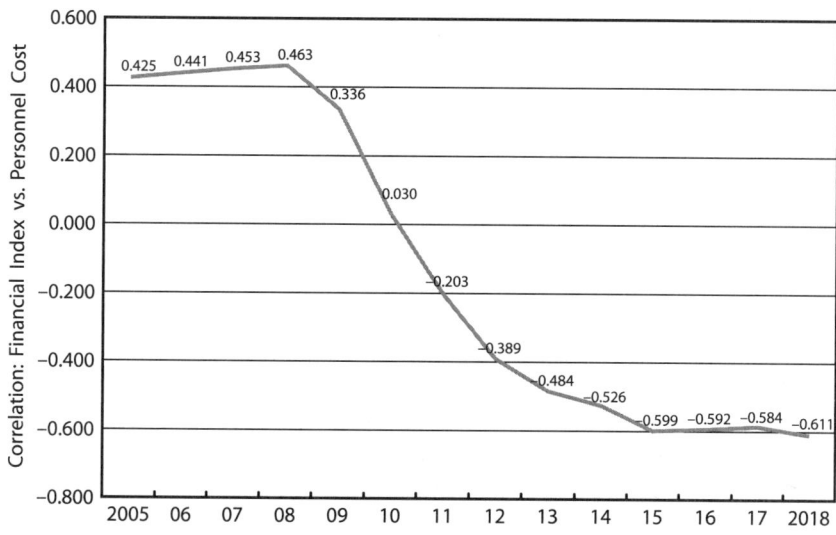

FIGURE 2.2 Correlations Between the Financial Index in 2001 and Increasing Rates of Predicted Total Personnel Cost for Compulsory Education (from 2005 to 2018, with 2004 as the base year)

tures will need more money to maintain the same quality of compulsory education compared with wealthier prefectures. This will occur because financially richer prefectures hired many teachers during the 1970s to accommodate geographical migrations to urban industrial areas and increased numbers of school age children. This movement created an increased demand for teachers earlier than in other prefectures. These teachers are retiring earlier (in the 1990s and 2000s) than those in other prefectures. The latter teachers were hired during the early 1980s, when the second baby boomers reached school attendance age. These teachers will reach retirement age after about 2010, which will increase the cost for compulsory education in those many prefectures in the future.

Finally, Figure 2.3 shows correlations between personnel cost per capita for the future and the percentage of schools designated as having special needs for education in remote regions. The correlation coefficients have positive signs and their absolute terms decline at first but increase after 2008. That is, prefectures with special needs for remote education will face increasing per-student costs for compulsory education in the future.

Of course, as long as the national government's subsidies continue, no serious problems might arise. However, if the subsidies are abolished or the amount is reduced, poorer prefectures must face a shortage of finances to maintain quality education. In addition, the highly skewed age distribution

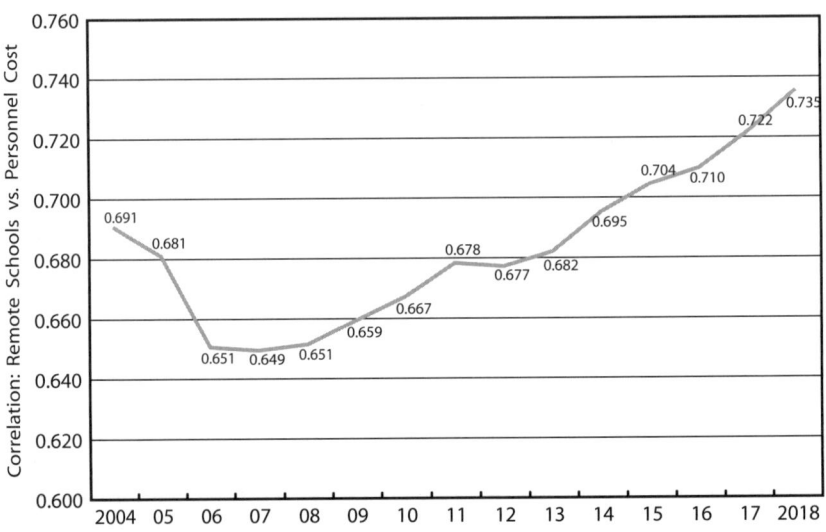

FIGURE 2.3 Correlations Between Percentage of Elementary Schools of Designated as Remote School in 2003 and Predicted Per Capita Personnel Cost for Compulsory Education (from 2004 to 2018)

of teachers means that in the near future there will be a great demand for teachers. Competition among prefectures for recruiting good teachers result from such a shortage. Poorer prefectures will be in disadvantaged positions in such competitions, because their limited budgets will weaken their bargaining power for hiring good teachers in competition with wealthier prefectures. Results of the competition for recruiting new teachers may worsen the inequality in compulsory education. Money will also count in terms of the quality of education. Where a child is born and educated will matter even more than it does today. Japan is just turning the corner.

CONCLUSION

Educational policies are now at a precarious point in Japan. If the nationally subsidized system is abolished in the name of decentralization, each local government may be given more discretion to decide how much should be paid for compulsory education. It is often misunderstood in Japan that issues of the State's control and regulation over education, on the one hand, and the centralized system of subsidies for education, on the other hand, are not necessarily linked. Some critics argue that the financial subsidies system of the State is linked with its power to control regional administrations, boards of education, and the curricula of schools. However, looking at the relations between these two elements carefully, one finds, strictly speaking, that the State Subsidies Law for Compulsory Education has nothing to do with other aspects of the State's control over education. Nonetheless, advocates whose goal is decentralization of education tend to regard it as a source of power of the State to control many other aspects of local education. Therefore, unless additional administrative decentralization follows, even if the budgetary system is decentralized, centralized control over national curricula or other regulations may be left unchanged. In a worst-case scenario, financial discretion will simply increase the "freedom" of local governments to implement budget cuts for compulsory education, leaving other controls of the State over local education as they are.

In a "high skills" society (Brown, Green, & Lauder, 2001), schools are given a more difficult and complicated task to provide "best practices" education for all students. To attain these goals, better learning environments and more skilled teachers are required than were needed previously. All of these requirements equal increasing costs for public education, particularly for the earliest stages of schooling. As human capital formation becomes more complicated—and its results become more crucial for individual life-chance determination—"equality" in education becomes more important. In particular, if inequality in education expands in the early stages in schooling (Kariya, 2001), people's belief in the fairness of meritocratic systems of educational competition will erode. To maintain this sense of fairness, the Japanese government has implemented a progressive distribution of resources for compulsory education. But now the system is in transition toward a more decentralized and, consequently, more unequal distribution. This shift not only will expand inequality in educational finances among different regions but also will deprive people of a sense of fairness in educational competitions. The Japanese myth of egalitarian education and society is on the edge of vanishing at the gates of a neoliberal-led "capitalist learning society" (Kariya, 2006).

REFERENCES

Brown, P., Green, A., & Lauder, H. (2001). *High skills: Globalization, competitiveness, and skill formation.* Oxford, UK: Oxford University Press.
Coleman, J. S., Campbell, E. Q., Hobson, C. J., McPartland, J., Mood, A. M., Weinfeld, F. D., & York, R. L. (1966). *Equality of educational opportunity* (DHEW Report No. OE-38001). Washington, DC: U.S. Government Printing Office.
Cummings, W. K. (1980). *Education and equality in Japan.* Princeton, NJ: Princeton University Press.
Esping-Andersen, G., Gallie, D., Hemerijk, A., & Myers, J. (2002). *Why we need a welfare state.* Oxford, UK: Oxford University Press.
Giddens, A. (1998). *The third way: The renewal of social democracy.* Cambridge, UK: Polity Press.

Hanushek, Eric A. (1986). The economics of schooling: Production and efficiency in public schools. *Journal of Economic Literature, 24,* 1141–1177.

Hanushek, Eric A. (1989). The impact of differential expenditures on school performance. *Education Researcher, 18,* 45–51.

Ishida, H. (1993). *Social mobility in contemporary Japan: Educational credentials, class and the labour market in a cross-national perspective.* London: Macmillan.

Kariya, T. (1995). *Taishu kyoiku shakai no yukue* [Mass education society]. Tokyo: Chuo-koron-shinsha.

Kariya, T. (2001). *Kaisoka nihon to kyoiku kiki* [Increasingly stratified Japan and the educational crisis]. Tokyo: Yushindo.

Kariya, T. (2006, February). *The ending of diploma society and where to go next? The answer is going towards a "learning capitalist" society.* Paper presented at the conference "Ending the Postwar?" Sheffield University, Sheffield, UK.

Sato, T. (2000). *Fubyodoshakai Nippon.* Tokyo: ChuoKoron-Shinsha.

MAMORU TSUKADA

Educational Stratification

Teacher Perspectives on School Culture and the College Entrance Examination

THIS CHAPTER examines how the college entrance examination system was constructed historically after World War II and how it has affected high school cultures, through an analysis of high school teachers' narratives pertaining to their experiences in various kinds of high schools in Aichi Prefecture, a region of eastern Japan in and around the city of Nagoya. The interview data for this analysis come from narratives described in *Jukentaisei to kyoshi no raifukousu* (*The entrance exam system and teachers' life course*) (Tsukada, 1998). All interview data quoted in this chapter are selected from interviews with 19 male high school teachers conducted between 1995 and 1996. The names of all teachers in this chapter are pseudonyms to the individuals' privacy. Except for Togo High School, the names of all high schools are also pseudonyms.

The discussion will focus on the political conflict between the teachers' union and the Department of Education of Aichi and how the conflict has affected educational policies there. In Aichi Prefecture this conflict was particularly intense due to increased socioeconomic development and shifts in educational policies, changes that contributed to shaping the hierarchical structure of high schools in Aichi. Second, the chapter describes the diversity of high school cultures by applying a two-dimensional typology in terms of school culture and dominant curriculum orientation. The characteristics of four distinctive types of high schools based on this typology are also illustrated by drawing on teachers' narratives. Finally, in conclusion, I argue that the ways in which the teachers viewed the different types of high schools may have contributed to maintaining the hierarchy of high schools and reproducing high school cultures appropriate for the school's relative position in the hierarchy.

HIGH SCHOOLS IN AICHI PREFECTURE

During the period of political upheaval of the late 1960s and 1970s, the teachers' union for high schools in Aichi Prefecture followed a Communist party–oriented political line, while the union for elementary and junior high school teachers followed a less radical, Socialist party–oriented political line. In following radical strategies and tactics, many high school teachers participated in various political activities, greatly intensifying the political conflict between the teachers' union and the Department of Education of Aichi Prefecture. Gradually, the Department of Education began to employ a series of policies to reduce the political influence of the teachers' union. One was the establishment in 1968 of Togo High School, which would serve as a model for all new high schools in the prefecture. The principal of Togo High School was given absolute administrative power over all educational processes, and a branch of the prefecture teachers' union was prohibited from being organized there. While a few of the teachers with administrative duties were in their 40s and 50s, the vast majority of teachers were in their 20s and were expected to follow their senior colleagues without questioning their authority. The high schools that followed the Togo High School model were called *Shinsetsukou* (newly established high schools). They had a different school culture from high schools established before 1968. The characteristics of the *Shinsetsukou* will be described in detail later in this chapter in connection with a discussion of the different types of high schools in Aichi Prefecture. The "comprehensive-equalizing policies" at the national level also affected Aichi Prefecture's entrance examination system but the effect there was not as drastic as in schools in Tokyo and Kyoto, where the policies were extensively implemented to equalize the academic levels of all of the public schools, which had traditionally had different levels of prestige.

In 1971, the Department of Education of Aichi announced the *Gakkougun* system for the purpose of eliminating the academic gaps between high schools and solving the problem of "examination hell." The Department of Education of Aichi explained:

> In 1956 the high school entrance rate was only 40% but in 1972 the rate became 92%. Students wanted to apply to so-called "prestigious schools," which had history and tradition. As a result, students with excellent academic achievement were likely to concentrate on applying to these schools and the gap between the public academic high schools, in terms of the entrance exam average scores of entering students, became more than 20 points, which shows a clear academic gap between the public high schools. The competition to enter these prestigious high schools has been intensified, and some students stay up until 1 a.m. or 2 a.m. to study for the entrance examination to the high schools. This phenomenon cannot be ignored because it is bad for growing children's health. (*Kyoikujihou*, 1972, p. 137)

After emphasizing the negative aspect of the academic gaps between high schools and overcompetitiveness for admission to certain prestigious high schools, the Department of Education of Aichi began to implement the *Gakkougun* system as an educational reform, as follows (*Kyoikujihou*, 1972, p. 128):

- The number of required subjects for entrance examinations changed from five to three.
- In the admission process, high school grade point average (GPA) and teachers' evaluations would be seriously considered. Subjects for which exams were not required would be evaluated on the basis of students' academic records and the record of school extracurricular activities. Teachers' evaluations of students as individuals in junior high schools would also be taken into consideration.
- Among the *Gakkougun* schools, the distribution of entering students to given high schools would be processed fairly and rigidly. Specifically, the academic record, GPA, and scores on the entrance exam would be used to equalize the academic level of students among the *Gakkougun* schools. This would be done without any subjective data but only with objective data so that students would be distributed by chance.

Through this program, the Department of Education intended to reduce the academic gaps among high schools and eliminate "examination hell." But actually these objectives reflected the formalistic egalitarianism that emerged in the 1970s. The system did not reflect the thoughts of parents and students. Moreover, the system was applied only to high schools in Nagoya city, the most urban area of the prefecture, and to high schools in medium-sized cities that had traditional prestige. All of the newly established high schools as well as the high schools in small cities and in the countryside were excluded from the reform. In this sense, there was a crucial difference between those high schools that were part of the *Gakkougun* system and all other high schools. This affected the nature of the hierarchical ranking of high schools in Aichi Prefecture because many high schools that had been established after the creation of Togo High School were excluded from the *Gakkougun* system. High schools in Aichi have had to compete for their relative position in the hierarchy of high schools since the early 1970s. In the 1980s, affected by the National Council on Educational Reform, the Aichi Department of Education regarded "multiple chances for entrance examinations," "the expansion of freedom in school choice," and "diversity of the selection processes" as key policy objectives and changed their entrance examination policy from "formalistic egalitarianism" to "meritocracy." Under this national reform in education, Aichi Prefecture implemented a new entrance exam system for public high schools in 1989.

The new system was intended to expand the options of school choice from one public school to two public schools and changed the selection process.

Under the new system, a policy of admission through recommendation was employed by all public schools, and individuality was positively evaluated by emphasizing the importance of the students' performance in interviews. Thus, this new system was intended to diversify the selection processes for all public high schools. However, newspapers reported that the new system promoted "revival of former elite high schools," "the intensification of the entrance examination to high schools," and "the enforcement of control over education." *Chunichi* Newspapers (November 12, 1989) reported in a special issue that public high schools with tradition and prestige had become more competitive than before and that more students entered private high schools with their safer orientation in evaluating exam and interview results. Three years after this new system was implemented, it was argued that the hierarchical structure of high schools had been reinforced, and traditional public schools had revived their successful results in the college entrance exam. In sum, the hierarchical structure of high schools was first intensified by the increase of newly established high schools in the 1960s and 1970s as a result of economic development and educational expansion, and then further strengthened by the reform of entrance exams late in the 1980s. Consequently, the high school entrance exam system has become the predominant influence in every high school in Aichi Prefecture (*Chunichi* Newspapers, April 6, 1992).

THE DIVERSITY OF HIGH SCHOOLS IN AICHI PREFECTURE: A TYPOLOGY OF HIGH SCHOOLS

The social changes and educational policy changes described in the foregoing discussion, especially those affecting the entrance examination system, have shaped the peculiar hierarchy of public high schools in Aichi Prefecture. In this section, the high schools in Aichi will be described in terms of their respective characteristics that have developed as a result of their relative positions in the hierarchy. For the sake of simplifying the later discussion of diversified high schools, a hypothetical typology of high schools is constructed here by drawing upon teachers' narratives. Based on an examination of these narratives, two dimensions that distinguish the types of high schools and characterize school culture and the dominant curriculum can be identified; these are shown in Figure 3.1. One dimension is control orientation versus freedom orientation, and the other is college entrance exam orientation versus life guidance orientation. In the first dimension, control versus freedom, one can categorize schools according to whether the school emphasizes its control over students or allows students the freedom to do anything at school. The meaning of control is not the one criticized by the mass media and expressed in a typical slogan of union teachers: "inhuman treatment of students and

Educational Stratification

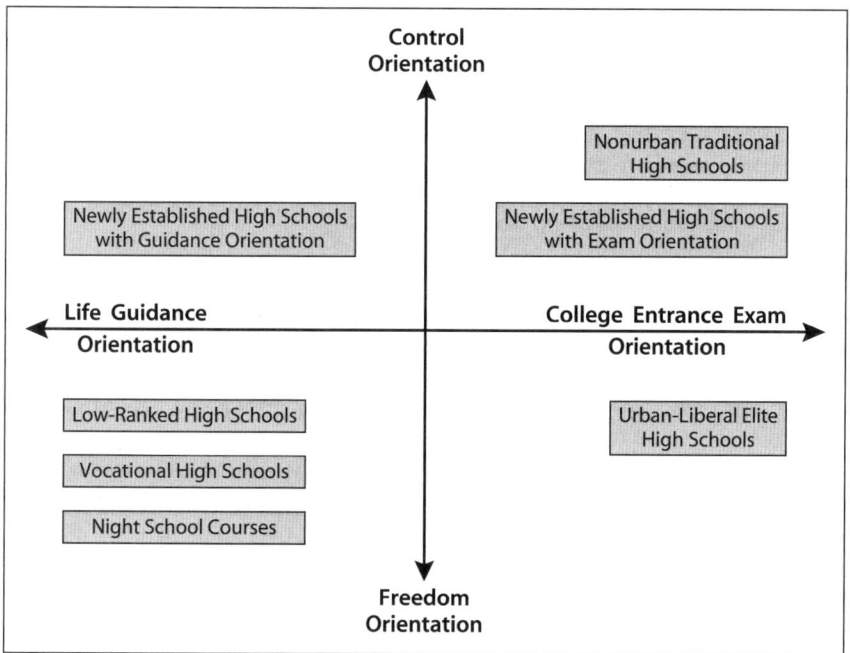

FIGURE 3.1 Hypothetical Typology of High Schools

neglect of their human right." Rather, control in this context means whether or not the school has any systematic educational arrangement. Freedom in this context means "democratic": The school does not provide its students with any systematic structure but instead emphasizes students' individuality and autonomy, and the students use their own initiative and autonomy for almost all aspects of school life. In the second dimension, college entrance exam orientation versus life guidance orientation, schools are categorized in terms of their dominant curriculum orientation: whether the school systematically prepares its students for the college entrance examination or emphasizes self-discipline for its students as an important matter in their curriculum and guidance.

Based on these two dimensions, there are four types of high schools. The schools in the first quadrant are characterized by both the college entrance exam orientation and control orientation; the schools in the second quadrant by both the life guidance orientation and control orientation; the schools in the third quadrant by both the life guidance orientation and freedom orientation; and the schools in the fourth quadrant by both the college entrance exam orientation and freedom orientation.

THE DIVERSITY OF HIGH SCHOOLS IN AICHI PREFECTURE AS EXPRESSED IN TEACHERS' NARRATIVES

In characterizing the features of the high schools in Aichi Prefecture, the discussion will begin with the urban-liberal elite high schools that have been affected by the political conflict between union teachers and the Aichi Department of Education. This type of school represents a typical urban high school in metropolitan areas of Japan.

Urban-Liberal Elite High Schools: Freedom and College Entrance Exam Orientation

Union Teachers' Dominance. Traditional high schools in Nagoya city are in this category. They have a long school history and have won social prestige. It is said that to work at traditional high schools in Nagoya city itself is regarded as respectable, and every teacher wishes to work at this type of high school. As a result, teachers with many years of teaching experience tend to teach at these schools. Mr. Imai, who worked at one of the most prestigious traditional high schools in Nagoya as a vice principal, pointed out the influence of the teachers' union and the older ages of teachers as two characteristics. He said:

> High School A seemed to be attached to the high school teachers' union of Aichi. There were a lot of former chairmen of local branches or former members of executive committees of the teachers' union. Thus, teachers there tended to criticize teachers doing overload work. They would not do anything for their students, saying that they respect the students' autonomy. They were academically good teachers and were excellent in class and would not make any mistakes in their daily duties ... since they were good at understanding a given situation, they would not make too much effort until the situation became critical for them.
>
> The average age of the teachers was 48 years. As a vice principal, I was almost at this age. Frankly speaking, half of the teachers were "elderly men." Four or five teachers would retire every year. There were many teachers who were waiting to work there for its social prestige, and union activists were transferred to work there. Then they would not make any official claim to the Department of Education. If such teachers were transferred to the other type of high schools, they would file a suit for unfair personnel transfer. It sometimes takes a couple of years to solve the suit but if they stayed in this type of high school, they would not file any suit for such a matter.

High Academic Level of Students. Students at this type of high school have high academic achievement because of the competitiveness of the entrance examination, and therefore these teachers do not have discipline problems with students. Teachers are not expected to prepare their students systematically for the college entrance exam because "students' autonomy" and "students' freedom" are respected most at this type of high school. At the same time, students tend to attend the *yobiko* (private university preparation classes) in Nagoya rather than taking the supplementary classes taught by the teachers at the high school. Imai explained how students do not participate in the supplementary classes at his school:

> Teachers give a few supplementary classes, but Kawai Yobiko announces its class schedule very early so students tend to ask when and how the supplementary classes will be offered at High School A. If possible, the students want to attend both classes at High School A and those classes for high school students in Kawai Yobiko. If the students' schedules are in conflict between the two, they are likely to go to Kawai Yobiko.

Thus, because there is a famous *yobiko* in Nagoya city, students are likely to turn to the *yobiko* for their exam preparation, not to their high schools. They may think that their teachers are not experts in exam preparation for college but the *yobiko* is.

"Democratic" School Management. Hayashi, who worked at one of the newly established high schools, thought the school management at the urban-liberal elite schools was peculiar in comparison with that at the newly established high school. The urban-liberal elite school is managed on the basis of "democracy." Hayashi said:

> In comparison with the newly established high schools, there is no order from the top.... In the newly established high schools, the principal had strong leadership and managed the school as he wished.... But [in the urban-liberal elite school] it is impossible for any principal to think of any plan and carry out it as he wishes. Union teachers would say that the staff meeting has the decision-making power. In such a high school the chair of the staff and the department chair groups are selected by members' votes. All the chairs are union teachers.... Any important decision is made by the majority vote. In a sense the school management is "democratic," but the principal cannot implement his vision in the school management.

Hayashi, who did not experience the era of teachers' union activism and is critical of the teachers' union, thought that it was difficult for principals to take leadership in the urban-liberal elite high schools in Nagoya.

In sum, traditional high schools in Nagoya are categorized as elite urban-liberal elite high schools. Senior union teachers have control over school management, and the principal is regarded as symbolic, without any power;

school management tends to be democratic. In such a high school there is no college entrance exam preparation system organized by the school; preparation depends upon individual students' "free will." Because of the schools' social prestige and competitive entrance examination, students in these high schools have relatively high academic achievement and study for the college entrance exam themselves while they attend supplementary classes in the *yobiko* in Nagoya. If these students obtain successful results on the college entrance exam, it is not the schools' effective education but the students' individual independent preparation and their study at the *yobiko* that are responsible.

Nonurban Traditional High Schools: Control and College Entrance Exam Orientation

Nonurban or local traditional high schools with prestige are strongly oriented toward college entrance exam preparation, but the school provides a powerful entrance exam–oriented curriculum rather than leaving it the students' individual efforts. These schools can be considered control oriented, unlike the democratic style of the traditional high schools in urban Nagoya.

Bright Students Can Do Anything Well Here. The nonurban traditional high schools where top students from the local area enroll employ a rigid college entrance exam–oriented system, but the students seem also to be active in their school life, with good academic achievement. Tanabe described this type of school in comparison with the middle-level high school at which his wife teaches:

> My wife teaches at High School B (the middle-level high school). Students are active in extracurricular activities such as cultural activities and school council activities, but they seem to be not necessarily trained to do them well. Students with leadership skills go to High School A (the traditional prestigious high school). . . . Teachers in High School B have to spend five times as much energy as teachers in High School A to keep up with the level of the activities done in High School A. Students in High School A can manage activities for themselves. . . . What I feel as a dilemma is that those students who are good at academics, have a high level of interest in cultural activities, have leadership, and have talent in sports all tend to come to High School A.

Top students from the local area tend to enter High School A by winning the competition in the unified entrance examination for public high schools, and they tend to do everything better than the students in the other high schools in the area. This happens because of the marked hierarchical structure of high schools in the entrance exam for high schools in a given area.

Oriented Toward Only One Goal: To Pass the Entrance Examination for Prestigious Universities. The students who fit the college entrance examination system best are those who have been successful in entrance exams throughout their school life. These students have been in the top strata since elementary school. Their parents are proud of them, as are their junior high school teachers who sent them to this top high school. Success on the entrance exam is the most important value in such a top high school. Regarding the emphasis on this value among students, their parents, and their teachers in this top high school, Aoki, a teacher at such a school, said:

> In High School A students, their parents, and their teachers all look in the same direction. Namely, it is the entrance examination. All three "actors" get their benefits, although not monetary benefits, from the entrance examination. The students will be satisfied if they pass the entrance examination to a prestigious university. Such students have been doing well since elementary school. As a good track and field athlete improves his or her ability in running, students who have been excellent in school naturally regard their academic achievement as the most important thing. They assume that students who are doing well in school are excellent as persons. The prestigious universities that they aspire to are what their parents and teachers want. The students' status will be raised in the school and their relationships with their friends will be enhanced while their future is also secured. The parents may think that this is good for their children but actually it satisfies their own ego. By guiding their students in this direction, teachers also are evaluated for their guidance ability.

The Special Entrance Exam–Preparation System in Schools. Special classes for college entrance exam preparation are organized in every exam preparation-oriented high school. However, the top school can have an extremely demanding system for these classes, because the students there are bright enough to do whatever they are expected to do. Tanabe, who taught such a course, Mathematics for Exam, said:

> In the third year I taught from six classes to eight classes in Mathematics per week, but in those classes students are supposed to solve four mathematics questions. Solving these mathematic questions for the college entrance exam may take 20 to 30 minutes. One class is 50 minutes long so that they can solve only two questions in class. But they are expected to solve four questions as an assignment at home. It is impossible to do so in the other high schools because of the academic level of the students there but almost all the students in this high school can do so.

A similar preparation for English for the college entrance exam is systematically organized by the teachers. Tamura, an English teacher, explained how he prepares his students for the college entrance exam:

In the first year, teachers teach English grammar thoroughly and make a faster curriculum in the second year; by the end of the second year their students will have finished all materials for the high school curriculum. Especially they push their students in order for them to read long essays in English and build their vocabulary. More specifically, whenever one lesson is over, a test on learned vocabulary is given. If they cannot make passing scores on the test, they have to stay in school until they pass. To build vocabulary systematically, students are given a group of words that have a certain theme, so they can understand related words and memorize them meaningfully.

Preparing students for the college entrance exam includes making them solve difficult exam questions, taking mock exams on a regular basis, and announcing the results of the mock exams of all the students by each homeroom on the bulletin board so that the homeroom teachers and their students experience a sense of competition among homeroom classes.

In sum, the prestigious traditional high schools in local areas outside Nagoya have special characteristics. First, students, parents, and teachers share a common goal: to succeed in the college entrance examination. Second, students tend to be selected from all the junior high schools in the given area so that they are likely to be top students who can handle social and cultural activities as well as academic activities. Third, the school is well organized for the college entrance exam in terms of its curriculum, supplementary classes, and yearly guidance by homeroom teachers. With a carefully tailored 3-year plan, teachers encourage their students to prepare for the college entrance exam, and the results of a series of mock exams taken by the students are analyzed "scientifically." The term "scientifically" refers to a peculiar system of estimating each student's chance of entering the university of his or her first choice. Each time students take the exam, they receive its result in the form of the standardized scores, which measure the relative position of each test taker in the mock exam. By examining the standardized scores, teachers estimate each student's chances to pass the university entrance exam of the student's first choice. This process is regarded as scientific by teachers and students even though it is a statistical analysis of the results of the mock exams.

Newly Established High Schools with Control and College Entrance Exam Orientation

The high schools established after Togo High School were called *Shinsetsukou*, which has a dual meaning of not only being newly established but also having a new administrative principle. Criticism was voiced by the mass media in the 1980s that these high schools carried out "control-oriented education" to catch up with other high schools that a longer history of prestige within the hierarchy of high schools. The newer schools had to do something to catch up with traditional high schools in the college entrance examination competition. A social ranking of high schools depends on the number of their graduates who enter prestigious universities. Yamada discusses his experience in a *Shinsetsukou* with "control-education" for college entrance exam preparation:

> High School G was just terrible then. For example, supplementary classes for the college entrance exam preparation were given until December 30 and began again on January 2 through the winter vacation. In the summer vacation, I had to teach three English classes of 80 minutes long per day for 20 days to those students ranging from the first year to the third year in the morning. Then in the afternoon I had to supervise students' club activities. I had to work all day even during summer vacation. Supplementary classes, supplementary classes . . . this is a key word for this type of high school.

This type of school emphasized "control-oriented education" in all other aspects of school life as well. Yamada described the students' school life in such a high school:

> When I was at High School G, the school festival was prohibited by the school. They said that the school festival was not necessary and the students should concentrate their energy on the college entrance exam preparation without participating in any cultural activities. The school did not allow the students to do anything that seemed to take away from preparation for the college entrance exam.

Anti–Teachers' Union Conditions. This emphasis on control-oriented education amounted to antagonism toward the teachers' union. Keeping union-oriented teachers busy with college entrance examination–oriented instruction and related activities was intended to indirectly destroy union activities. One of the union teachers said:

> By emphasizing the college examination system, teachers simply become very busy so that even union-oriented teachers are likely to lose their energy in doing union activities. The strongly union-oriented schools are likely to be the traditional high schools. But if the newly established high schools exceed the traditional high schools in the competition for the college entrance examination, even those teachers in the traditional high school are blamed by the principal for their record of sending their graduates to prestigious universities, with comments such as "While you are talking about your own rights, our school loses the competition." Or "We have to concentrate on preparation for the college entrance exam without criticizing the competition for the college entrance examination."

The Academic Level of Students Is Not Very High. The academic level of students in the newly established high schools is not as high as that of students in the traditional high schools, even though college entrance exam preparation is well organized. The students are not the top students selected by the competitive entrance examination for high schools; they enter this type of high school knowing their relative position in academic achievement in the junior high schools. Ootani, who organized the special summer camp for the college entrance exam in the traditional high schools, was expected to do the same thing in the newly established high schools. But he found something different there. He commented about his experience in the newly established high school:

> It is a quite different atmosphere there. Especially the students' attitude toward the training camp itself was quite different. We began to hold such a camp for the students without considering their intention. Actually, they were forced to participate in the camp against their will. It was organized by the school. Many of the students quit the camp after a couple of days, and there was serious absenteeism among the participants. The students thought that they were forced to attend, and they were not having as exciting a time as the students in the traditional prestigious high school did.

This is due partly to the low level of the students' academic achievement in this type of school and partly to a lack of the teachers' collaboration.

In sum, the newly established high schools with college entrance exam–preparation emphasis are characterized by a lower level of students' academic achievement than is found in traditional high schools. This type of school tries to organize its curriculum for college entrance exam preparation by providing its students with supplementary classes without allowing the students to have social or cultural activities, because they are thought to be a disturbance to its goal. Teachers must conduct so many supplementary classes in this college entrance exam–oriented curriculum that they may lose their energy for union activities, which is a policy of the Aichi Department of Education. This type of school is criticized as employing control-oriented education by the mass media, but the school may claim that the teachers have been doing so for the sake of the students' future. The students may also feel appreciation for the teachers' efforts toward them, even though their high school life seems to be stressful under the strong pressure of the college entrance exam.

Newly Established High Schools with Control and Life Guidance Orientation

The newly established high schools with life guidance orientation are usually ranked lower in the hierarchy of high schools than are the newly established high schools with college entrance exam orientation. This type of school cannot control its students by providing them with the college entrance examination–oriented classes. In fact, the students in this type of school are not necessarily interested in going to college or university. This type of school exercises its control over the students by strict school rules.

Corporal Punishment. Teachers at this type of school use corporal punishment to maintain order. This corporal punishment has been criticized by the mass media. One of the teachers who taught at such a school said:

> The corporal punishment at the school was reported in the newspapers because a student was killed by some sort of corporal punishment at a junior high school in another prefecture so that the Department of Education of Aichi sent all high schools an official notice to prohibit any corporal punishment by any teacher over students at any school. It no longer happens but it was very severe. The school was very strict with the dress code and imposed certain types of school bags and shoes on the students to wear. There was no freedom with anything. While I was critical of such strict school rules, I became accustomed to them. I myself exercised my authority to control my students. I think that I wanted to be positively evaluated by the administrators. I slapped my students on the cheek on some occasions. Such teachers received positive evaluation from their administrator. Slapping the students on the cheek was a corporal punishment for sure.

Corporal punishment might take a different form that sounds like power harassment by teachers. Students in Japan are expected to clean their classroom and other places on campus as part of their educational activities. But such activities are organized in a military-like manner. All of the students begin to clean with music, and students in charge of cleaning get together to check the list of students in the group by shouting, "one, two, three." The assignment of cleaning places would be announced; some students take care of the toilet, others clean the sinks, and others clean students' shoe shelves. In the classrooms one person is in charge of sweeping the room with a broom while others are expected to move the desks and chairs. Every detailed assignment is given and the students function according to their roles. This kind of activity is designed to discipline students morally and educationally. The school intends to create a school culture in which students behave themselves.

A Peculiar Scolding System. This type of school has a peculiar method of disciplining students when they engage in any deviant action. They have to see several teachers to make an apology for their action. Ueda, who taught at this type of school, explains how a student was treated by teachers there when he made a mistake:

> In scolding a student that committed a deviant action, more than one teacher was involved. The student has to see teachers of different roles in turn. For example: One male student stepped on a steel bookshelf for fun and made a hole in it while he was cleaning. As a result, first he had to see a teacher in guidance counseling and then went to see his homeroom teacher to make an apology about his conduct. And then he went to see the chairing teacher of the grade and finally he came to see me, who was in charge of discipline. The student said to me, "Please don't scold me again because I was scolded four times before coming here." I thought that he was right. But such a method of scolding was an ordinary thing at that school.

In sum, a newly established high school with discipline control emphasis is ranked lower than that with the college entrance examination–oriented control emphasis. In such a school, instruction for the college entrance exam does not function as a method to keep students in order; the school needs to have strict school rules to discipline the students. Without such discipline control, students at this type of school would not lead a normal school life.

Schools with Freedom and Life Guidance Orientation: The Bottom High Schools

The "Combined Pollution" Phenomenon at the Bottom High Schools. The hierarchical structure of high school rankings is so strict that academically poor students gather in the bottom high schools. One of the teachers labels the situation in the bottom high school as "combined pollution" that stems from multiple negative factors, one of which is the students' family background. Nishida, who teaches at one of bottom high schools in Nagoya city, said:

> Students there come from poor families as well as being very poor in academic performance. If their problem is only with their poor economic status, the school can work with them but if they also have a very poor academic record in junior high school, it is much more difficult. In terms of their GPA, the minimum on a five-scale grading system is "one." Because the distribution of grading is by percentage, any student can get a "two" in PE or music but we have 11 students with a "one" in all nine subjects in junior high school.

The "combined pollution" phenomenon happened after the educational reform of the entrance examination for high schools in Aichi Prefecture in 1989. Because any student is allowed to take the exams for two public high schools, he or she ends up entering the preferred one. Students in the middle strata of academic achievement tend to be accepted by private school recommendations. As a result, the bottom high school in the hierarchy of public high schools cannot fill its official seats. Once a high school is recognized as the one with unfilled seats, then any student, regardless of his or her grade, can enter, resulting in the acceptance of the lowest strata of all students.

In such a school the dropout rate is about 30%. By the end of the first year about 80 students, which is equivalent to the number of two homerooms, drop out. The students' attitude toward their learning is quite different from that of students in other types of high schools. One of teachers in this type of school said:

> In each classroom there are a few students who cannot sit at a desk for more than 20 minutes. Whatever teachers do, their attitude will not change. They will go out of the classroom regardless of what the teachers say. Those who do not go out of the classroom tend to sleep during the lesson. Some others read comic books or magazines and others are listening to music; another group may drink juice and eat snacks. Though I visited several American high schools, our school is much worse than them.

Teachers have given up control over their students. Facing such problem students in their daily teaching, teachers there seem to have a "cultural truce" with the students. As they begin to work with such difficult students who have cultural values different from their own, they are likely to adjust themselves to the school culture. The teachers in this school accept the real situation of the school as it is and seem to give up exercising their educational guidance of the students. Nishida, who teaches in such a high school, describes the teachers' attitude:

> The staff meeting usually ends within an hour. We sometimes have a longer meeting about problem students whom teachers on the students' affairs cannot handle. But our school tends to accept any problems as reality without handling them. The other day a student caused some trouble. There is a bus route between Atsuta Shrine and our school. The bus was late for its schedule. The student hit the bus driver, saying "Why was the bus late for its schedule?" The incident was reported to the police immediately. The driver was kind enough to allow the student to go back to school when his homeroom teacher and a teacher in charge of guidance went to the police to apologize on behalf of the school. The homeroom teacher gave special guidance for the student for only a week and then the student returned to regular class. At the staff meeting the teacher reported that the student's behavior has been corrected. If I were on the guidance committee, I would continue to give special guidance to the student. But the current committee members would not carry out the complete guidance.

The disciplinary guidance in general is not strict with students. The teachers seem to have given up controlling their students. Even though some teachers try to discipline the students strictly, the students' logic undermines what the teachers do. According to the school's official rules set by the Department of

Education, the maximum limit for absenteeism is 11 days. In the other schools, no students would be absent from school more than 11 times whether the school's rule is set as such or not. But some students may ask, "How many classes can I be absent from?" Such students took the limiting number of absences and additionally had to be absent from school because of sickness, or some dishonest students excused their absence because of a delayed bus. When such cases occurred, their homeroom teachers could not avoid approving their excuses. By knowing the homeroom teacher's nonrigid attitude, students are likely to easily violate the school's rules. The teachers in this type of school lose control over the students.

In sum, this type of school, without either control or the college entrance exam orientation, has three distinctive characteristics. First, students come from families with low economic status. Second, they came from the lowest strata in academic record at their junior high school, so they are not likely to have the basic habit of studying. Third, teachers at this type of school tend to give up controlling their students and let them do whatever they want without any rigid punishment.

High Schools for Vocational Education

In the 1960s, during the rapid economic development, the high school entrance rate was only 60% and many bright students in local areas went to high schools for vocational education. However, after the 1970s, as the demand for higher education increased and the status of agriculture diminished, a new hierarchical ranking of high schools was established. Academic high schools were at the top of the hierarchy, schools for commerce were the second, high schools for technology were next, and high schools for agriculture were at the bottom, as measured by the entrance examination scores of entering students.

The academic level of the high schools for technology is low. Because high schools for technology are located outside the college entrance examination system, it is difficult to motivate the students. Instead of college entrance exam preparation, teachers use a variable certificate system to motivate their students, as described below. One of the teachers said:

> Teachers at high schools for technology seem to have invented some ways to motivate their students. For example, the certificates that students are encouraged to obtain include abacus, drafting, information, and electricity. In the case of high schools for commerce, they promote certificates in word-processing, personal computer, and accounting. They started such a system by thinking that if the students obtain such certificates, they would be able to have some advantage in the job market. But now the teachers can have control over their students by letting them study for such certificates.

The teachers do not necessarily question whether or not such certificates are useful in the job market, but they motivate their students to study seriously by awarding such certificates at schools for vocational education.

Night Schools

The function of night schools has changed from that of a school for serious workers to that for problem students such as maladjusted students, those with school phobia who had a personal history of many absences at their junior high schools, or those who fail to enter regular high schools in the daytime. In the rapid economic development of the 1960s and early 1970s, many young people who could not go to high school for economic reasons went to metropolitan areas and attended night school while they worked in the daytime. Night school functioned as a school where the serious children of poor families could study while holding jobs. Such low-cost young laborers were welcomed by small and medium-sized companies in Aichi Prefecture. Night schools then were very active places, where students even engaged in club activities for an hour after school, staying until 10 p.m. But the nature of night school has changed. One of the teachers who worked at night school said:

> Night schools are schools for those students who work in the daytime. They are changing now essentially. The general tendency for night schools is the increase of students who are school refusals. For example, I know that at High School J one third of the students are school refusals. In our night school we have three students who got "1"s (grading system from 1 to 5) in all the subjects in their junior high schools. Besides such students with the lowest GPA in junior high school, we have those students who committed some sort of deviant conduct in junior high school. We have these two groups: those who have the lowest academic record and those who committed some sort of deviant behaviors.

In a sense, night schools have become the same as difficult high schools or bottom high schools in the daytime. They consist of similar students with low academic performance and difficult behavior patterns.

INTERPRETING TEACHERS' PERSPECTIVES AS EXPRESSED IN THEIR NARRATIVES

This chapter first described the historical changes in educational structure and policies that took place along with the economic development in Aichi Prefecture of Japan. With this understanding of the historical background, the diversity of high school cultures has been described by using two dimensions: control orientation versus freedom orientation and college entrance exam orientation versus life guidance orientation, drawing on teachers' narratives about their experiences in various kinds of high schools in Aichi Prefecture. From these descriptions it is apparent that there is no typical Japanese high school, but rather a diversity of high schools occupying different relative academic positions in the hierarchy of high schools. This hierarchy has been established by dynamic interaction among factors such as the political conflict in education, economic development in the industrial area of central Japan, and educational reforms, especially changes in the high school entrance examination system.

In the concluding discussion I examine how teachers' perspectives, as expressed in their narratives about their experiences in various kinds of high schools in Aichi Prefecture, indicate that once the hierarchy of high schools was established, the teachers contributed to maintaining and reproducing it by adjusting themselves to the high school culture in which they work. There are typically two political orientations among teachers: the teachers' union orientation, which tends toward left-wing political positions favoring reform; and the administration orientation, which tends toward conservative political positions favoring maintenance of the status quo. Not all teachers in a school take an extreme political position. Teachers' political orientation seems to be related to their attitudes toward teaching. Typically, teachers' union–oriented teachers tend to criticize the college entrance examination system. They may say that the college entrance exam undermines students' personality, individuality, and creativity. These teachers are not supposed to encourage their students to aspire to prestigious universities but to educate the students as balanced persons. Thus, they refuse to provide special supplementary classes as preparation for the college entrance exam. In contrast, administration-oriented teachers tend to think that they should prepare their students for the college entrance exam for the students' own sake. They train their students for the college entrance exam so that the students will be able to enter the universities of their choice, which may lead the students to a promising future. The teachers regard high school days as a training period for entry to universities. Such teachers may also feel that by preparing their students for the college entrance exam they will increase the number of students who enter prestigious universities, and thus raise the social prestige of the school where they work. In a sense, they train their students for the exam for the sake of their own prestige.

The clear division between the union-oriented teachers and the administration-oriented teachers has been fading as a result of the development of the entrance examination system after the 1970s. In Aichi Prefecture the number of high schools has nearly doubled since 1968, when Togo High School, a new school without the political influence of a teachers' union, was established. Many high schools, especially local traditional prestigious high schools and the newly established high schools, began to engage in severe competition on the college entrance exam. As a result, even union-oriented teachers had to participate in the competition once they began to teach at any high school with the college entrance exam orientation, partly because they wanted to increase their school's prestige and partly because they had to survive in the school culture. Regardless of their political orientation, they had to contribute to promoting the college entrance exam preparation system within the school where they worked. Teachers in the local traditional prestigious high schools and the newly established high schools with college entrance exam emphasis thus contribute to reproducing the hierarchy of high schools.

In contrast, teachers in the urban-liberal elite high schools tend to distance themselves from the college entrance examination system. Many of the teachers who are union-oriented and middle-aged place importance on their individual rights as teachers. They teach what they are expected to in the fixed high school curriculum, and do not want to teach more than that. They are not willing to provide special supplementary classes for the college entrance exam for their students, partly because they do not feel obligated and partly because they think that promotion of the competition in the college entrance exam is not good for their students. They also think that the college entrance exam is the students' private matter, not the school's matter. These teachers do not have to make an effort to raise the school's prestige, because the school has already won its prestige as a result of the academic level of the students who enter the school. Even though the teachers in the urban-liberal elite high schools do not contribute to reproducing the hierarchy of high schools directly, they live on the basis of the hierarchy of high schools.

Teachers in the newly established high schools with control and life guidance emphasis and the other types of high schools located at the bottom of the hierarchy of high schools tend to "cool-out" their students, with poor student performance reinforcing the schools' low ranking in the hierarchy. Teachers in the newly established high schools with life guidance orientation make use of the schools' rules to control their students without encouraging the students to aspire to prestigious universities. Instead, they maintain a social order in the students' daily school life and feed their students into social positions appropriate for their respective educational level. As the population of the college-bound age-group has decreased, more of the students in this type of high school can enter universities, colleges, and technical schools at the postsecondary level. Teachers in the high schools for vocational education also seem to reproduce the hierarchy of high schools by accepting their students as they are. They usually do not encourage their students to aspire to apply to college and universities. Instead, the teachers encourage their students to obtain a variety of certificates fitting their specialty subjects. These basic certificates are good for middle-level workers but not for professionals.

Teachers at night schools often work with students who were maladjusted in junior high schools or in daytime high schools. They just want their students to function as ordinary adults in society by providing them with a minimal high school education.

To conclude this analysis of the teachers' narratives, I would argue that high school teachers, regardless of their political orientation, contribute to maintaining and reproducing the hierarchy of high schools both directly and indirectly. The teachers do so by insisting that they should work for the students' sake. But they seem to do so for the sake of their own interest as well, in the sense that they work best by adjusting themselves to the school culture. The question is whether or not the hierarchical structure of high schools can change in the future. I would say that the structure may continue for as long as teachers can maintain order in their schools successfully.

REFERENCES

Chunichi Newspapers. (1989, November 12). Tokai local section, p. 28.
Chunichi Newspapers. (1992, April 6). Tokai local section, p. 19.
Kyoikujihou [*Educational current news*]. (1972). Nogoya, Japan: Department of Education of Aichi Prefecture.
Tsukada, M. (1998). *Jukentaisei to kyoshi no raifukousu* [*The entrance exam system and teachers' life course*]. Tokyo: Tagashuppan.

AKIRA SAKAI

Educational Selection, Career Decisions, and School Support

The Case of an Urban Commercial High School

COMMERCIAL HIGH SCHOOLS occupy an intermediate space in Japan's academic hierarchy of high schools. Given their position they can play a powerful role in student social mobility, educating students for clerical jobs in business and industry or for further education. In this chapter, I describe and analyze the career consciousness of students at an urban commercial high school (with the pseudonym "Nozomi Commercial High School") and explore measures that might motivate them to attend high- or middle-level universities. For the past 5 years, my colleagues and I, in collaboration with undergraduate and graduate students, have been working as a nonprofit voluntary organization (NPO) to help students enter university. This study flows out of the reciprocal relationship that was constructed between Nozomi and the research team (two graduate students who have been engaged in the activities of our NPO). This relationship enabled us to collect data from a variety of sources: school records, interviews with teachers and students, and observation of school activities.

Our findings provide insight into how the economic recession of the 1990s influenced the school's policy on career guidance and the career consciousness of its students. Recent career guidance policy has emphasized giving priority to the opinions of students. However, in schools like Nozomi, it has been demonstrated that this kind of guidance serves to encourage student choices that have "little chance for success" later. What current theory lacks is the idea that certain socially disadvantaged people, or people who are discriminated against, should receive special benefits or need to be offered support to help them achieve success in society. Our study leads to the conclusions that the students' consciousness lacks a concrete future perspective and that providing support to help them gain this perspective is, in fact, consistent with the management strategy of the school in coping with economic difficulties.

TYPES OF HIGH SCHOOLS IN JAPAN

In Japan, high schools are broadly classified into two categories: general or academic and specialist or vocational. Vocational schools are further divided by track of study, most typically into commercial and industrial high schools. Commercial high schools are regarded as institutions for the instruction of students who wish to be employed in clerical positions after graduation. In addition to the academic curriculum, students are taught the fundamentals of business, bookkeeping, and computer processing. Since the economic recession of the 1990s, however, the employment rate for these students has been decreasing as companies have become less interested in recruiting high school graduates and have increased their labor outsourcing. Banks, the most prestigious employers for commercial high school students, have stopped hiring high school graduates altogether, indicating just how difficult it has become for students from commercial high schools to find stable jobs. In line with these changes, the percentage of commercial high school students who feel the need to go on to universities or "specialized training colleges" has increased over the past 10 years. Commercial high schools were most directly affected by the changes arising out of the economic recession in the 1990s, and they are an ideal subject for studying how social change has influenced the direction of career guidance in high schools and student awareness of their career choices.

Given these research problems and interests, our study examined an urban commercial high school. Nozomi's status was quite low even compared with other commercial high schools nearby, and it was a school that had directly suffered from the economic recession. We examined the career perspective of students under these conditions and it was clear that in response to uncertain guidance, their attitudes were being formed without much focus on the future. The second component of this study addresses the content and effects of a college entrance support program on a group of students at Nozomi. The program was administered by myself and Mr. Kawai, a teacher at Nozomi who began in the year 2000 (all names of students and teachers of Nozomi are pseudonyms). University student volunteers were sent to Nozomi to encourage motivation among students and help them advance to higher education. Forming project teams, we participated in support activities and attempted to get to know the students and their everyday behavior and attitudes. Over the course of our interaction, we were able to deepen our understanding of why these students shrank from the idea of going on to college. We also observed how their career perspectives changed and how much gender played a crucial role in these changes. By focusing on the two research topics—future perspectives of students and their response to support—we sought to better understand how economic conditions, problems with high school structure, gender, and poverty are involved in career decision-making and perspectives among low-track high school students, *and* to understand how best to support these students and motivate them to resist their adverse circumstances.

OVERVIEW AND TRANSFORMATION OF COMMERCIAL HIGH SCHOOLS

Commercial high schools have their roots in pre-war vocational schools, or *jitsugyo gakko*. Following the democratization process after World War II, secondary education was reorganized and new 3-year high schools were set up according to the American school model. The General Headquarters (GHQ of the Allied Occupation) enforced the so-called "Three Principles" of small attendance districts, coeducation, and comprehensive schools. As a result, many secondary schools were urged to reform and (or) combine. Apart from coeducation, however, the policy was repealed in many regions a few years after the end of the Occupation. Districts were enlarged and tracks were separated. The new high schools that had been comprehensive in form only were soon operated separately as either vocational or academic high schools.

In the history of high school education in Japan after the end of World War II, vocational education received the most attention for about three decades. In response to the rising numbers of students continuing on to high school, the Ministry of Education in 1960 announced a basic policy for secondary school expansion. In the national income-doubling plan, announced the same year, the industrial sector aggressively proposed that the subject tracks in high schools should be evenly divided 5:5 between general and vocational tracks, as opposed to 6:4. The policy of the Ministry of Education was written along these lines, and the enhancement of industrial tracks was given top priority, followed by agricultural and commercial tracks (Tomie, 1999). In reality, however, this shift in emphasis did not take place. Due to pressure from parents and students wishing to advance into academic schools, the general track was increased. With both the government's policy of expansion of vocational tracks and citizens' expectations for academic tracks, the 1960s saw enormous growth in the high school enrollment rate overall. A drop in the percentage of vocational tracks has continued since the mid-1970s.

Table 4.1 shows a number of important statistics regarding high school education in Japan between 1955 and 2003. The second column in the table indicates the high school enrollment rate: It increased more than 34% in the 15 years between 1960 and 1975, reaching 90% enrollment in the early 1970s. The columns across the middle of the table show the percentage of all students enrolled in each subject track. At first glance, it is clear that most students were enrolled in the academic (general) track. On the other hand, while showing

TABLE 4.1 Specialization of High School Students by Subject Track

Year	Rate of advancement to high school (%)	Enrollment rate by subject track (%)									Total number of students	Rate of new graduates entering employment (%)
		General	Commerce	Industry	Agriculture	Home economics	Fishery	Nursing	Others	Integrated		
1955	51.5	59.8	14.3	9.2	7.8	8.2	0.5		0.1		2,571,615	47.6
1960	57.7	58.3	16.5	10.0	6.7	7.8	0.5		0.2		3,225,945	61.3
1965	70.7	59.5	16.9	12.3	5.2	5.5	0.4		0.2		5,065,657	60.4
1970	82.1	58.5	16.4	13.4	5.3	5.2	0.4		0.8		4,222,840	58.2
1975	91.9	63.0	14.5	11.8	4.5	4.5	0.4	0.6	0.7		4,327,089	44.6
1980	94.2	68.2	12.5	10.3	3.8	3.5	0.4	0.6	0.7		4,616,339	42.9
1985	93.8	72.1	11.3	9.3	3.0	2.7	0.3	0.5	0.8		5,171,787	41.1
1990	94.4	74.1	10.4	8.7	2.7	2.4	0.3	0.4	1.1		5,616,844	35.2
1995	95.8	74.2	9.5	8.8	2.8	1.9	0.3	0.5	1.9	0.1	4,717,191	25.6
1999	95.8	73.4	8.7	8.8	2.8	1.7	0.3	0.5	2.4	1.4	4,203,750	20.2
2000	95.9	73.3	8.5	8.8	2.8	1.7	0.3	0.5	2.5	1.7	4,157,269	18.6
2001	95.8	73.0	8.3	8.8	2.8	1.7	0.3	0.5	2.6	2.0	4,053,627	18.4
2002	95.8	72.9	8.1	8.8	2.8	1.7	0.3	0.4	2.7	2.3	3,921,141	17.1
2003	96.1	72.8	7.8	8.7	2.8	1.6	0.3	0.4	2.8	2.8	3,801,646	16.6

Sources. http://www.mext.go.jp/english/statist/xls/012.xls, http://www.mext.go.jp/english/statist/xls/040.xls, and http://www.mext.go.jp/english/statist/xls/050.xls.

no increase during the rapid expansion period of the 1960s and early 1970s, the commercial track held about 15% of the share. Since that time, the fraction has dropped dramatically, to the point that fewer than 10% of all students have been enrolled in the commercial track in recent years.

The far right column shows the percentage of students who found employment after graduation from high school. In 1960, 61.3% found jobs immediately after graduation. The percentage held at over 40% in the 1980s, but began to decline rapidly in the 1990s to arrive at 18.6% in the year 2000. Of course, behind these figures is an increase in university enrollment, but it is important also to look at changes in the employment environment to explain the sudden drop in the 1990s. The commercial high school my colleagues and I have been studying and supporting since 2000 experienced the same trends as are illustrated in Table 4.1. Next, I will address how these kinds of conditions penetrated individual schools.

Nozomi Commercial High School

Nozomi Commercial High School is located in the Tokyo metropolitan area. It was established in 1934 as a women's commercial school and was transformed into a commercial high school after World War II. With only 300 students, it is small for a high school. Like most commercial high schools, most of its students are girls, with a 1:2 or 1:3 male to female ratio. Nozomi is clearly at the bottom level, ranked lower than other neighboring traditional commercial high schools, and the academic achievement is poor. As explained by Mr. Kawai, the students who are accepted are usually ranked the fourth or fifth lowest in their junior high school classes, which typically have 30–40 students.

Over 20% of Nozomi students drop out before graduating. Many students come from complicated family backgrounds, with about 10% living in one-parent households and many receiving public assistance. Over 10% of families apply for remission of school fees. Postgraduation status of Nozomi students from 1980 to the present is shown in Figure 4.1, according to data compiled by Kazama (2005).

Up until the end of the 1980s, the employment rate of Nozomi graduates was over 80%. In comparison, the percentage of students going on to universities or postsecondary vocational schools was relatively low, as was the ratio of undecided graduates. Beginning in the first half of the 1990s, however, the employment rate at Nozomi dropped drastically, to less than 50%. Conversely, the percentage of undecided students jumped up, creating a stratum of graduates who either did not work after finishing school or worked only part-time. While more graduates went on to higher education, most went to postsecondary vocational schools. Of the 10% who went to 4-year or 2-year colleges,

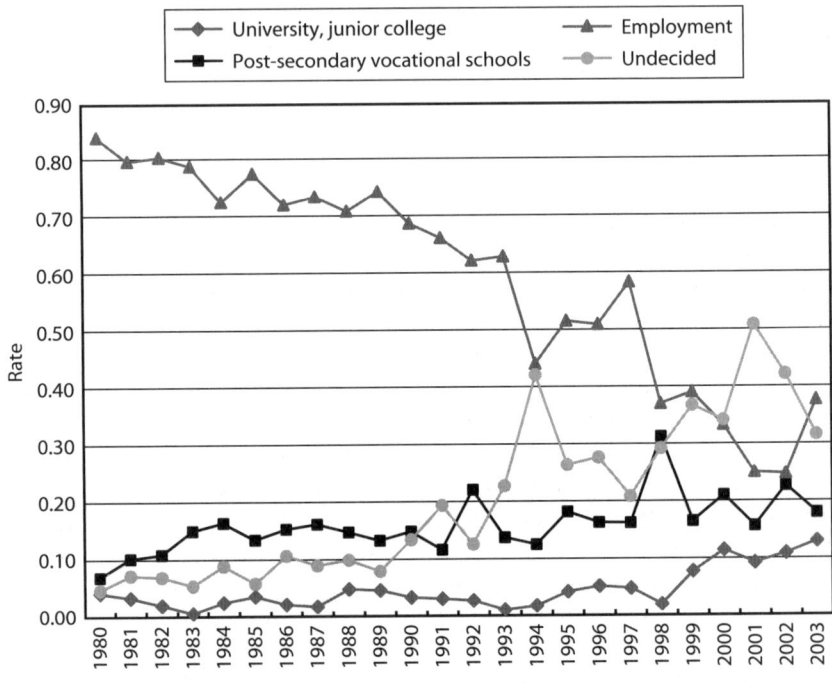

FIGURE 4.1 Changes in Postgraduation Status of Nozomi High School Graduates, 1980–2003

Source. Compiled from "*Shinro no Tebiki*" Guide to Post-graduation (Kazama, 2005).

most were admitted only to low-status schools that would accept anyone who took the entrance exam.

The worsening employment situation becomes even more apparent when looking at job recruitment data. At the height of Japan's economic bubble in 1991, there were 2,088 job postings for the 300 students at Nozomi. When the bubble burst, demand for labor decreased overall and companies began a switch over to using part-time workers and nonregular employees. Job openings dropped in the latter half of the 1990s, and by 2000 there were only 248 recruitment postings (Kazama, 2005). This deterioration in conditions also brought down student morale. The dropout rate until the 1990s was around 10%, but it had risen to almost 30% by 2000.

"Here and Now": Students' Postgraduation Career Perspectives

In a drastically changed job-seeking environment, what kinds of career perspectives do students hold, and how can we as educators help them to have a chance at success by actively making career choices? Before one can offer them support, it is necessary to first grasp the particular characteristics of students' career perspectives, for which a theoretical framework becomes necessary. For our purposes, the research team has chosen to rely on the life story approach, which has developed out of social constructionism and its theoretical foundations. Social constructionism as advocated by Berger and Luckmann (1966) has been taken up recently in Japan in the fields of sociology and psychology. Students' career perspective awareness is organized as part of a continuing narrative intertwined with their life and school experiences. Ascertaining how this narrative is constructed, and knowing how it can be changed, is essential to being able to support these students.

One of my graduate students used this theoretical construct and interviewed 17 students at Nozomi and 6 students at an academic high school (Sugihara, 2004). She compared how "career stories" were told and constructed. The most significant difference between the two groups of students was where the "start" of the story fell. Sugihara concluded that these narratives could be divided into three main types based on whether students began by telling about the future, the present, or the past, and by the clarity of the theme. In the first type, students began their narratives with clear statements of career and personal goals, and continued with these throughout their storytelling.

Students with the second type of narrative did not have clear goals for their futures; their first priority was to decide what to do after graduation. It was difficult enough for these students to handle tasks immediately at hand, let alone think about what they would need to do afterward. They did not have a specific theme for the paths they would take after high school, but this also gave them the quality of being flexible and able to adapt to changes in their lives and surrounding conditions. The third type of narrative placed emphasis on past life experiences. Students began their stories by telling about their past and explaining how it shaped them. They strongly felt a need to value their present selves.

When comparing postgraduation storytelling between Nozomi students and the academic high school students, Sugihara (2004) found that the Type 1 narrative was more common among the academic high school students while the Type 3 narrative was typical of the Nozomi students. Many of the Nozomi students had poor grades in junior high school, and they thought, as expressed by one student, that they did not want to work at a "regular company" where they would be judged on the basis of their grades, but rather at a company that would value them "as a person." Another student at Nozomi had a Type 2 narrative and explained that his grades were so low that it was enough for him to worry about the tasks immediately in front of himself. High school graduation was the goal, and it would not be bad to live as a *freeta* (part-time, nonregular employee) after that.

The majority of students at Nozomi had either Type 2 or Type 3 narratives and went on to become nonregular employees. For these students with low grades and limited career choices, it may not be surprising that they simply wanted to be accepted for who they were, or that they could not think much about their postgraduation plans because graduating in itself was difficult enough. Of course, there were also commercial high school students with very distinct goals in mind. For example, to achieve her dream of becoming a hair and makeup stylist, one student incorporated into her postgraduation narrative plans for going to a postsecondary vocational school of cosmetology and getting a license. This is the type of student that the vocational high school curriculum is supposed to cater to but, in reality, very few of these students exist.

Postgraduation Career Support Program

Summary of the Program. It was certainly difficult for graduates of Nozomi to find regular, stable employment. However, these students were not being actively encouraged by the school to exercise their choice to take college entrance exams as an alternative. Mr. Kawai, a science teacher who was transferred to Nozomi from an academic high school in 1999, expressed concerns about the situation and decided that a number of students needed to be introduced to the choice of college as one of their postgraduation options. After coming up with ideas for activities to support the efforts of these students, Mr. Kawai contacted me to collaborate on the project.

When this project first began in 2000, Mr. Kawai described the atmosphere of the entire school as one that encouraged "cooling out." He explained, "At the time, there was a shared consciousness among teachers that 'our students would never get into college.'" With low student motivation to learn and high absentee and tardiness rates, there was an implicit understanding at Nozomi that graduation was the only goal, and that becoming a nonregular employee was inevitable. To change this situation, Mr. Kawai thought that it would be necessary to give support to students in making choices at their own pace. For this support, Mr. Kawai and I began to enlist the help of undergraduate and graduate student volunteers in 2000.

Project Goals and Operation. The support project brought undergraduate and graduate student volunteers to Nozomi Commercial High School to meet with interested students after school about two or three times per week. Students at Nozomi could consult with the volunteers about their postgraduation career options or get help with their studies and test strategy. At the conclusion of each session, the volunteers would write a summary of their activities and observations on the students. This summary served as a reference for the next volunteer as well as a record of the project. In addition, Mr. Kawai and I met with the volunteers in conference meetings once a month to discuss the activities in detail.

Our purposes were:

1. To get students to know what college students are like
2. To have students spend time with college students while working toward their goals
3. To encourage students to study at home
4. To collect college application information and assist with application forms

However, there were very few students who joined of their own volition. Most students participated after strong encouragement from Mr. Kawai, who told them that college should be a goal.

The Transformation Process of Students' Postgraduation Outlooks

Based on the cases of two girls who graduated in March 2003, and on support activities covering up to 7 months, in this section I examine the transformation of career perspectives in students and the factors involved in the change (Sakai, 2007; Sakai, Chiba, Hamano, & Hirosaki, 2004). Table 4.2 shows the profiles of the two girls. Approximately 10 undergraduate and graduate student volunteers participated. On average, two volunteers visited the school at a time; some volunteers participated as few as 2 or 3 times and others made as many as 20 visits.

Case 1: Hiromi. This student lived in a five-person household with grandparents, an older sister, and a younger brother. The mother was divorced and did not live with the children; the father was hospitalized and was not on

TABLE 4.2 Profiles of Two Students Participating in a Postgraduation Career Support Program

Name	Absent days in a year	Grade	Postgraduation plans before participation	Postgraduation plans after participation	Career after graduation
Hiromi	A few days	A	Employment	College	College (night course)
Rie	10 days	C	Employment	College	College (night course)

Source. Sakai et al. (2004).

speaking terms with Hiromi. She wrote, "Since I started falling behind in junior high, I decided to just go to a commercial high school and then find a job." Her postgraduation plans were to finish school and either work or go to a specialized training college. Her grade point average (GPA) was 4.4 (out of 5.0), and she ranked first or second in her class. The family's financial situation was not good, and Hiromi worked at a part-time job until midnight on weekends to help pay for school and household expenses. These financial concerns were the biggest factor causing her to hesitate about going to college.

Hiromi continually stated that she was not going to take college entrance exams, but her actions showed that she was working hard to prepare. She had the highest participation rate of any student involved in our support activities. Even if she had to go home after school to take care of errands, she would come all the way back just to participate in support activities, and she always did her homework thoroughly no matter how difficult she felt it was. Although she showed a very active commitment to the program, however, she continued to say that "Actually I don't really want to go to college myself" and that she was participating in the activities "because Mr. Kawai got me [convinced]." Her attitudes also changed off and on: for example, one week she excitedly said to a volunteer, "I found a really cool-sounding major at a law college" (student volunteer notes, 2002, 9.18), but the next week she said, "I don't want to go to college, I'm not even interested, so it's not like I have any aspirations to go" (student volunteer notes, 2002, 9.25).

It is important to note how Hiromi's career perspective wavered back and forth as she considered how aiming for college would be a financial burden added to her already stressful family situation. Even though her grades were good and she had a desire to go to college (after Hiromi had decided on her postgraduation plans, we found out from a parent interview that she had told her mother that she wanted to attend college), she was unsure of her "self-will" when she thought of her family situation or, more directly, when her older sister said "why don't you work [instead of going to college]."

Not knowing initially what was later revealed in the parent interview described above, the volunteer, whose role it was to support Hiromi, was uncertain whether or not Hiromi was expressing her true self-will when she said, "I don't even want to go to college." After consulting numerous times with Mr. Kawai and the project supervisor (Sakai), the consensus was that "if Hiromi truly did not have an interest in going to college, then she would not be joining the activities. After all, there were students we encouraged who did not join and ended up opting for specialized training colleges or other things. The fact that she comes at all has to mean that she wants to go," and that "so long as she keeps participating without being forced, we should keep encouraging her to prepare for college even if she says 'I don't want to go.'"

Although Hiromi had stated that she would "change directions and find a job if I fail [the exams for the first time]," she ended up entering the night course program at a university after overcoming two failed admission attempts.

Case 2: Rie. This student lived in a four-person household with her parents and younger brother. Her parents ran a business, but their finances did not leave much to spare. The mother had stated that with some effort they probably would be able to pay for college, but she maintained that unless Rie had something that she really wanted to study, she would be better off working instead. Rie's GPA was 3.0. Rie explained:

> When I first started high school, I wanted to get a lot of certifications for business, but actually haven't gotten any. I'm always tardy at school, so I thought I wouldn't be able to find a job—that was around the end of my second year. Then, when Mr. Kawai said, "So, you want to go to college too?" I thought, oh, right, there's college.

When she first started participating in the support activities, however, Rie was unwilling to do much on her own. When searching for possible schools, she asked the volunteer, "I don't know what to do so can you just tell me?" As the activities progressed, she was able to engage more actively in searching for schools and studying for the entrance exams, and she reported that her wish to go to college was "getting stronger and stronger." Because Rie was unable to write short essays on her own at first, a volunteer carefully explained the basics as they wrote a paper together. After writing down each word, Rie would look at the volunteer as if to say, "Is this okay?" Eventually, Rie was able to write on her own without having the volunteer respond. However, Rie had poor study habits and found it difficult to do her assigned homework. She was always concerned about her family's finances, and she seemed distressed about choosing college, especially after hearing that her younger brother had said, "If Rie is going to go to college, then I won't go."

Rie was also worried about convincing her mother, who was opposed to Rie taking the exams, about her motivation to go to college. The volunteers responded by sharing their own experiences with Rie and telling her that she could "decide what she wanted to do once she got to college," and that at college, "you meet a lot of different people and learn lots of different things, and you might be able to discover something that you want to do with your future there."

Rie's mother had said that Rie should look for a job if she did not pass the entrance exams for her first-choice school. Rie in fact failed the exam and was conflicted over whether to keep trying or look for work. At that time, a student who had participated in our support program 2 years earlier told Rie about night course options and explained, "If you take night courses like I did, the tuition is cut in half, and since you can work during the day, it's not a burden on your parents. If you really want to go, you should think about it." Rie had not considered this possibility before, and she decided to study for the exams again. Finally she was accepted into the night course program at a university. During an interview conducted after Rie had decided to go to Toyo University, she showed strong motivation, saying, "I want to study hard so that when I graduate, I won't regret not having studied more [at college]."

Rie's school performance was not particularly high and she did not have good study habits. Consequently, she did not have confidence regarding exams and schoolwork in general, and she was unsure of her future. She was also unable to offer a concrete "this is want I want to do" explanation to her parents, who maintained that "unless there is something that you really want to do, there is no point in going to college"; in addition, concern for her family's finances also made her think that it would be better to work rather than to go to school. However, by talking with her friends, former students in the program, and volunteers, and by preparing for the exams, Rie's desire to go to college grew stronger.

FACTORS DETERMINING CAREER CHOICES

The most direct factors affecting the career choices of students are more often than not poor grades and the lack of good study habits. Apart from these individual factors, however, economic recession and the transformation of the employment system also influence students' career choices. Family relationships and family finances are involved, as well. At a school like Nozomi, many students come from complicated family situations and, more often than not, relationships with parents and siblings play a part in how a student views his or her future options. Even regarding family finances, we observed that students did not simply say, "I don't have money so I won't go to college." Rather, they demonstrated concern for their parents, stating, "I don't want to be a burden on my parents" or "I want to pay off my parents' debts." It was not infrequent that these students would say they were voluntarily choosing not to go to college. In this way, family is often a concern when students consider their career plans. However, rather than perceiving simply that family is a factor for these students, it is important also to understand that there may be a certain power mechanism at work that makes students connect their own difficulties with those of their family when trying to make career plans.

For example, when students raise their family's financial situation as an obstacle to going to college, and state that they do not want to be a burden on their parents, the statements must be considered in the context of weak government support. As Miyamoto comments in her translation of Jones and Wallace's *Youth, Family, and Citizenship* (1992/1996) while drawing a comparison with England, "In our country [Japan], it is left up to parents to provide the support necessary for youth to become independent. Compared to industrialized countries in the West, the role played by the government is minimal" (p. 271). Students blame their difficulty in choosing an educational or career path on "personal failure" or "family issues," and never on the problem of insufficient scholarship programs for college.

Further, students did not once mention their family's social class as a factor when talking about postgraduation plans. Unlike the "lads" described by Willis (1977), who had a group consciousness about being part of the working class, no one in our study expressed any sentiments against the middle class. These conditions seem to reflect what Beck (1986/1998) has referred to as the individualization of social inequality and social risk.

A final observation drawn from our project was that students have little information about higher education. Based on research by Kariya (1991), Shimomura (2002) writes, "high school students are able to judge fairly accurately what kind of career options they have based on their grades and attendance" (p. 96). While this is true, students' use of information about applying for college is extremely low. They are able to access information about different subjects and exams from sources such as examination magazines, but they have no concrete idea of what college life and classes are like. Selecting a school or a major out of so many choices is a very difficult task for the kinds of students who participated in our project. Furthermore, if their parents are not college graduates, the image of college these students have is the one promoted by the mass media: leisure land. One student said, "I've already done all the kinds of fun things you do in college anyway, so there's no reason for me to go," clearly indicating how the college experience is viewed.

Turning Points and Gender

As a factor in determining postgraduation career plans, gender should be given particular consideration (Sakai, 2007; Sakai, Chiba, Hirosaki, & Saito, 2006). In our support activities, we found that the students who experienced a turning point in their postgraduation thinking were all girls. Denzin (1989) has described this kind of turning point experience as an "epiphany," one of the central elements of storytelling. Of course, Denzin's concept of epiphany is one born out of problematic situations such as abuse or alcoholism, and it is not quite the same as the turning point experience for students. In the current context, a turning point, though perhaps not so dramatic as Denzin's epiphany, is an experience that significantly changes a student's postgraduation career perspective and motivation.

Why is there a difference between boys and girls in the way that they experience a turning point? Analysis of our support project at Nozomi shows that once girls decided that they wanted to continue to higher education, they had higher aspirations and worked harder than boys. This phenomenon has not been addressed in previous "gender and career" research. Such studies have analyzed what path each gender chose out of the options available in their particular situation but ignored cases that deviated from the norm. Certainly, these deviations should be explained if they are to be considered as a construct of gender. Moreover, they contradict the premise on which all previous studies have been based. What has become clear through the cases we studied in this project is that previous research has been overly dependent on socialization theory. It was assumed that girls chose options thought to be ideal for girls, and that was the topic of study. However, even when girls choose options that differ from what is expected by others, a gender factor still exists. What role, then, does gender play in mediating career decision-making of students?

Gender Identity in Mediating Career Decision-Making

Go-Getter Girls. Of the students introduced earlier, Rie experienced turning points. She did not have much approval from her mother about going to college. When Rie failed the entrance exam to her top-choice school, she seriously debated whether to try again for school or to find work instead. A conversation with a former student who had participated in our program 2 years earlier provided the turning point for Rie. When the former student asked her, "Do you want to work, or do you want to study a little more," Rie said that she thought, "I want to study a little more."

Rie was carrying feelings of regret over not having studied harder when she was in junior high school and not getting any certifications for computer processing while she was in high school, even though that had been her goal. For Rie, going to college was her chance to take a second shot at the studying she had not done up until then. She asked her father for permission to take the college exam for the last time, and even though there were not many days left before the exam date, she put together her statement of purpose for the application and practiced writing essays and doing interviews. She was accepted into the night course program at a university.

Case 3: Kazumi. Another student I will introduce here is a girl named Kazumi, who graduated in March 2004. She lived in a four-person household with parents and a younger sister in seventh grade. In her third and last year of junior high school, Kazumi did not go to class often. Her attendance record was poor and her GPA was low. Her advisor had said, "You're not going to get into high school so you better starting thinking about looking for jobs." She panicked and studied enough to get into Nozomi. When she first started high school, Kazumi thought that she would not be able to keep up with her studies, so her goal was to at least graduate. Perhaps all of her studying for the high school entrance exams had proven effective, however, because she scored highly on her first-term test and continued to get high marks thereafter. In her third year of high school, Kazumi even became class president. She had also actively participated in volunteer activities with her school, starting in her first year. As a freshman, Kazumi had planned to find a job after graduation because her mother had told her, "You're a girl, and it's a commercial high school, and you'll get married anyway, so going to college would be a waste," and that "working at a bank would be good."

Kazumi stated that she became interested in going to college herself after she watched a senior student participate in our support program and get into college. However, until the student festival held in October had passed, Kazumi was not able to devote her attention to thinking about her postgraduation options. She said, "After the festival was over, it was as if I had finally opened my eyes and I started to panic about what I was going to do after graduation." At that point, there were only 10 days until the deadline to submit purpose statements for application. Although Kazumi stayed late after school every day to put together her paperwork, she said, "I was really not too excited about the first application I sent out," and she said that she knew nothing about the subjects she had chosen for her exam.

However, in the process of compiling her application paperwork, Kazumi said that she reflected on the various volunteer activities she had participated in while at school, and thought, "I want to work hard!" after realizing how she had had the opportunity to meet so many people and have the support of Mr. Kawai and the volunteers in this project. Finally, when Kazumi began drafting essays seriously, she worked with a volunteer to search the internet and read books on continuing education in the subject she planned to take for exams. She realized that she would be able to connect her high school volunteer activities to her studies in college. This was a big turning point for Kazumi, and she began to study actively. After passing the first round of exams, she participated in our support activities almost every day. She read books in her field and practiced answering numerous high-level essay problems. As a result, she was accepted at one of the most prestigious universities in Japan.

Boys Bound by Expectation

We found that the boys at Nozomi did not necessarily choose their postgraduation course independently. Rather, they were bound by a general atmosphere that assumed, "Nowadays, boys should go to college." Although these boys showed a desire to go to college early in the process of choosing what they would do after graduation, they did not study or prepare for exams. For this reason, many ended up becoming part-time, nonregular employees. These kinds of students could get into college if they were given postgraduation decision-making support. In 2004, more boys than in any previous year participated in our project. Here, two of them are presented as case studies.

Case 4: Makoto. Makoto lived a 15-minute walk from Nozomi in a high-rise Tokyo public housing complex. He lived with his parents, and was the oldest of three sons. He had attended local schools for both elementary and junior high school. After finishing junior high school, Makoto entered high school but withdrew midway through his first year because of truancy. When he entered Nozomi, he was 1 year behind. His advisor of 3 years commented, "That kid is just lazy, he doesn't like to work hard. He's fairly smart, but he doesn't make an effort, can't get up in the morning, goes home if he's bored in class, basically he doesn't have much self-control. That's why his friends from junior high didn't take him seriously."

On the postgraduation plans survey given by the guidance division at Nozomi, Makoto wrote that he planned to go to college. During the year before graduation, however, Makoto went from being decided to being discouraged each term about his postgraduation plan to go to college. At the beginning of his senior year, in April, Makoto said to Mr. Kawai, "I haven't been late to class at all up through today [3 days]. I'm going to keep it up, I swear, this time I really will, so watch me, okay?" The next week, though, he started coming late to school.

Mr. Kawai advised Makoto to participate in the essay-writing support activities of this project, and Makoto attended five times over the course of summer break. However, when instructed on how to write on typical college topics, he insisted on his own opinions or said, "I'll do it at home," and started talking with friends. He also did things such as invite his friends and the volunteers to go camping, showing no sign of the commitment he had made to study for exams before the break. Still, he was accepted into the night course program at a university.

Case 5: Yusuke. Yusuke's family ran a kimono business. His older brother had graduated from a private high school and had gone on to Komazawa University. Yusuke's parents wanted him to attend college like his older brother, and in response to the postgraduation plans survey given in June, Yusuke wrote that he planned on continuing to college. However, he had not thought about exactly which colleges and which exams he wanted to apply for until summer break of his senior year. Worried, Yusuke's advisor phoned him and had him come to school to meet with a career guidance counselor.

The counselor recommended that Yusuke apply to a less competitive university through the business enterprise and management course of the "Admission Office" entrance exam, without any achievement tests. One of the requirements for this exam was that the applicant had to be planning to take over a family business. The application was complicated and required a statement of purpose, consent forms from a guardian, and essays. Yusuke finished his admission application over the summer, but starting in September, he did not participate actively in the twice-weekly support activities until right before the exam date approached. He also did not seem to think that he needed to be making any special effort. Finally, 2 weeks before his exam date, Yusuke seriously engaged in the remaining activities.

After his admission exam, Yusuke complained, "I was shocked—during the interview they said something about my hair. Why didn't anyone warn me?" Actually, Yusuke had been warned three times by the volunteers and by his teachers, but he had not taken them seriously, saying, "It's going to be a breeze so don't worry about it," or "I know, I know." The volunteers and teachers had managed to persuade Yusuke to get a haircut, but his hairstyle remained more or less the same. He understood in general that to get into college he would need to make an effort and to bear certain things he did not like, but he was unable to translate the knowledge into action. Still, he was admitted into the college of his choice, and he went around saying to the volunteers and teachers, "I thought I would never get in after they said all that [about my hair], but this is great! I swear I'm going to do well once I start!"

Gender Differences in Postgraduation Plans at Multiple-Track Schools

The study revealed clear differences between girls who reach a turning point and become go-getters and boys who never actively reach that point. One of the volunteers who worked mostly with boys stated, "Boys don't swing back and forth or worry the way girls do, but they don't have any ambition to work hard." Still, their parents approve of them going to college. If girls had the same approach, it can be assumed that their parents would not permit them to go to college. Moreover, girls themselves tend to self-regulate and think that they should not go to college with an irresponsible attitude. To state it simply, boys can go to college with a complacent attitude if their parents are able to pay for it, but girls have to have a clear goal in mind that is convincing not only to their parents but to themselves as well.

This gender and postgraduation issue can best be understood as a problem of discrimination. The biggest difference between female and male students is whether or not they bear the burden of "proof of existence" shouldered by all of those who are discriminated against. As Ishikawa (1992) pointed out, all people at one point in their lives must prove their identity and who they are. However, those who tend to have their value denied—that is, those who are discriminated against—become vehement about proving their existence in an effort to protect their self-worth. Ishikawa used the term "identity issue" in describing this structural problem of people bound to their proof of existence.

Deciding on postgraduation plans is one of life's major turning points. The task that girls attending multiple-track schools have, even beyond deciding what to do after graduation, is the identity issue cited by Ishikawa (1992). Attending multiple-track schools, and being female, they are doubly devalued as students for which there is "no point in going to college." For boys, college is expected even at multiple-track schools, and it is hardly necessary for them to explain the reasons why they would choose the option of going to college. In contrast, girls at multiple-track schools have to explain their purpose in going to college not only to others but to themselves as well, and they must do it convincingly. This becomes one part of their identity issue.

DISCUSSION

In commercial high schools, those who rank highly among their classmates and have good attitudes have chances to find work, but the vast number of students are left with working odd jobs or attending relatively easy-to-enter specialized training colleges and low-level colleges. They choose to take a path with a low possibility for success in society, dictated by their low achievement, family financial situations, or low expectations from their parents, and this becomes the basis for their career narratives. For them, it is difficult to envision a narrative where they have a goal and they work hard to achieve it. Instead, these students have a desire to be recognized and accepted as they are, "as a person," or they only want to finish high school and do not give much thought to what they will do afterward. Based on various rationales, they opt not to work full time, instead becoming part-time, nonregular employees.

Through the strategic intervention of our volunteer support activities, we attempted to aid students in an escape from the structural difficulties that inhibited them. First and foremost, our objective in supporting students was to figure out how best to loosen their hardened postgraduation career perspectives. Labeled as low-track, and with few employment possibilities, most students had more or less given up on any dreams or aspirations for a better life after high school. Of course, they did not express this directly, instead talking about how they wanted to do something that would accept them as they were. In negative statements such as "college is pointless so I'm not going," we detected "the other voice" of students who had no choice but to give up on further education because of their low prospects and a dearth of information.

Our activities focused on challenging this thinking and getting students to reconsider their postgraduation plans. As a result, there were students who still chose not to go to college, but we believe that this decision was a product of their own careful thinking.

One of the major sociological problems we encountered in our project was the influence of gender. Through our activities over an extended period, we found that discrimination toward women in Japanese society is imposed quite heavily on girl students at low-track high schools. To contend with the discrimination against them, these girls were pressed to have clear reasons for wanting to go to college, and they had to convince their parents and teachers to support them. Because of this, girls experienced significant turning points in their career perspectives.

CONCLUSIONS

In our research and through undertaking these support activities, my colleagues, the volunteers, and I observed the "plasticity" of young people of high school age. Due to frequent testing and examination, high schools in Japan are precisely divided by academic level, and students judge their own abilities based on the rank of the school they attend. They tell their career narratives accordingly. These narratives are further reinforced by a downturn in the hiring market for high school graduates. In fact, there are a number of chances for young people to recover in society after high school, but few of them attempt it actively. The tracking system moves students along, and their grades at the end of junior high school largely determine their futures. Many of these young people do not have anything to look forward to, or they become *freetas* (part-time, nonregular employees) because they say they want to maintain their personal identities. The reality is that life is not easy for most of them, but they take on their problems and try to solve them on their own. In many societies, youth who are angry over their social system and status will incite political crisis. But, in Japan, nowhere in the past 10 years has there been a rebellion by youth unhappy with bad treatment. There have been calls to address this problem collectively surrounding Japanese youth with support from sociological standpoints or political measures, but there has been little true action. As demonstrated in this chapter, it is a worrisome issue.

ACKNOWLEDGMENTS

I wish to acknowledge the assistance of the following colleagues: N. Otawa, a research assistant at Tokyo University; S. Chiba, a vice principal for a Tokyo high school; J. Hirosaki, a high school teacher, formerly on the staff at Waseda University; A. Kazama, formerly a graduate student at Ochanomizu University and now a family court probation officer; H. Sugihara, formerly a graduate student at Ochanomizu University; and R. Hamano, formerly a graduate student at Tokyo University.

REFERENCES

Beck, U. (1986). *Risikogesellschaft: Auf dem Weg in eine andere Moderne.* Frankfurt: Suhrkamp. [Translated edition: (1998). *Kiken shakai: Atrashii kindai eno michi.* Tokyo: Hosei Daigaku Shuppan Kyoku.]

Berger, P., & Luckmann, T. (1966). *The social construction of reality: a treatise in the sociology of knowledge.* Garden City, NY: Doubleday.

Denzin, N. K. (1989). *Interpretive interactionism.* Newbury Park, CA: Sage Publications.

Ishikawa, J. (1992). *Sonzai shomei no shakaigaku* [*Identity game: Sociology of identification identity game*]. Tokyo: Shin Hyoron.

Jones, G., & Wallace, C. (1992). *Youth, family, and citizenship.* Buckingham, UK: Open University Press. [Translated edition: (1996). *Wakamono wa naze otona ni narenainoka: Kazoku, kokka, citizenship* (M. Miyamoto, Trans.). Tokyo: Shin-Hyoron.]

Kariya, T. (1991). *Gakko, syokugyo, senbatsu no shakaigaku* [*Sociology of school, occupation, and selection*]. Tokyo: Tokyo University Press.

Kazama, A. (2005). *A sociological study of functional change of career guidance and organizational process in a commercial high school.* Unpublished master's thesis, Ochanomizu University, Tokyo.

Sakai, A. (Ed.). (2007). *Shingaku shien no kyoiku rinsho shakaigaku: Shogyo-kohko ni okeru action research* [*Clinical sociology of education on supporting students' advancement to university: An action research in a commercial high school*]. Tokyo: Keiso Shobo.

Sakai, A., Chiba, S., Hamano, R., & Hirosaki, J. (2004). A clinical educational research on student's career choice: A report on a support project at 'A' commercial high school. *Bulletin of the Research Center for Child and Adolescent Development and Education, Ochanomizu University, 2,* 85–100.

Sakai, A., Chiba, S., Hirosaki, J., & Saito, R. (2006). A clinical educational research on student's career choice (2): Turning points and gender. *Bulletin of the Research Center for Child and Adolescent Development and Education, Ochanomizu University, 3,* 97–112.

Shimomura, H. (2002). Freeter no shokugyo ishiki to sono keisei katei [Occupational attitude of freeter and its formative process]. In R. Kosugi (Ed.), *Jiyu no daisho/freeter* (pp. 75–100). Tokyo: Nippon Rodo Kenkyu Kiko.

Sugihara, H. (2004). *A qualitative study of students' "career stories" in two high schools.* Unpublished master's thesis, Ochanomizu University, Tokyo.

Tomie, H. (1999). Increase and decrease of the vocational tracks in high school education: Focusing on the cases of the rural areas. *Bulletin of the Graduate School of Education, the University of Tokyo, 39,* 203–211.

Willis, P. E. (1977). *Learning to labour: How working class kids get working class jobs.* Farnborough, UK: Saxon House.

PART II

Educational Inequalities and Marginalized Groups

YOSHIRO NABESHIMA

Invisible Racism in Japan

Impact on Academic Achievement of Minority Children

*D*OWA MONDAI (or *Buraku Mondai*) signifies the issues concerning a castelike minority group unique to Japanese society. *Burakumin* are the people whose ancestors were relegated to an outcaste status in the premodern era. Having no distinguishing physical or cultural traits, *Burakumin* are distinguished by their addresses in communities called *Buraku* (or *Dowa* districts), which were segregated in the premodern era, or by their ancestral backgrounds. *Burakumin* still face discrimination and suffer from generally below average socioeconomic status today.

In 1966, when the first edition of *Japan's Invisible Race* by George DeVos and Hiroshi Wagatsuma was published, it was quite difficult for a researcher to find written information on *Buraku* issues. The significance of the book was great, because it was the first academic report on *Burakumin* by a non-Japanese researcher. The publication of *Invisible Race* coincided with dramatic changes in the lives of the *Burakumin*. These could be described in many ways, but the best place to start would be the obvious changes that occurred in the study of *Buraku* issues (Fujita, 1987; Kurokawa, 2004; Nabeshima, 1998, 2003; Noguchi, 2000; Uesugi, 1997).

Osaka City University, which founded the first academic research facility devoted to the *Buraku* issue in 1969, has one of the richest book collections on *Buraku* in Japan. Among its collections, only 14 titles were published in the 1950s. The number grows slightly (to 58) for publication in the 1960s, then it steps up to 280 for the 1970s and 407 in the 1980s. In the 1990s, the number declines to 324. The researchers of the original studies in *Japan's Invisible Race* were doing their work with scarcely any information, and they just missed the information boom that occurred in the few years after their work was published.

As a researcher in educational sociology, I started my research career studying the academic achievement of *Burakumin* children in the late 1980s. I was an undergraduate student in aesthetics when, in 1982, I volunteered to work as a tutor for after-school activities offered at a *Buraku* community near the university I attended. I still remember the shock of first seeing children who lagged so far behind their peers in standard academic achievement. This experience led me to convert my career plan from aesthetics to educational sociology. In this chapter I will present some facts on the academic achievement of *Burakumin* children whom I have studied over the past 20 years. Through my explanation I hope to provide an understanding of the range of characteristics associated with "racism" in Japan. I will begin with a short introduction to the *Burakumin,* followed by a review of the *Dowa* measures that began in 1960s and their impact on *Burakumin.*

THE *BURAKUMIN*

The *Burakumin,* who number approximately 1,170,000, or 1% of Japan's national population (Ministry of Public Management, 1992), are one of the largest minority groups in Japan. There are no physical or outward cultural differences between *Burakumin* and other Japanese. Discrimination against *Burakumin* has been long-lasting, though declining gradually. Their socioeconomic status is still lower than that of other Japanese. The direct originators of this group are the outcaste people of Japan's feudal society. In the late 16th century, the ruling class established a rigid caste system in which the top castes were the warriors (*Bushi*) and the nobility (*Kuge*), followed by peasants (*Hyakusho*) and artisans and merchants (*Chonin*). The ancestors of the *Burakumin* were below these four categories, and were viewed as outcastes who were segregated and bound to many "caste codes" that forbade them from participation in society or interaction with another caste. (See Berreman, 1960, and his comments in DeVos & Wagatsuma, 1966, about the usage of the term "caste." Ogbu, 1974, 1978, further utilizes this term for comparative minority studies.)

The Meiji revolution of the mid-19th century changed Japanese society into a "modern" society based on "Western" values. Freedom and equality were declared by the new government, and the Emancipation Order in 1871 abolished the legal basis for the outcaste status. But, naturally, traditional attitudes toward these people did not change. Moreover, drastic changes in the economic system started to leave them behind as they lacked enough economic and political power to participate in the modern system. Despite many efforts, by individuals and groups of both *Burakumin* and non-*Burakumin,* to raise public concern, Japan's government did not officially create a measure to remedy these conditions. Relevant academic study was also neglected. On the other hand, the growing, overheated nationalism among Japanese people narrowed the door for them to see their own inner diversity. Thus, the caste minority in Japanese society was covered up, made a taboo subject, and kept a secret from the outside world, leaving the *Burakumin* to suffer (Inoue, 1969; Mahara, 1973; Ryoke, 1996; Shindo, 1977; Uesugi, 1990).

During the half century after the Emancipation Order of 1871, *Burakumin* fought back against discrimination and demanded equality. Because most of those struggles were by individuals or by a single community, they usually did not end successfully (Uesugi, 1993; Wada, 1994; Yoshinami, 1987). However, these struggles did lead to recognition among *Burakumin* and a realization that there were many people around Japan who suffered from the same conditions. In 1922, this increased communication finally resulted in creation of the first nationwide political organization for and by *Burakumin*: the *Suiheisha* (the Levelers). *Suiheisha*'s influence grew rapidly among *Burakumin*, and branches were opened in many *Buraku* communities (Kurokawa, 1999).

Suiheisha was known by its tactic of thorough denunciation. When they found an incident of discrimination, they went to the source and demanded an apology, usually published in a newspaper. The government began to fear that *Suiheisha* might become a trigger for radical political movement. In 1925, the government established the Central Harmony Project Organization and began to give aid to *Buraku* communities. In 1933, a militaristic cabinet took over the Japanese government. Ironically, the official antidiscrimination campaign was reinforced by this government because they cared about discrimination among soldiers. "Ordinary" Japanese soldiers did not recognize *Burakumin* soldiers as fellow Japanese, and they treated them by traditional caste codes. *Burakumin* Soldiers Associations were organized among some troops to fight against these situations. Jiichiro Matsumoto, one of the leaders in these associations, became the first chairperson of the *Buraku* Liberation League, which was established after World War II. Matsumoto is known as "the father of *Buraku* liberation." *Suiheisha* itself was suppressed by the government. Many members were imprisoned on charges of violating the Peace Preservation Law, and the organization was forced into dissolution in 1943 (Buraku Mondai Kenkyu Sho, 1986; Inoue, 1969).

The National Law for Dowa *Measures*

Post–World War II *Buraku* liberation movements have been critical about usage of the term "*Dowa*" because of its connection to militarism and the emperor system. *Dowa* is a combination of two characters: *Do*, meaning "same," and *Wa*, meaning "harmony." These characters were picked up from the emperor's imperial edict issued at the enthronement in 1926 to signify *Buraku* issues within an imperialist scheme. *Dowa* replaced the term "*Yuwa*" in 1941. *Yuwa* meant "integration," which was the term the government had used since the 1920s in designating *Buraku* issues. In 1941, the government started to force any kind of *Burakumin*-related organization, whether it was governmental or nongovernmental, to be reorganized into *Dowa Houko Kai* (*Dowa* Serving Society) and placed *Burakumin*-related activities under the control of the national government. Such centralization was used by the military government to control social movements. Although there were many criticisms of using the term *"Dowa"* after the war, the government decided to use this term to designate *Buraku* issues in establishing a new governmental scheme in relation to the *Burakumin* in the 1960s.

The Dotaishin-toushin *of 1965*

One of the most dramatic events in *Buraku* history (which was not reported in the first edition of *Japan's Invisible Race*) was the report by the *Dowa* Council to the Cabinet issued in 1965, known as *Dotaishin-toushin*. This report expressly stated that both the government and the people bore responsibility for the past and present suffering of *Burakumin* (namely, the *Dowa* issues). The report also precisely designated a vast number of issues that should be solved and described the required budgetary measures needed to eliminate discrimination and the underprivileged status of the *Burakumin*. Wagatsuma reports on intensive interviews with the main personnel of this council in *Japan's Invisible Race*. The *Dotaishin-toushin* became the major weapon used by *Burakumin* to seek equality and solutions for their conditions. The BLL (*Buraku* Liberation League) organized several huge demonstrations after the issuing of the *Dotaishin-toushin,* including the Grand March of 1961, demanding the "full enforcement of the *Dotaishin-toushin,*" which finally led to the enactment of the *Dowa* Measures Special Law of 1969. The law was planned for a 10-year fixed period. Under pressure from the BLL, the national government extended the law for 3 years in 1979, and then again for 5 more years in 1982. At the second extension (1982), the name of the law was changed to the Community Improvement Special Measure Act. The intention of the name change was to hide the word *Dowa* and, it was hoped, avoid provoking a "jealous mind" against the special treatment toward the *Burakumin*. In 1987, another 5-year extension was made, cutting several areas of subsidies to reduce the budget. The final extension of 5 years came in 1992.

Along with a few original projects of the national government, the *Dowa* measures laws focused mainly on encouraging local governments to operate *Dowa* projects (*Dowa Jigyo*) by subsidizing two thirds of their budget. The usual subsidy of the national government to local governments had been only one third under similar laws. Being twice as supportive, monetarily, the *Dowa* Measures Special Law successfully activated many local efforts. Applications submitted by local governments were required to meet several criteria. The most basic criterion was that projects had to be aimed at a "*Dowa* district," which meant that the national government had to verify that the districts in question were truly *Dowa* districts. However, the national government took a shortcut and left this authority to the local governments, thus keeping out of local controversies about which districts should be designated *Dowa* districts.

Quite a few local governments that were eager to solve *Buraku* issues worked to figure out where the *Burakumin* lived, consulting researchers, the BLL, or other organizations. After determining where the supposed *Burakumin* were living, the local governments then asked people living in the supposed *Dowa* districts whether they approved of the designation as a "*Dowa* district" and asked the local legislatures to approve the designation. Some districts approved and some did not, and in some cases the issue led to political arguments involving various politicians and political parties. Local governments had to deal with these sensitive situations in order to adequately enforce the law.

The positive side of this situation was that it made *Buraku* much more visible and public than they had been previously, as local governments were literally revealing *Buraku* to the public. It was no longer taboo—at least for local governments—to talk about *Buraku* issues. *Dowa* education became formally promoted by the Ministry of Education, reinforcing the trend toward more revelation and discussion. However, many *Burakumin* were excluded from the measure because they did not live in an officially designated *Dowa* district. Researchers presume that approximately 1,000 districts were excluded from the *Dowa* measures (Kita, 1989). These *Buraku* were referred to as *mishitei-chiku,* literally "nondesignated district." Some local governments, such as the Tokyo Prefecture government, refused to designate any *Dowa* districts for political reasons. Many people even today share a perception that revealing the whereabouts of *Buraku* would encourage discrimination against *Burakumin.* These people believe that the best way to solve this problem is to totally eliminate the word *Buraku* and related terminology from people's minds. That, they believe, can only be accomplished by hiding information about *Buraku.* For these people, the official designation of *Dowa* district only awakens discrimination in people's minds and causes those living in designated *Buraku* to be victims of discrimination. Some governments decided not to enforce the national law for these reasons. Most of the prefectures and cities/towns/villages that did not designate any *Dowa* districts were in eastern Japan, though the reasons for not doing so varied from area to area. *Buraku* that were isolated among non-*Burakumin* populations and (or) *Buraku* with a very small populations tended to refuse designation in an attempt to discourage an environment that might call attention to their identity.

A Case Study of the Lived Reality of the Dowa *Measures: Asaka*

Asaka *Buraku,* located on the bank of the Yamato River, is a village with a population of 1,300. Among 48 *Buraku* in Osaka Prefecture, Asaka was one of the latest to install *Dowa* measures. Asaka was one of the typical *Buraku* in which residents were divided into "for" and "against" groups regarding *Dowa* measures, which caused a delay in implementation (Buraku Kaiho Asaka

Chiku Sogo Keikaku Jikku Iinkai, 1991; Yamamoto & Buraku Kaiho Asaka Chiku Sogo Keikaku Jikku Iinkai, 2002). Examining the implementation of *Dowa* measures in Asaka demonstrates how the measure and concomitant controversies actually played themselves out in public.

Establishment of Asaka *Buraku*. Asaka is a relatively young *Buraku*, developing 280 years ago, whereas many *Buraku* are assumed to have a history of more than 500 years and some are documented as going as far back as the 15th century. Formal documents from the Edo period show that Asaka, which was called *Sugimoto Shinden* at the time, was developed in 1721 by several outcaste families who happened to occupy the location because of their prescribed caste duties. Outcaste people were obliged to do construction work whenever their landlord needed it done. At that point in the early 18th century, the Edo *Shogunate* decided to change the watercourse of the "wild" Yamato River and called up outcaste people to carry out their feudal duties. After the construction, some of the workers decided to remain at the former construction site and cultivate their own rice fields, and the landlord permitted them to do so, which was unusual for outcaste people at that time. They started to plow the land, perhaps dreaming of a life as ordinary peasants (Asaka no Rekishi wo Tsukuru Kai, 1979).

Although *Burakumin* were outcastes under Japan's feudal system and were presumed to be impure under the dominant ideology, that did not mean they were all economically poor. Most of them had the privilege of monopolizing their "menial" businesses—such as tanning, gardening, low-rank police work, and so forth—which not only secured their economic livelihood but also allowed a few to make a good fortune through such monopolies. They were also immune from taxation (Uesugi, 1997). The reason why the first-generation Asaka inhabitants left their original *Buraku* as well as their privileged vocation is unknown, but the challenging project of developing the land soon proved to be too difficult. The land was not fertile enough for rice; the only crop that would grow was *konjak*—an easy-to-grow but less profitable vegetable. Facing an economic crisis, they asked the neighboring *Buraku* to give them a share of the privileged outcaste vocation to collect dead cattle, but they were refused (Asaka no Rekishi wo Tsukuru Kai, 1979).

In the 1860s, the Meiji government replaced the Edo *Shogunate* and started to liberalize the economic system. The government stripped the vocational and taxation privileges from outcaste people and, in turn, declared that "they should be treated as commoners." The Emancipation Order of 1871 soon became a disaster for former outcaste people. The behavior of non-*Burakumin* toward the *Burakumin* did not change, other than that they began to be called "special villagers" (*Tokushu-Burakumin*) or "new commoners" (*Shin-Heimin*). Indeed, offenses toward them became harsher to the point that, in many areas, non-*Burakumin* started to protest against the government, demanding restoration of the caste system. These social agitations often resulted in attacking and burning of the *Buraku* and in some cases killing of the residents (Uesugi, 1993; Wada, 1994; Yoshinami, 1987). In addition to a tax burden they had never before experienced, *Buraku* businesses were now threatened by many competitors from both within and out of the community. With the exception of a handful of successful businesses, the *Buraku* people's economic situation was far more fragile after the Emancipation Order due to the economic deflation policy in the late 19th century. As a result, *Burakumin* sought jobs outside their districts, but employment discrimination left them with only low-paying positions, such as day laborers or tenant farmers (Mahara, 1973).

Asaka in Modernization. After the Emancipation Order, Asaka residents faced more difficulties than they had faced before enactment of the law. In addition to growing *konjak* or collecting and selling river sand, they started to collect junk for recycling. Even young women carrying babies on their backs pulled a cart through the streets of Osaka City calling out, "sell me junk!" which inevitably raised more discriminative gazes toward *Burakumin*. Most of the Asaka residents lived in very poor wooden houses jammed side by side. It was obvious that the slightest negligence with fire could be disastrous for the whole village. No sewage system was installed, nor was there a water supply pipe. People used a common bath and toilet, drawing water from wells, while other Osaka citizens enjoyed modern waterworks (Buraku Kaiho Asaka Chiku Sogo Keikaku Jikku Iinkai, 1991, 2002; Yamamoto & Buraku Kaiho Asaka Chiku Sogo Keikaku Jikku Iinkai, 2002).

Riverbed Life. Life was even worse for the approximately one third of Asaka residents who lived on the riverbed. Many *Buraku* are located by rivers and suffer from flooding and other inconveniences. The Asaka case is typical. National law prohibits people from living on a riverbed, and usually the riverbed is owned and controlled by the government. But in the Asaka case, the riverbed was registered as owned by the Asaka residents, which meant that the government left Asaka people on the riverbed even as they embanked the Yamato River. Riverbed houses were built in a unique way, leaning up against the bank of the river, which served as the back wall of the house. Whenever it rained, water would ooze out into the house from the bank wall. When the river rose as high as the bank, houses were swallowed into the river. Starting in the late 1970s, the riverbed houses of Asaka were removed and the Osaka City government provided apartment complexes for the people who had once lived on the riverbed. Today the riverbed has been renovated into a public park.

The Train Depot. Another injustice Asaka residents suffered from was the huge train depot built right in front of Asaka village in 1960. Train depots, garbage plants, dog pounds, and other public facilities that people do not want near their homes tend to be built near *Buraku*. Moreover, because *Buraku* were situated in relatively isolated areas, non-*Burakumin* would not complain if these facilities were built in such areas. Therefore, developers and governments faced less pressure in negotiating construction of these troublesome facilities. Whether through talking, threatening, or bribing, isolated *Buraku* that had low populations and little political power were easy to persuade. The train depot brought significant noise pollution to Asaka. Train after train coming into to the depot made loud, irritating braking sounds, which continued until long after midnight. But much more serious for the people of Asaka than the noise was the geographic isolation. Located behind the train depot, Asaka was totally isolated from the surrounding area and was dubbed *riku-no-kotou* (an inaccessible corner). On the south side of Asaka runs the Yamato River, while the east side of Asaka was blocked by the huge campus of Osaka City University; the west side is cut off from the neighboring area by the Greater Abiko Bridge. Then came the tall walls of the train depot, closing every inch of the northern border of Asaka. This environment magnified Asaka residents' feelings of social isolation. They felt as if the Osaka City government and the majority of its citizens had deliberately tried to disconnect Asaka from the city (Buraku Kaiho Asaka Chiku Sogo Keikaku Jikku Iinkai, 1991, 2002; Yamamoto & Buraku Kaiho Asaka Chiku Sogo Keikaku Jikku Iinkai, 2002).

The Struggle. *Dowa* measures do not start automatically. Many local governments were passive in approving the need for a measure because of the financial burden. Even though the local governments received subsidies from the national government, they still had to contribute one third of the costs. Thus, *Burakumin* had to send strong messages to their local governments to make them initiate the measures. Local governments began to face tough negotiations with the BLL and other groups, who came armed with a new strategy called *gyousei-tousou* (government struggle). In 1965, 5 years after the train depot was built, the Asaka branch of the BLL was organized by a number of residents who thought the troubles that Asaka had been suffering should be understood as "consequences of discrimination" (Yamamoto & Buraku Kaiho Asaka Chiku Sogo Keikaku Jikku Iinkai, 2002). Since the time of the "*All Romance* incident" in Kyoto in 1959, the BLL had been using a consequences-of-discrimination theory to convince the government to take responsibility for the troubled situation of *Burakumin* life.

The *All Romance* incident was an epoch-making event in the *Buraku* liberation movement. A public servant of Kyoto City published a story called "Tokushu *Buraku*" ("A Special *Buraku*") in a journal named *All Romance*. Not only was the title seen as offensive, but the descriptions of poverty, prostitution, and other illegal acts surrounding the *Buraku* were also considered condescending, upsetting many *Burakumin*. The BLL took immediate action to denounce the author and Kyoto City. A common component of BLL's denunciation tactic at that time was to force the relevant people to make a public apology through the media and to take compensatory actions, such as dismissing one or more persons. But Zennosuke Asada, the leader of BLL Kyoto at the time and in charge of the denunciation process, took a different approach. He rejected the proposal by the Mayor of Kyoto City to fire the author as a settlement between BLL and the city. Instead, Asada requested that the Mayor call the section directors of the city together to analyze whether the situation in the *Buraku* described in the story was true or not. Furthermore, he asked them to determine whether such situations are typical of other *Buraku*. Finding that the poor situations in the concerned *Buraku* were commonly observed in other *Buraku* in Kyoto City, the Mayor and his men had to admit that those situations were probably generated as the consequence of lack of policy and (or) intentional neglect by the city government. Asada called this connection between governmental neglect and the existing poor situation of *Buraku* "consequences of discrimination" and argued that the true compensation for discrimination has to be a definite governmental policy to remove poor situations among the *Burakumin*. This logic of consequences of discrimination has worked very powerfully since that time to bring governmental attention to *Buraku* issues. Once a government agrees that a given situation is a consequence of governmental action (or inaction) and is thus its responsibility, the BLL then asks for a measure to solve the problem to compensate for the discrimination. This denunciation tactic was named "government struggle."

In 1968, Asaka branch of the BLL succeeded in convincing the Osaka City government to start the *Dowa* special measure after a long, exhausting course of negotiation. However, there were several people in Asaka who did not want their town to be labeled as a *Dowa* district. These people neither joined nor opposed the BLL's political actions. The BLL persisted in communicating with the opposing residents the importance of not splitting the community and finally succeeded in making them understand the need for the measure. Other efforts like those of the Asaka residents led to the installment of the national *Dowa* measures policy, and afterwards made it possible for many *Buraku* to receive resources, such as subsidized housing, from their local governments. In the case of Asaka, governmental compensatory action included relocation of the train depot, which was placed underground in 1982. And while Asaka now enjoys a clean environment with facilities for its residents, there were *Buraku* communities that split into two or more groups due to controversies over the *Dowa* measures. In some cases, this conflict ended in refusal of the government's *Dowa* measures proposal, which has left those areas in very poor conditions even to this day.

Mobilization and Negotiation

As discussed, in the late 1960s and early 1970s the *Burakumin* began negotiations with local governments to compensate for the long history of discrimination and segregation. Tough campaigns, including sit-in demonstrations, were necessary in the early stages, leading to the establishment of communication frameworks including such features as periodic meetings between the governments and the BLL, which helped late-comers in starting their own negotiations (Ueda, 1974). Among the many possible outcomes of the measures, those exercised under the control of the Ministry of Construction (MOC), such as housing projects, and those of the Ministry of Health and Welfare (MHW), such as establishing nurseries and clinics, were in high demand. In 1981, expenses incurred by the *Dowa* measures approached their peak, with 40% of the national subsidy going to MOC operations and 25% to those under MHW. Operations under the Ministry of International Trade and Industry and the Ministry of Agriculture, Forestry and Fisheries shared approximately 10%. Although other ministries, such as the Ministry of Education, had a relatively small share of the funding, their role was significant (Teraki & Noguchi, 2001).

Through the *Dowa* measures projects starting in the late 1960s, the lives of the *Burakumin* have changed. Community improvements include apartment complexes, paved roads and walkways, nurseries, kindergartens, hospitals, welfare centers for the elderly, youth education centers, and other facilities, as well as scholarships, literacy classes, special rate loans for business, and other economic and cultural supports. The need for such improvements differed from *Buraku* to *Buraku*. For example, urban *Buraku,* which were usually densely populated, needed new apartment complexes to reduce overcrowding in housing. On the other hand, rural *Buraku,* which had very small populations, did not need such large housing projects. They needed relatively small projects to stabilize businesses, renovate specific houses in poor condition, and so on. To plan projects for the diverse range of *Buraku*, local governments had to gather specific information from the residents; to monitor the projects, they needed to continuously communicate with the residents. Thus, the local governments inevitably found themselves engaging in various forms of partnership with the *Buraku* communities.

Most of the governments expected the BLL and other social movement bodies to become representatives and coordinators of community demands in the early stages of implementation of the measures. Those representative bodies were referred to as "reception windows" (*mado-guchi*) because they were the bodies that initially received individual residents' concerns and claims and carried them on to the government. As a consequence of this situation, such organizations began to gain influence over governmental policies. *Burakumin* leaders began to establish personal relationships with governors and other important agents who were concerned with policymaking. In some cases, personal relationships went beyond the public interest and created scandals. The best known scandal was the arrest of a vice governor and other top officials of the Kochi Prefecture government in 2001. Prosecutors claimed that the funds officials had been awarding as *Dowa* measures to a private sewing company had been illegally taken as profit by a BLL leader. The sewing company had been established through a BLL initiative to promote jobs among *Burakumin* in 1996. The BLL leader had asked the official for funding under the *Dowa* measures to modernize the factory, but the modernization was never done. Officials were arrested on suspicion of aggravated breach of trust and the BLL leader on suspicion of fraud.

Termination of the Dowa Measures

National legislation for the *Dowa* measures was enacted in response to the many voices of *Burakumin* who enthusiastically fought for it under the leadership of the BLL during the 1960s. Then why was the law terminated after 22 years, and why did the BLL agree to its termination? The main cause was the shift in policies affecting public projects. In the 1990s, nonprofit organizations started to take over governmental projects. The collapse of the "bubble" economy in early 1990s provided the political trigger to reverse policy, as most governmental bodies faced a serious shortage of funds for maintaining public projects. Instead of costly and inflexible government projects, private sectors were encouraged to take over public welfare projects in more flexible, diverse, and inexpensive ways. The NPO (Non-Profit Organization) Act of 1998 gave these groups public authority to have access to public resources and preferential treatment on taxation.

However, there were other forces working to end the *Dowa* measures. A Cabinet Council report in 1996 recommended termination of the *Dowa* measures and gave four major reasons. One was the claim that the projects had successfully accomplished their intention, with the exception of eliminating discrimination against *Burakumin*. In response to this issue, the national government established a new law called the Human Rights Education and Enlightenment Promotion Act in 1997. The second reason was repeated illegal or unfair transactions that took place in relation to the *Dowa* projects, such as bribery, leakage of inside information, and a murky decision process that profited some people. In addition, law enforcement agencies were alerted to complex extortion schemes carried out by organized crime groups against private companies. Some criminal groups exploited the fact that most of the private companies did not fully understand *Buraku* issues and the *Dowa* measures, and they attempted to trick these companies into buying ridiculous information books sold at exorbitant prices. The third reason was the problem of the "jealous mind" (*netami-ishiki*). Special measures passed exclusively for

Burakumin created jealousy toward *Burakumin* among non-*Burakumin* citizens, sometimes fulminating into claims of counterdiscrimination. The fourth reason was that a project-dependent lifestyle had spread among some *Burakumin* after the *Dowa* measures. Parts of the measure attempted to alleviate the effects of poverty by reducing expenses for housing, education, and so on. This support for poor *Burakumin* families was intended to create solid family financial bases from which individuals would seek upward social mobility, but instead it provided a route into dependency.

Each of the *Burakumin* organizations responded differently to the Cabinet Council's views. However, a political consensus developed for terminating the *Dowa* measures. The BLL, which had a history of fighting for extension of the law whenever it came close to expiration, was expected to oppose termination once again, but this time they did not. The reason the BLL did not call for extension was because they also were worried about social welfare dependency. In the beginning, the BLL had not considered the measure as potential welfare, but rather as "compensation for the 400 years of discrimination." The basic goals of self-sufficiency and self-determination, however, were undermined by dependency on governmental subsidies. The BLL thus established a new policy on *Dowa* measures in the mid-1990s and agreed with the government to terminate the national law.

Citizens' Actions Instead of Governmental Aid

During the *Dowa* measures policy era, *Burakumin* activists faced the reality that they needed more support than the government could provide and needed to cooperate with neighboring non-*Burakumin* to carry out *Dowa* projects more efficiently. Government projects related to education, welfare, employment, or livelihood support had limitations in terms of quantity, quality, and methods. For example, the government could place extra teachers in schools with *Burakumin* children, but that resource alone was not sufficient to make *Burakumin* children do more homework. The government needed to educate and empower parents in order to improve their child rearing. Many *Burakumin* communities started to organize civil activities, mostly by volunteers, and some even sought to start community businesses. These independent activities inevitably led to cooperation with neighboring non-*Burakumin* communities to seek better ways of providing quality services. After the Non-Profit Organization Act of 1998, many community activity–based organizations enrolled themselves as NPOs. For *Burakumin* residents, the means for seeking support for their lack of resources gradually shifted from collective and political struggles to mutually supporting specific civil activities.

The shift in community services observed in *Buraku* communities was not an isolated phenomenon. In Japanese society, governments had been the major provider of community services until the late 1990s. From nationwide systems of health, education, and welfare to specific projects to support minorities, as long as a given project was defined as "public," it was considered the responsibility of the government. The *Dowa* measures were a typical case. Also, there was a social consensus that government was the only body that could deliver resources fairly. But, given the limited nature of governmental projects, incidents of governmental agents' corruption, or the difficulty of defining "fairness" through governmental procedures, many started to look for their own way to seek "public" missions began to rethink the notions "public" and "fairness." These social changes led to the establishment of the NPO Act of 1998, which was one of the very rare cases in Japanese history of legislation being initiated by a House member of the Diet.

Limitations of Dowa Measures: Focus on the Educational Attainment of the Burakumin

The *Dowa* measures dramatically changed the outlook of many *Burakumin*. Apartments were supplied, nursery schools were built, and medical facilities and welfare facilities were provided by governments. People outside of the *Buraku* assumed that these changes must have stabilized *Burakumin* life. But improvement in the physical aspects of life does not necessarily improve the socioeconomic status (SES) of the group. Relative discrepancies in SES have been maintained despite the *Dowa* measures. In the pages that follow I will examine the educational attainment of *Burakumin* children and consider the weak side of the special measure.

Dowa Education. The term "*Dowa* education," which chiefly refers to teaching about *Buraku* issues, has been used by the government since 1941. The *Dowa* Special Measure Law of 1969 identified many areas of educational activity other than teaching of *Buraku* issues, such as scholarships for *Burakumin* children and improvement in high school enrollment rates. Even before enactment of the law, many teachers were devoted to supporting *Burakumin* children. In the late 1940s, there were many independent teacher groups that designated themselves "*Dowa* education research societies." In 1953, these groups united as the *Zen-Do-Kyo*, the National Committee of *Dowa* Education Research. Despite the problematic roots of the word *Dowa* discussed earlier, these teachers' efforts were highly respected by *Burakumin* and their organizations.

The *Dowa* education movement of teachers in the 1950s and 1960s revealed the serious problems that *Burakumin* children faced. *Burakumin* children's nonenrollment rate and long-term absence rate in elementary and secondary schools were significantly higher than those of non-*Burakumin*. Teachers called for additional school resources to support *Burakumin* children's academic achievement. In planning *Dowa* projects under the 1969 *Dowa* Special Measure Law, the Ministry of Education adopted many practical ideas from local projects that had been developed through the initiative of teachers who belonged to these earlier research groups. Such projects included additional teachers for *Dowa* schools, financial support for *Burakumin* children to buy textbooks and stationary, scholarships for *Burakumin* senior high school and college students, special budgets for *Dowa* schools to develop *Dowa* education, placing youth- and children-supporting facilities and tutors in *Buraku* communities, and so on. These resources from both national and local governments dramatically improved *Burakumin* children's situation from what was once called "Again their seats are empty today" (Kochi Shi Fukushi Bukai, 1954; Nara Ken Dowa Mondai Kenkyusyo, 1957).

However, simply increasing attendance rates did not solve the problems *Burakumin* children faced. Classroom misbehavior, delinquency, and low academic achievement among *Burakumin* students have been frequently reported. Figure 5.1 shows a comparison of senior high school entrance rates of *Burakumin* and all students in Osaka Prefecture (Nabeshima, 1997). The graph shows that *Burakumin* students' entrance rate grew dramatically from the early 1960s to 1975. The wide discrepancy between the two groups in the 1960s had narrowed to less than 10% in 1975. Marks of improvement were also seen in other figures such as the college entrance rate. These improvement marks had been regarded as an effect of the *Dowa* measures and *Dowa* education. However, there had been a misreading of the data.

The Invisible Barrier. The Japanese senior high school education system was established in 1948 as 3 years of optional and additional secondary education after 9 years of compulsory education. Its mission was to provide educational opportunity more widely to the nation. Different from the Japanese senior high schools in the pre–World War II period, which were very elitist (enrollment rate less than 10%), postwar senior high schools started accepting 50% of the junior high school graduates and continuously expanded their capacity until 1975, reaching more than 90% acceptance. College capacity also expanded after World War II; higher education in Japan now accepts nearly 70% of senior high school graduates. As shown in Figure 5.1, the overall high school enrollment rate grew dramatically until 1975; this was true for *Burakumin* students as well as non-*Burakumin*. It is quite plausible that the *Burakumin* students' improvement was not necessarily due to *Dowa* measures. Nabeshima (1991) has argued that this "improvement" was caused by the expansion of *opportunity* in the postwar period and that relatively low *achievement* for *Burakumin* was sustained. Since the government fixed the high school entrance rate at 95% in 1975, the discrepancy between the rate for *Burakumin* and the overall rate has been the same. This shows that *Burakumin* children's attainment has not been promoted beyond that due to the change

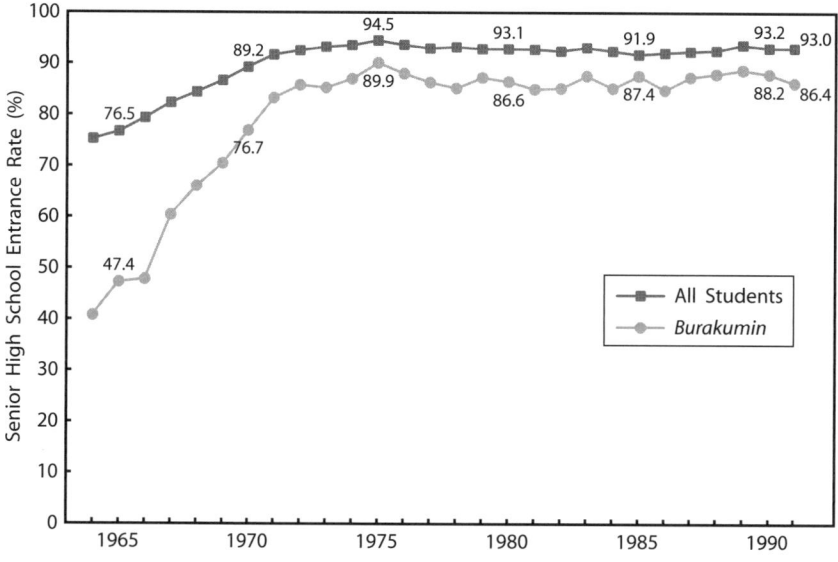

FIGURE 5.1 Entrance Rates to Senior High School

of opportunity structure. The continuous and stable discrepancy between overall students' and *Burakumin* students' figures observed in the high school entrance rate after 1975 is the most compelling evidence of an underlying factor that inhibits *Burakumin* children from attaining academic success. This "invisible barrier" has been widely observed among minority populations around the world, especially among nonimmigrant minorities. The difficulties in academic achievement among *Burakumin* children served as evidence for Ogbu's (1987) rejection of the heredity theory to explain the achievement gap between races.

Inefficacy of *Dowa* Measures. Despite the rapid growth of the national *Dowa* education budget after 1975, high school and college entrance rates of *Burakumin* children have stagnated. The Ministry of Education's *Dowa* education budget was only 338 million yen in 1970, but it expanded to 2.8 billion yen in 1975 and to 11.3 billion in 1985. It is clear that the budget growth did not have a significant effect on the *Burakumin*'s educational attainment. Many people point out that lower SES among the *Burakumin* on average is one of the problems that the *Dowa* measures could not solve. A controversy exists as to whether this was a methodological failure or a limitation rooted in the very concept of the measure itself. Some have called for quota systems in schools, but few have supported them. Quotas have been quite unpopular as a policy approach for improving minority status in Japan.

TABLE 5.1 Test Scores Comparison, *Burakumin* Versus Non-*Burakumin*, 1989–2001

	Non-*Burakumin*		*Burakumin*		Difference	
	Score	n	Score	n	Score	p
1989 Survey	(a)		(b)		(a – b)	
Fifth-grade math	81.4	1,115	72.9	255	8.5	.029
Fifth-grade language	75.2	1,124	64.6	257	10.6	.001
Eighth-grade math	76.2	1,827	58.2	297	18.0	.000
Eighth-grade language	80.4	1,830	65.0	297	15.4	.000
2001 Survey	(c)		(d)		(c – d)	
Fifth-grade math	61.0	716	41.7	156	19.3	.003
Fifth-grade language	67.7	718	50.6	160	17.1	.000
Eighth-grade math	66.6	952	45.2	177	21.4	.000
Eighth-grade language	72.8	950	60.8	176	12.0	.001
Change 1989–2001	(a – c)		(b – d)			
Fifth-grade math	–20.4		–31.2			
Fifth-grade language	–7.5		–14.0			
Eighth-grade math	–9.6		–13.0			
Eighth-grade language	–7.6		–4.2			

Sources. Osaka University (1989), Tokyo University (2001).

Recent Research on Burakumin *Education*

Burakumin children are at more risk now than they were 10 years ago. Table 5.1 shows a comparison of scores on scholastic achievement tests conducted at the same schools in 1989 and 2001 using the same set of examination questions (Nabeshima, 2004). Mean scores of both primary school fifth-graders and junior high school second-graders (the equivalent of eighth-graders in the USA) have dropped significantly, with *Burakumin* students scoring the lowest. Discrepancies between *Burakumin* scores and overall average scores have widened, except for the eighth-grade language score. Given the fact that large investments of resources by the government could not change *Burakumin* children's educational attainment, we might consider other causes in an attempt to understand why the *Burakumin* children are failing at school as a group. Thus, research on *Burakumin* children's educational attainment since the mid-1980s has begun to focus on the psychological and cultural aspects of *Burakumin* children's lives.

Hiroshi Ikeda, the late professor at Osaka University, adopted the term "self-concept" in determining the effects of children's psychological status on academic scores. He developed psychological scales to measure children's self-esteem and discovered that *Burakumin* children had lower self-esteem scores than others. He concluded that self-esteem had significant effects on academic study (Ikeda, 1989). Later surveys by Ikeda's group found that self-esteem scores were not as low as expected among *Burakumin* children. Self-esteem scores do affect academic test scores in general, but *Burakumin* children have unique features in relation to self-esteem and academic scores (Ikeda, 2000).

Yoshimasa Nishida, a professor at Osaka Prefecture University, has pursued Ikeda's idea in a different way. He conducted fieldwork in a *Buraku*, observing children's everyday life to uncover the cultural framework that affects children's perception of school, education, labor, and society. His early ethnography of a small fishing *Buraku* in Kochi Prefecture found that children's behaviors were strongly affected by the fisherman ethos shared among adults of that community (Nishida, 1990). His later interviews with members of three generations from 21 families in urban *Buraku* of Osaka Prefecture revealed that *Burakumin* families tend to value short-run profits and opportunities over long-term success and that these tendencies carry on from generation to generation (Nishida, 2001). He describes the lifestyle as a "flow" life, which differs from the "stock" life observed especially among middle-class non-*Burakumin*. He also reports that child-rearing strategies and perception of school and education among *Burakumin* families could be interpreted as derived from the flow lifestyle.

I have also been doing empirical studies on *Burakumin* children, collecting reports from surveys conducted by schools and boards of education after World War II, and have found that *Burakumin* children consistently lagged behind in academic scores (Nabeshima, 1991). I also have conducted quantitative surveys to explore what areas of life have more effect on *Burakumin* students' achievement based on John Ogbu's cultural model theory (1974, 1978, 1987, 1990, 1991). My findings indicate that besides parents' SES, which had the largest effect on *Burakumin* children's relatively low achievement, *Burakumin* students' and parents' perception toward discrimination, ambition for social promotion, and desire for early marriage had unique and significant effects on achievement (Nabeshima, 2003). These findings suggest that *Burakumin* have developed a particular interpretation of education, schooling, labor, marriage, and other institutional aspects of society as a group under the unique conditions in which they have been placed, which leads them to unique decisions and behaviors in facing those institutional features.

Kokichi Shimizu of Osaka University has been applying an interpretational approach in analyzing the interrelationship between minority groups and school systems. He gathers information on school policy, teachers' understanding of students' backgrounds, teachers' ethos, and other aspects of school, as well as students' behavior and voices, to interpret how the school and students are interrelating. He suggests that in changing the relationship between school and community, the family might have a considerable effect on minority children's achievement (Shimizu, 2005).

Nabeshima, Shimizu, Nishida, and other researchers have cooperated in conducting a set of surveys to explore school effectiveness in relation to academic achievement of poor and minority children. These analyses are based on school effectiveness research in both the United States and the United Kingdom (Bliss, Firestone, & Richards, 1991; Edmonds, 1980, 1986; Edmonds & Frederiksen, 1979; Rutter, Maughan, Mortimore, & Ouston, 1979; Sammons, Thomas, & Mortimore, 1997). We have found several primary and junior high schools that have succeeded in promoting academic achievement of poor and minority children above typical levels. We have concluded that effective schools exhibit seven key characteristics (Nabeshima, 2006):

1. Precautions against students' misbehavior and classroom disorder
2. Empowerment of each student through collective activities
3. Regard for teamwork among teachers as a decisive factor in school management
4. Active and positive school culture
5. Active liaison with parents, community, and other educational facilities
6. Maintenance of an explicit and reliable curricular system to improve students' academic achievement
7. Explicit leadership in school management

THE MYTH OF IMPROVING SOCIETY

Frankly speaking, Japanese society has been insensitive to issues of minority status throughout its modern history. Except for the period of militarism and its aftermath (from the 1930s to the 1940s), the Japanese economy has expanded greatly, and Japanese legislation has been successful in controlling the overall socioeconomic gap among the Japanese population since its modernization in the late 19th century. Because of this continuous overall improvement in the quality of life in Japanese society, including most of its subgroups, people were blinded to the need for specific legal controls over opportunity structure (especially in the areas of education and employment) designed to raise the socioeconomic status among minorities. Both minorities and majorities have spontaneously assumed that lower SES among minority groups was due to relative lack of resources on an individual basis to invest in upward mobility—and not that the problem arose from within the opportunity structure on a collective level. It seemed plausible for many people until the early 1990s that their quality of life and equality in opportunity would keep growing, although many sociological surveys had raised doubts about this (e.g., The National Survey of Social Stratification and Social Mobility conducted by members of Japanese Society of Sociology every 5 years; Hara & Seiyama, 2005; Seiyama, 2000). Then came the collapse of the bubble economy in 1992. During the ensuing economic depression, the national law for *Dowa* measures was terminated. It was like opening the window to get some air in the midst of a storm. But some might also say that the window wasn't working anyway, at least not as a device to raise *Burakumin* socioeconomic status.

CONCLUSION: FUTURE BEYOND HOMOGENEITY

The *Burakumin* are the people who live the diversity hidden beneath the myth of a homogeneous Japan. *Japan's Invisible Race* (1966) was a monumental study, conducted by outsiders, that succeeded in exploring the diversity of the Japanese cultural experience. Unfortunately, the diversity that DeVos and his colleagues made public has not been welcomed by the majority of the Japanese people. As I have argued, the perpetuation of the *Burakumin's* lower socioeconomic status is caused by a difficulty to adapt in mainstream education. This phenomenon is produced not only by poverty but also by the *Burakumin's* perception of the society. Self-identification as *Burakumin* does not necessarily motivate taking advantage of institutional opportunities, such as formal education. Thus, to promote academic success among *Burakumin* children, we need not only the resources to compensate for the poor economic and cultural conditions of their living environment, but also opportunities within and adjoining the formal education system to connect *Burakumin* identity with academic success. This idea might also be effective for working-class children who suffer from both poor living conditions and low expectations.

While school effectiveness research demonstrates that school efforts that focus on academic discrepancies work to narrow the gap, it also shows that a gap remains even in the most effective schools. More resources are needed to explore the potential of schools to encourage children living in a diverse society, such as out-of-school educational programs. Combining community activities instigated by minority people to better their living conditions, or to raise their self-esteem, with child education activities might be a good path for connecting their unique experiences with high expectations toward children's academic success. I have observed many cases where people who failed in school have been able to recover their academic ability through participating in civil rights, community, or parent activities. Sometimes these activities can serve as a strong force for motivating participants to learn in those contexts but, unfortunately, we lack empirical studies in this area.

The idea that minority children need a different way to connect themselves to the world has been studied little, but has been put into practice in many cases. One obvious example is Afro-centrism. When I observed an African-centered school in Washington, DC, in 1995, I was surprised by the unusual "radical" method used by the public school system and envied the American governance system that provides for such opportunities. At the same time, I have found much similarity between an African-centered approach and "*Buraku* liberation education" in Japan, which was promoted by local

Buraku movements and responded to by public school teachers in the 1970s to 1990s. To raise *Burakumin* children's self-esteem, *Buraku* liberation education taught *Burakumin* children the history and experiences of the *Buraku* and its movements in after-school and out-of-school programs. These activities have now mostly vanished because of a backlash in the late 1990s. Teachers involved were accused of serving a "specific benefit" instead of the public benefit. Most of the *Buraku* community facilities, such as youth centers, have been abolished and programs that emphasize *Burakumin* identity are now prohibited, especially since the expiration of the *Dowa* measures law in 2002. While African-centered schools and *Buraku* liberation education are eye-catching and often regarded as separatist, other relatively quiet methodologies based on the idea that some children might need a different path to connect themselves to the world should be studied more.

I personally think that supporting the uniqueness of minority experiences and self-concepts benefits the public in many ways, though the policymakers rarely agree with this idea. Especially under the influence of the myth of homogeneous Japan, people tend to be intolerant of diversity, and public policies are rarely given a chance to focus on our different identities. Whether radical or moderate, a diverse society needs a variety of paths for different people to join with the rest of the world. Although there is less overt discrimination or segregation in Japanese society these days than in the past, and although *Buraku* communities have been considerably improved by the *Dowa* measures, intolerance toward diversity in the development of public policy stands in the way of equity. Japanese society needs a legal framework that respects diversity and devotes a certain amount of resources and opportunity to promote diverse paths toward success for every child. The *Burakumin* will not be able to move socially or physically from where they are if they lack ability or motivation to move. This is one of the major reasons that segregation continues. Achievement and identity of minority peoples are closely related to each other, and both are vulnerable to the political and cultural atmosphere of the surrounding majority. Thus, educational efforts in schools and communities to raise minority achievement and self-esteem, as well as political and cultural efforts to respect diversity, are needed to resolve this long-standing issue of caste in Japan.

REFERENCES

Asaka no Rekishi wo Tsukuru Kai (Ed.). (1979). *Asaka no rekishi to seikatsu 1: Asaka no okori* [*History and life of Asaka 1: Origin of Asaka*]. Osaka: Asaka no Rekishi wo Tsukuru Kai.

Berreman, G. D. (1960). Caste in India and United States. *American Journal of Sociology, 66*, 120–127.

Bliss, J. R., Firestone, W. A., & Richards, C. E. (Eds.). (1991). *Rethinking effective schools: Research and practice.* New York: Prentice Hall.

Buraku Kaiho Asaka Chiku Sogo Keikaku Jikko Iinkai (Ed.). (1991). *Buraku Kaiho Asaka Chiku Sogo Keikaku undo to Asaka no Jittai: Chiku kengaku no tebiki* [*The movement for Buraku lib-*

eration and comprehensive planning of Asaka and the reality of life in Asaka: Guide book for community tour]. Osaka: Buraku Kaiho Asaka Chiku Sogo Keikaku Jikko Iinkai.

Buraku Kaiho Asaka Chiku Sogo Keikaku Jikko Iinkai (Ed.). (2002). *Asaka story*. Osaka: Buraku Kaiho Asaka Chiku Sogo Keikaku Jikko Iinkai.

Buraku Mondai Kenkyu Sho (1986). *Buraku no rekishi to kaiho undo: Kingendai hen* [History of Buraku and its movement: Volume of modern age]. Kyoto: Buraku Mondai Kenkyu Sho.

DeVos, G., & Wagatsuma, H. (Eds.). (1966). *Japan's invisible race: Caste in culture and personality*. Berkeley: University of California Press.

Edmonds, R. R. (1980, June). *Search for effective schools*. Paper presented at Strategies for Urban School Improvement Workshop Series, Washington, DC, June 12, 1980. ERIC ED 212 689.

Edmonds, R. R. (1986). Characteristics of effective schools. In U. Neisser (Ed.), *The school achievement of minority children: New perspectives* (pp. 93–104). Mahwah, NJ: Lawrence Erlbaum.

Edmonds, R. R., & Frederiksen, J. R. (1979). *Search for effective schools: The identification and analysis of city schools that are instructionally effective for poor children*. Cambridge, MA: Center for Urban Studies, Harvard University. ERIC ED 170 396.

Fujita, K. (1987). *Dowa wa kowai kou: Chitaikyo wo hihan suru* [Inquiry of Dowa fear: Criticism on Community Improvement Policy Council]. Tokyo: Aunsha.

Hara, J., & Seiyama, K. (2005). *Inequality amid affluence: Social stratification in Japan* (Stratification and inequality series, Vol. 1) (B. Williams, Trans.). Melbourne: Trans Pacific Press.

Ikeda, H. (1989). Jikogainen to gakuryoku [Self concept and academic achievement]. *Kaiho Kyoiku No. 2*. Tokyo: Meiji Tosho.

Ikeda, H. (2000). *Gakuryoku to jikogainen: Jinken kyoiku kaiho kyoiku no aratana paradigm* [Self concept and academic achievement: A new paradigm of human rights education and Buraku Liberation Education]. Osaka: Buraku Kaiho Jinken Kenkyusho.

Inoue, K. (1969). *Buraku no rekishi to kaiho riron* [History of Buraku and theories for Buraku liberation]. Tokyo: Tabata Shoten.

Kita, K. (1989). *Houchi sareta 1000 Buraku* [The abandoned 1000 Buraku]. Osaka: Kaiho Shuppansha.

Kochi Shi Fukushi Bukai (Ed.). (1954). *Kyomo anoko ga tukue ni inai* [Again that kid is absent today]. Kochi: Kochi Shi Fukushi Bukai.

Kurokawa, M. (1999). *Ika to doka no aida: Hisabetsu Buraku ninshiki no kiseki* [In between alienation and assimilation: The locus of Buraku perceptions]. Tokyo: Aoki Shoten.

Kurokawa, M. (2004). *Tukurareta shirusi* [The artificial marks]. Osaka: Kaiho Shuppansha.

Mahara, T. (1973). *Nihon shihonshugi to Buraku Mondai* [Japanese capitalism and Buraku issue]. Kyoto: Buraku Mondai Kenkyusho.

Ministry of Public Management. (1992). *Dowa Chiku Jittai Chosa* [Survey on Dowa districts]. Tokyo: Ministry of Public Management.

Nabeshima, Y. (1991). Sengo gakuryoku chosa ni miru hisabetsu buraku no kodomotachi [Buraku children appeared in post World War II period achievement surveys]. In *Buraku Kaiho Kenkyu, No. 78* (pp. 71–101). Osaka: Buraku Kaiho Kenkyusho.

Nabeshima, Y. (1997). Kyoiku [Education]. In Buraku Kaiho Kenkyusho (Ed.), *Zusetsu kon nichi no Buraku sabetsu* [Buraku discrimination in charts and figures] (pp. 78–95). Osaka: Kaiho Shuppansha.

Nabeshima, Y. (1998). Buraku no gakuryoku mondai ha sabetsu no kekka ka? [Is academic failure among Buraku children consequence of discrimination?]. In *Datsu jyoshki no Buraku Mondai* [Overturning of Buraku issue common sense]. Kyoto: Kamogawa Shuppan.

Nabeshima, Y. (2003). *Miezaru kaisouteki fubyoudou: High school wars 2* [The hidden social class inequality: High school wars 2]. Osaka: Kaiho Shuppansha.

Nabeshima, Y. (2004). Darega ochi kobosareru no ka? [Who are forced out of schools?]. In T. Kariya & K. Shimizu (Eds.), *Gakuryoku no Shakaigaku: Chosa ga simesu gakuryoku no henka to gakko no kadai*. (pp. 197–215). Tokyo: Iwanami Shoten.

Nabeshima, Y. (2006). *Gakuryoku no kaisoukan kakusa wo kokufuku suru gakko kouka ni kansuru rinshouteki kenkyu* [A clinical study on school effectiveness to overcome academic achievement discrepancy between social classes]. Osaka: Osaka City University.

Nara Ken Dowa Mondai Kenkyusyo. (1957). *Choki kesseki fushugaku jido seito no seitai chosa* [Survey on long term absent and not enrolled pupils/students]. Nara: Nara Ken Dowa Mondai Kenkyusyo.

Nishida, Y. (1990). Aru gyoson *Buraku* ni Okeru field study [A field study of a fisher folk *Buraku*]. In H. Ikeda & A. Nagao (Eds.), *Gakko bunka: Shinsou he no perspective*. Tokyo: Toshindo.

Nishida, Y. (Ed.). (2001). *Buraku no 21 kazoku* [21 Families of Buraku]. Osaka: Buraku Kaiho Jinken Kenkyusho.

Noguchi, M. (2000). *Buraku Mondai no paradigm tenkan*. [Paradigm change of Buraku issue] Tokyo: Akashi Shoten.

Ogbu, J. U. (1974). *The next generation*. New York: Academic Press.

Ogbu, J. U. (1978). *Minority education and caste*. New York: Academic Press.

Ogbu, J. U. (1987). Variability in minority responses to schooling: Nonimmigrants vs. immigrants. In G. Spindler & L. Spindler (Eds.), *Interpretive ethnography of education at home and abroad* (pp. 255–278). Mahwah, NJ: Lawrence Erlbaum.

Ogbu, J. U. (1990). Cultural models, identity and literacy. In J. W. Stigler, R. A. Shweder, & G. Herdt (Eds.), *Cultural psychology: Essays on comparative human development* (pp. 520–540). Cambridge, UK: Cambridge University Press.

Ogbu, J. U. (1991). Immigrant and involuntary minorities in comparative perspective. In M. Gibson & J. U. Ogbu (Eds.), *Minority status and schooling* (pp. 3–33). New York: Garland Publishing.

Rutter, M. J., Maughan, B., Mortimore, P., & Ouston, J. (1979). *Fifteen thousand hours: Secondary schools and their effects on children*. Cambridge, MA: Harvard University Press.

Ryoke, Y. (1996). *Nihon kindaika to Buraku Mondai* [Modernization of Japan and Buraku issue]. Tokyo: Akashi Shoten.

Sammons, P., Thomas, S., & Mortimore, P. (1997). *Forging links: Effective schools and effective departments*. London: Paul Chapman.

Seiyama, K. (Ed.). (2000). *Nihon no kaisou system* (Vols. 1–6). Tokyo: Daigaku Shuppankai.

Shimizu, K. (2005). *Gakuryoku wo sodateru* [Nurturing academic achievement]. Tokyo: Iwanami Shoten.

Shindo, N. (1977). *Kaihourei to Buraku Mondai: Fukken doumei no rekishi teki kenkyu* [The Emancipation Law and Buraku issue: Historical study on Fukken League]. Kyoto: Buraku Mondai Kenkyu Sho.

Teraki, N., & Noguchi, M. (Ed.). (2001). *Burakumondai heno shoutai: Shiryou to kaisetsu* [Invitation to Buraku issue: Documents and explanation]. Osaka: Kaiho Shuppansha.

Ueda, T. (1974). *Buraku ha tatakatte iru*. Tokyo: San Ichi Shobou.

Uesugi, S. (1990). *Meiji Ishin to senmin haishirei* [Meiji restoration and the outcaste status abolition order]. Osaka: Kaiho Shuppansha.

Uesugi, S. (1993). *Buraku wo osotta ikki* [Riots attacked Buraku]. Osaka: Kaiho Shuppansha.

Uesugi, S. (1997). *Burakushi ga kawaru* [A shift in Buraku history]. Tokyo: San Ichi Shobou.

Wada, K. (1994). *Hisabetsu buraku isson dokuritsu shi: Edago taisei to meiji shoki no kaiho undo* [A history of discriminated-against Buraku that sought independence: Buraku liberation movement in early Meiji period and the branch-village system]. Osaka: Kaiho Shuppansha.

Yamamoto, Y., & Buraku Kaiho Asaka Chiku Sogo Keikaku Jikko Iinkai (Eds.). (2002). *Ningen no Machi he Asaka* [Asaka toward a town of human beings]. Osaka: Buraku Kaiho Asaka Chiku Sogo Keikaku Jikko Iinkai.

Yoshinami, T. (Ed.). (1987). *Meiji Shonen kaiho rei hantai ikki no kenkyu* [Study on Anti-Emancipation Order riots in early Meiji period]. Tokyo: Akashi Shoten.

HARUHIKO KANEGAE

Schooling of *Buraku* Women

Life Histories in Eastern Japan

*B*URAKU is a Japanese word referring to "village" or "hamlet." The word began to acquire a new connotation after the Meiji government (1868–1912) started to use *tokushu Buraku* (special hamlet) in order to clearly distinguish former outcaste communities from ordinary villages. More than a century has passed, and the word *Buraku* is generally recognized today as having to do with the outcaste communities. *Buraku* people are the largest population facing discrimination in Japan (the *Buraku* Liberation League insists that there are about 3 million *Buraku* people now in Japan). They are not a racial or an ethnic minority, but a castelike Japanese minority. They are generally recognized as descendants of outcaste populations from the feudal days. Outcastes were assigned such social functions as slaughtering animals and executing criminals, and the general public perceived these functions as "polluting acts" under Buddhist and traditional religious beliefs.

The discrimination against *Buraku* people is often characterized today as "racism within the same race" because these are native Japanese people and indistinguishable from non-*Buraku* populations. Still, however, *Buraku* people are sometimes perceived as a different "race." *Buraku* people have suffered from social ostracism and generally have lived in extreme poverty. Educationally, *Buraku* people remained at a low level even at the time when Japanese society was heading toward an achievement orientation based on educational success. *Buraku* children were deprived of the chance for an education due to a paucity of schooling facilities in their communities or through discrimination that discouraged their academic achievement. As a result, many Japanese believe that *Buraku* people's schooling experience is uniformly poor and miserable. They think that most old or middle-aged *Buraku* people failed to finish even the 9 years of compulsory education or did not have advanced schooling because of poverty. But, as each non-*Buraku* individual's schooling experience is different depending on the time period and personal circumstances, the school experiences of *Buraku* people are also different depending on the time period and region in which they lived. This chapter, based on the life histories of *Buraku* women spanning the 20th century, identifies the characteristics in eastern Japan of discrimination, bullying, and exclusion that made life there so very different from schooling in western Japan. The situation of *Buraku* students varied by region, despite the common shared experience of segregation into special districts and occupations.

The research presented here addresses only the women from *Buraku* communities and therefore is focused on the combined problems of *Buraku* discrimination and sexual discrimination. Geographically the chapter looks at the differences in school experiences of *Buraku* women who live in eastern Japan (the greater Tokyo region of Kanto, Nagano, and Niigata) and those of *Buraku* women who live in western Japan (the greater Osaka region of Kansai, Kyoto, and Kobe). This is not research on the general problems of women who are *Buraku* people.

Since 2001 I have been researching the life histories of *Buraku* women living in eastern Japan who were born during the 20th century along with Ms. Asako Hattori, a graduate student of Senshu University. In the following discussion, all quotes without reference citations are taken from our own interviews. Interviewers are identified by the letter A. In discussing life history with these women, we noticed that the older (born pre-1930) and middle generations (born between 1930 and 1950) did not talk much about their school experiences. It is not only because school experiences have become old memories for them, but also because the importance and weight of school life, from the perspective of their entire lives, were not very significant. There was a trend in the interviews that indicated that education was not necessary for girls right up until the 1940s.

During the early part of the 20th century, the proportion of students who went beyond primary education was low throughout the nation. Moreover, access to education for most *Buraku* women in the eastern part of Japan in the first half of the century was hampered by poverty, discrimination, and exclusion. *Buraku* women generally had less schooling than either *Buraku* men or non-*Buraku* women. As a result of these conditions, memories of schooling for these *Buraku* women have remained remarkably clear. The following excerpt illustrates both the discrimination these women experienced and the recollection that they have of their educational experiences. Y.N. is now more than 70 years old but remembers her experience vividly:

> There were four or five *Buraku* students in our school. . . . At that time we cleaned the floor of the class with a damp cloth on chilly winter days; students put water in the bucket and wiped the floor. Other students used water but we used ice-covered water (used for fire prevention that was put in a bucket the previous day) and our task was just to rinse the cloths out. Our hands got chapped and we put a black plaster on our hands, so our hands always were black. In my little mind, I thought that my parents had

worked hard to get me to go to school. Knowing that they had really worked hard for me, my intention was to go to school every morning, but in my heart I didn't want to go.

And then one day my teacher said to me, "N, you don't have to wash the floor today. Dust the window frames." I was so happy to hear this and thought that my teacher finally understood me because my teacher told me to dust the frames this time. Dusting the frame is easier, if you compare it with washing the floor. I thought that maybe I finally had become like the others. I felt like I had finally become normal. I thought my teacher was not altogether a bad person. I was in a happy mood. The windows were arranged with latticework with four or five or six pieces of glass. There is no person in the world who dusts frames from the bottom. So, it might be wrong to think ill of my teacher of that time, but I dusted frames from the bottom. I imagined that I was doing a good thing. My teacher kept a very close watch without a word about what I was doing. I thought again my teacher was not altogether a bad person. I said to myself, "My teacher is nicer to me, so I surely have to come to school tomorrow." I kept thinking my teacher surely thought that I was doing a good job. I felt so happy. Then my teacher suddenly came near and took a duster like this. I'll never forget it. And he hit me three or four times with the handle. He said to me, "You don't even know how to dust."
I really didn't know how to dust. He should have told me that the way I was doing it was wrong and then taught me how to dust. If he had brought this matter to an end there, he would have been clever. But then he said to me, "There is no help for it, since you live in a house without a paper sliding door." I was a small child then but I could understand he considered my parents cheap. What he said was right. But there is no one who wants to live in a house without a paper sliding door for preference. At that time, I didn't even shed tears and ran back home but no one was there. I knew it. Then I cried and cried, and finally I fell asleep from vexation and fatigue.

Y.N. was born in 1931 in a *Buraku* family in Chiba Prefecture. This discrimination by her teacher occurred when she was in the third grade. During cleaning of the classroom, she was told to dust the window frames of the class. When she was incorrectly dusting the frames from the bottom, her teacher reproved her severely and hit her with the handle of the duster. Her teacher insulted her, saying that she did not know how to dust the window because she lived in a house without a paper sliding door. She felt that her parents had been insulted by her teacher's words and deed, and she ran away from school. This is but one example that illustrates the difficulties *Buraku* women experienced during their educational experiences in the eastern part of Japan. The remainder of this chapter will examine the different educational experiences of *Buraku* women in both eastern and western Japan.

SCHOOL EXPERIENCES OF WOMEN BORN BETWEEN 1900 AND 1930: THE OLD GENERATION

We call people who were born before the 1930s "the old generation." Eastern Japan was not necessarily the worst region for the *Burakumin*; the educational opportunities for old-generation *Buraku* women in eastern Japan were better than those in western Japan. From reading several transcripts based on interviews with *Buraku* women from both western and eastern Japan, most of the school experiences of *Buraku* women in the old generation of western Japan showed that they could not finish elementary school or they had poor attendance records because of poverty. In a booklet published in 1984 of interviews from old *Buraku* people in Nara Prefecture, the following story was written:

> Among old people whom we interviewed, many couldn't go to school fully in a period of four to six years of compulsory education.... Especially among women, it was not a rare case that they said, "We have never passed through even the gate of school." Girls went to school but not everyday, because they had to make *zori* (Japanese straw sandals) or had to 'take care of a baby.' Some teachers said to me, "Come to school carrying a baby on your back." But I had to go out of the class when the baby cried. It is certain that about half of *Buraku* children finished six years of elementary school, but the truth is that they went to school reluctantly. Most of them went to school and saw the teacher, and then went back home. Many children left school when they were in the 4th or 5th grade. (*Buraku* Liberation Research Institute in Nara, 1984, pp. 33–36)

These interviewees were born during the beginning of the 20th century and now are in their late 80s to early 100s. Among people in their 70s, there are many in western Japan who could not go to school because of poverty. For example, one woman living in Fukuoka, who was born in 1926, said:

> When I started going to school, my family became poor. After my grandfather was stricken with paralysis, my family was finding it hard to make a living so I stopped going to school and began to work. In the spare moments when I was done with my farm work, I would go to a coal mine and work as a construction laborer. (Central Women Headquarters of *Buraku* Liberation League, 1993, pp. 49–50)

A woman from Osaka in her 70s said:

> When I was 8 years old, I met a teacher at a festival. He said, "Come to school." I said to him, "I can't go to school, because my mother died and my family became poor." ... I didn't go to school for even a day. (*Buraku* Liberation and Human Rights Research Institute, 2001, p. 81)

Contrary to these scenarios, when we conducted interviews with *Buraku* women in eastern Japan, few stated that they could not go to school because of poverty, even in earlier times. For example, T.T., born in 1919 and brought up in the town of Tokura in Nagano Prefecture, graduated from secondary school even though she was often absent from school because she was taking care of small children or working on the farm.

> A: You said that you didn't go to school but you worked on the farm whenever it was a fine day. Did you work like that since you started going to school?
> T.T.: When I was small, I didn't. It wasn't until I was in my first or second grade or maybe third grade. I didn't do farm work very often. But at that time, there were small children, so I often took care of them.
> A: Did you continue beyond elementary school?
> T.T.: I went on to the second grade of an advanced course.
> A: Did you often work on the farm when you were in an advanced course?
> T.T.: Yes, I did. I went on to an advanced course helping with farm work.

I recognize that there were a small number of *Buraku* people in the eastern part of Japan who could not go to elementary school because of poverty. Most of them were born before 1910 or were of a generation that attended elementary school in a state of confusion after World War II (Association of Teachers of *Dowa* Education in Nagano, 1986; Kanegae, 1996). However, in western Japan, even though *Buraku* women had access to school, they could not fully participate because they were too poor to purchase school supplies and materials needed to study properly. Comments from the old *Buraku* women interviewees include:

> I went back home to eat at lunch time because I couldn't take a lunch box with me. (*Buraku* Liberation Research Institute in Nara, 1984, p. 40)

> I couldn't buy articles of stationery such as textbooks, a pencil, a sheet of plain paper or paints. (Women Headquarters of *Buraku* Liberation League in Osaka, 1993, p. 44)

> I couldn't go to school in a rainy day, because I didn't have an umbrella. (Women Headquarters of *Buraku* Liberation League in Osaka, 1993, p. 52)

In contrast to the discrimination and poverty identified by *Buraku* women in western Japan, *Buraku* women born during or before the 1930s in eastern Japan talked mostly about bullying or discrimination by children from other neighborhoods. For example, U.M., who was born in 1932 in Asakusa in Tokyo and moved to her relative's house in a rural district in Saitama Prefecture for safety during World War II, talked about her experience of being bullied by children from a non-*Buraku* district. She was called *Chourinbo* (a derogatory name *Buraku* people were called in eastern Japan in general) and stones were thrown at her. When she got high marks, other children said, "How can *Chourinbo* get such high marks?" so she deliberately stopped writing the correct answer on her tests. Her teacher was considerate toward her when she was bullied, and then the other children said, "Teacher shows favor to *Chourinbo*." She talked about bullying as the first type of discrimination she experienced as a *Buraku* child:

> **U.M.:** We went to school in a group. On the way to school, mischievous boys were waiting for us and they started throwing stones at us saying, "*Chourinbo* came!!" We went forward, driving them away. A stone often hit me, because I walked naively. When I went to school with a lump on my head, my teacher asked me what happened to me. A child of my relatives said to the teacher, "She was hit by a stone on the head by mischievous boys." And then the teacher scolded. My teacher was in charge of our district. Every teacher was in charge of their own district.
>
> **A:** Yes, every teacher took charge of their own district, didn't he?
>
> **U.M.:** The teacher in charge of our district was my classroom teacher, so he scolded the boys. We went to school and went home together in a group of about 10 children. We did everything together. . . . That was the first time I was called "*Chourinbo*." "When I got high marks on the test, other children said, "How can *Chourinbo* get such high marks?" Then I gave up and didn't study at home and wrote nothing when the teacher handed out a blank answer paper. I just was looking at the paper and turned it in. Other children were pleased if my marks were low. I recall I often escaped out of disgust. I did every mischief. I climbed on to the roof of the school or went to the toilet. Soon after that, the word "*Chourinbo*" came out of mouths of other children. They jeered, saying, "*Chourinbo* studied very hard"; then I decided not to study and pretended to go to the toilet and then I ran away out of the lower window of a toilet. The teacher scolded and pretended to hit me in front of other children. Maybe he felt sorry for me. He said to them, "She is an evacuated child, so you have to be kind to her" In old times, the way of scolding was like the military. He forced us to sit here and there and he walked beside us hitting with a club. Since I was skinny and small, the teacher hit me mildly. Then other children bullied me again saying, "Teacher showed favor to *Chourinbo*!"

Another example of bullying or discrimination by non-*Buraku* children is the following. K.Y., who was born in 1931 in a *Buraku* in Chiba talked about her experiences. At that time there was a slaughterhouse of homeless dogs in her district, so other children said, pointing at her lunch box with meat, "Isn't it dog meat?" Her father made a special satchel of cowhide for her. The children taunted, "It is made of horse hide out of an already dead horse. Or it must be made of dog skin." Then she couldn't take it to school. She also talked about using flattery in order to be allowed to play with other children:

> Around the end of my third grade, I recalled it as the first discrimination. I opened my lunch box and found meat in it and then a girl who was sit-

ting beside me said to me, "Isn't the meat dog's meat?" Since then I hated lunchtime. Why did I hate lunchtime? Because in my district . . . well. . . . People in my district slaughtered homeless dogs. So, children said that meat in my lunch box was dog meat. I was taunted like that and then I wouldn't like to eat lunch after the next day. So, I opened my lunch box secretly and if I found something like meat, I ate only rice leaving a side dish in my lunch box and threw it away on the way home. I really hated it. It was the beginning. And then my father died young. He was 37 and I was in 5th grade. Before then, in the first term of 5th grade, my father had dealings with a bag store named Saito located on the opposite side of Juntendou Hospital in Sakura City and made a special satchel made of cowhide for me. It wasn't dyed like ones now. It was natural skin, since it was the old days. It was white like back skin, or you might say a sort of beige color, and I put ointment to make it shine. It means the more you use it, the more it shines. My father made it. But when I carried it to school on my back, children in my class told me that it was made of dead horse skin or dog skin. I couldn't carry it any more. But I couldn't say to my father that I didn't like it, because I knew he made it at great pains. I couldn't turn it down. But I didn't carry my satchel to school. I made an excuse of my shoulder or neck being pained. My father told me that nobody had such a good satchel, so it was good for you to carry it to school. But I had never carried it even once since then. It was so regrettable for me. My friends were limited. If they didn't let me play together with them, I made up flattery and tried to curry their favor: for example, a bud of camellia. At that time it was very popular at school to peel a bud of camellia and make it round and look at it. There was a tree of camellia in my garden, so I picked some without telling my grandfather and brought them with me to school and gave some to girls to get them to play with me.

Y.N., an eastern *Buraku* woman who was mentioned earlier in the chapter, also discussed experiences of belittling slander like "You eat horse meat" or "You eat dog meat," and was excluded by other girls or bullied by children from non-*Buraku* districts. In addition, she recounts how teachers would ignore the bullying and derogatory remarks made by other students:

Y.N.: In winter other children made their lunch box warm on the stove but I never made my lunch box warm. They said, "Your lunch box has dog meat. Or your lunch box has horse meat."

A: But in those days there were no children who brought a lunch box with meat inside.

Y.N.: No, no. And nobody kindly told me to make my lunch box warm. I tried to bring my lunch box near the stove but my teacher wouldn't ask other children to make my lunch box warm. When I recall the scene, I think it was cruel. I just kept crying. I looked at my teacher's face and expected him to say something like, "You shouldn't say such a thing. Since you are friends of her, make her lunch box warm." I gazed intently at his face but he looked the other way.... In my school, there were four or five *Buraku* students. During recess nobody joined us. I expected my teacher to tell other children that they should join us. But even teachers excluded us. Now I understand, because I belong to a movement group. Maybe teachers were afraid of being involved in it, so they often took an attitude that they didn't know anything. I often saw them ignoring us with my own two eyes.

Buraku women born during and before the 1930s in western Japan recounted experiences of discrimination by teachers (*Buraku* Liberation and Human Rights Research Institute, 2001; *Buraku* Liberation Research Institute in Nara, 1984), but what they mainly identify as the obstacle to school attendance was the poverty that prevented the purchase of school materials even when they did get a chance to go to school. Another difference in the experience of *Buraku* women in western Japan from that of their eastern Japanese counterparts is that those in western Japan did not talk much about bullying and discrimination by children in other districts. This is probably a result of the size of districts: in western Japan, *Buraku* districts were larger than those in eastern Japan and institutionalized segregation such as "*Buraku* schools" remained strong in western Japan, making the proportion of *Buraku* children in one school or one class in the district relatively high compared to that in eastern Japan.

SCHOOL EXPERIENCES OF WOMEN BORN BETWEEN 1940 AND 1960: THE MIDDLE GENERATION

Women who were born in the 1940s to 1960s were called "the middle generation." The school experiences of women in western Japan in general varied vastly, depending on the district in which they lived; however, the variation in school experiences of *Buraku* women in this group is even greater, depending on the period in which they were born. There are differences for those born in the early 1940s, from the late 1940s to the early 1950s, or after the late 1950s. Among women born during the early 1940s in western Japan, many could not finish compulsory education because of poverty. For example, a woman who was born in Kyoto in 1942 entered elementary school 1 year later than other children because her parents could not provide money for preparing her to enter school. In the fifth grade she began to take care of the neighborhood children to earn money to live, so she could go to school only when she was not minding them. Middle school attendance was compulsory, but she did not go on to middle school and instead worked in a factory (Central Women Headquarters of *Buraku* Liberation League, 1993, pp. 58–59).

Similarly, a woman born in Osaka in 1943 said that only children in her *Buraku* district did not receive a notice for entrance formalities, so their entrance to elementary school was delayed for 1 week. She had a poor attendance record because she could not buy textbooks and articles of stationery for drawing or calligraphy. She began to work part-time in a factory when she was in the fourth grade. She recounted that during her elementary school years, the number of teachers who outspokenly discriminated against *Buraku* students decreased after World War II, but most teachers did not care about children in the *Buraku* district and did not understand or try to understand them:

> My teacher didn't mind that I was often absent from school, because I couldn't buy stationery. He seemed to want to say, "The reason why you can't come to school is in you. It is your failure." Home visits in my district were a preposterous thing. [*Editor's note:* Japanese homeroom teachers typically visit student homes once a year.] Maybe teachers had never stepped in our district. Such teachers told us that *Buraku* children often forgot something at home or *Buraku* children took a bad attitude and then made us stand in a passageway for long periods of time. I had little memory of sitting in class to study. (Women Headquarters of *Buraku* Liberation League in Osaka, 1993, p. 65)

Women born in the late 1940s to the early 1950s mostly had compulsory education even in western Japan. However, many who wanted to go on to high school could not. For example, a woman born in 1947 in Tokushima Prefecture said that, beginning in the second or third grade, she worked when school was off and bought stationery with the money she earned. She asked her parents to send her to high school but her parents said, "We want you to go to high school but we can't." She felt mortified (Central Women Headquarters of *Buraku* Liberation League, 1993, pp. 71–72).

A woman born in the early 1950s in Osaka said that she studied hard and got high marks, but she could not ask her parents to let her go on to high school. Then she began to think it was absurd to study hard when she was at the end of ninth grade. She also recounts that she was sure that teachers in those days had discriminatory feelings against *Buraku* students:

> I was sure that teachers were aware of *Buraku* in their mind. I had heard one teacher saying, "Children from *Buraku* are violent," when *Buraku* children did something violent or did mischief. Conversely, I couldn't help suspecting a teacher's true intention, when my teacher said to me, "You got high marks, didn't you?" I guessed it meant that I had high marks for a *Buraku* child. I could feel teachers were aware of *Buraku* in their mind after I heard teachers speaking to *Buraku* children who played a prank. (*Buraku* Liberation and Human Rights Research Institute, 2001, p. 49)

In the 1960s, *Dowa* education—systematic educational efforts to eradicate prejudice against the *Buraku* people and to improve *Buraku* academic achievement and literacy levels—began in some schools in western Japan. However, *Dowa* education was incomplete, and as a result many *Buraku* children suffered harassment. One example is O.K., whom we interviewed in Arakawa ward in Tokyo. She was born in 1952 and was brought up in Kochi Prefecture in western Japan until graduation from high school. O.K.'s high school was designated as a research high school for *Dowa* education. All of the students went to see the movie *A River Without a Bridge* (which described a *Buraku*/village in western Japan in the 1910s). O.K. could not endure watching it and wept so bitterly that friends asked her what was happening to her. During the movie, she recalled, she learned for the first time about the past of her district, as miserable scenes in the movie and the circumstances of her own district overlapped. After the screening, there was a supplementary lesson in which students discussed the movie. The following excerpt is O.K.'s memory of that discussion:

> After the movie, there was a class discussion of the movie. The discussion was so disgusting. It was lucky that I wasn't called on to say my opinion in the class. Some students stated their impressions, which were "I felt sorry for them." There were such impressions as "I thought it merciless but if I tell my parents that I am going to marry a person who came from *Buraku*, parents will feel sad, so I wouldn't marry him." Or "I am glad that I wasn't born in the *Buraku*." Or "They are poor people." I was afraid of being called on to say something. I was lucky not to be pointed at by the teacher to say my opinion. I was worried to death about what to say when I was asked to say something. I had no courage to tell the truth. I was just looking fixedly at my desk to avoid the teacher's eyes. Then one of the students said, "You all brush the embarrassing facts under the carpet. If you really marry a *Buraku* person, what will you do? Think seriously!" Then some said, "I won't marry him." "Parents will discriminate against him or I feel sorry for my parents." Many students said such opinions. I was greatly shocked to hear that and I was determined not to tell where I came from. (Hattori, 2004, pp. 74–75)

Buraku women in western Japan born in the late 1950s to early 1960s mostly received scholarships to attend high school as a result of the *Dowa* policy, which was intended to compensate for the disadvantage experienced by *Buraku* people. Through participation in children's liberation clubs or the Association of High School Scholarship Students (an organization of *Buraku* scholarship students), *Buraku* students gradually studied about *Buraku* issues and accepted an identity as *Buraku* people. For example, a woman born in 1958 in Sakai City in Osaka Prefecture started attending children's liberation gatherings because her friend went there. It was through her participation in this club that she first became aware that the place where she lived was considered a *Buraku*. Her family received public assistance because her father was ill, so she was able to go to high school with a scholarship and with the help of teachers who belonged to the Future Course Securement Council. She took an active part in the Association of High School Scholarship Students (Women

Headquarters of *Buraku* Liberation League in Osaka, 1993, pp. 75–76). As a result of these clubs and scholarships, poverty became less of an obstacle to *Buraku* women in western Japan who were born during the late 1950s to early 1960s, compared with women born earlier.

In contrast, school experiences of *Buraku* women of this age cohort in eastern Japan whom we interviewed did not suggest changes in educational access between generations. These *Buraku* women had equal access to a normal school life throughout and were not subjected to overt discrimination. The main difference was that there was a complete omission of the *Buraku* issue in the school curriculum of eastern Japan. A.T., who was born in 1943 in Komoro City in Nagano, said that there was not any outstanding discrimination except in a few cases of children in the district, especially boys, about whom it was often said, "You see, again it is this or that boy from D [the name of the *Buraku* district]," when they did mischief. And she stated plainly that she would not go to high school because her family was poor:

> A.T.: There were five or six *Buraku* children among the 40–50 students in the class. If one *Buraku* boy treated another child harshly, it was said about him, "He is from D, he is a child of D." When some student was bullied, parents came to school. But if they found it was a child of D who bullied, they thought it was better not to be involved.
>
> A: Was there any more concrete discrimination in your elementary days besides it being said, "A child from D"?
>
> A.T.: There was no other obvious discrimination. I was a vigorous girl and I was not good at studying, or I can say that I was in the middle level. So, I had never been made fun of by others. I was cheerful and I sometimes helped the weak children. I had never been bullied.
>
> A: What sort of student were you in middle school?
>
> A.T.: Well, I liked sports, so I took a lot of exercise. I didn't have difficulty in studying. But my family was poor, so I couldn't go on to high school. My teacher encouraged my parents to make me go to high school, but I decided not to go to high school. I was the oldest child in my family, so I thought I had to work as soon as possible when I finished middle school.

Y.A., born in 1957 and a daughter of Y.N., had never been bullied until graduation from high school. However, she felt something different in her district, something different from other districts. But nobody mentioned the fact, so she did not know that her district was *Buraku*:

> A: What was your middle school life like?
>
> Y.A.: I was not good at sports. Until lower grades of elementary school, I liked running but I didn't belong to a club activity and I liked studying. I often read books or listened to the radio at home. I liked staying at home alone. From around that time, I began to notice something. That is most of the children who were called to go to the principal's room or

who were hit by the teacher in the class because they did mischief were boys in my neighborhood or my cousins. If some trouble happened, the cause was always from M [the name of the *Buraku* district]. Since then I started wondering why children from M were so violent and they bullied. I didn't know the reason. I didn't know why there were so many adults who didn't have a job and were playing mah-jongg outside their house or under a tree during daytime. I had to pass an alley when I went to school and when I walked in the alley in my district with school uniform, they all paid attention to me. I became disgusted with their eyes. I was sorry for my mother or other people in the district, but I began to think that I wanted to get out of that district. I had been thinking that when I grew up, I would surely get out of the district.

A: You still didn't know that the district was *Buraku*, you didn't know anything, did you?

Y.A.: I didn't know anything. Nobody would tell me about that.

SCHOOL EXPERIENCES OF THE YOUNG GENERATION

For *Buraku* women born after the late 1960s in western Japan, the educational experience was far different from that of women born in the oldest generation or even the middle generation. By the time these women attended school, the *Dowa* educational experience had been fully implemented—some prefectures in eastern Japan even had *Dowa* education programs, although most were only a formality—and these children were nurtured by the *Dowa* education. They belonged to children's liberation gathering clubs, studied *Buraku* issues in the curriculum, and their *Burakumin* identity developed as they grew older. Children's liberation gathering clubs are community-based children's organizations in the *Buraku*, and participants carry out such activities as studying *Buraku* issues and other issues of discrimination, doing homework or extra lessons, and various recreational activities. They are supported by school teachers, leaders of *Buraku* liberation movements in the community, and parents. Descriptions of the clubs can be found in *21 Families of Buraku* (*Buraku* Liberation and Human Rights Research Institute, 2001), *Interview: "People from Buraku"* (Kaiho Publisher, 2003), or *Youth in Buraku* (Kadooka, 1999).

The discussion and interviews that follow highlight some of the characteristics of the children's liberation gathering clubs. Most of the children born after 1970, some even from the time they were younger than the age of 1, went to *Dowa* nursery school and then went on to a school promoting *Dowa* education. They belonged to *Buraku* children's gathering cubs from the first grade of elementary school. Children often studied about the *Buraku*, *Buraku* discrimination, and the case of *Sayama* (a famous false accusation about a *Buraku* person) (*Buraku* Liberation and Human Rights Research Institute, 2001, p. 377). In the following selection, a women born after 1970 talks about her encounter with *Buraku* issues:

> In elementary school, I studied a history of *Buraku,* the passage of how *Suiheisha* (Levelers Society—the first organization for *Buraku* liberation) came into being and played in some dramas about the history of *Buraku.* We learned naturally without knowing anything. Maybe adults or leaders taught us with much care. They had an awareness of the issues, so we could acquire the problems before we were aware of *Buraku.* Maybe we could feel it naturally. (*Buraku* Liberation and Human Rights Research Institute, 2001, p. 378)

Conversely, the young generation in eastern Japan did not get any education about *Buraku* issues, and they spent their entire school life without becoming aware of themselves as *Buraku* people. A woman born in 1972 who is a member of the Youth Association of *Buraku* Liberation League in Chiba Prefecture talked about it in specific terms:

> A: When did you participate in the movement?
> S: I didn't know anything about *Buraku* issues until high school. My high school was a school promoting *Dowa* education, and I was called to come to a teacher to talk about a scholarship. After I entered high school, I noticed there were surely teachers of *Dowa* education in both elementary and middle schools. I knew there was a class for improving *Buraku* students' ability both in elementary and middle school, but I didn't even know the name of *Dowa.* A teacher who called me to talk about a scholarship was a *Dowa* education teacher and he laid stress on *Dowa* issues. At that time, things were incomprehensible to me. I studied the movement against giving students the loan or the subsidy of a scholarship and went to the Education Bureau to see government officers of prefecture. Friends who got together at that time started the movement. (*Buraku* Liberation Research Institute in Eastern Japan, 2003, p. 18)

You could say that the school experience of K.K. in Komoro City in Nagano, the only person who belongs to the young generation among our interviewees (she was born in 1979), was special, because she was born and brought up in Nagano Prefecture, where *Dowa* education became exceptionally active even in eastern Japan. In addition, K.K.'s father was an activist of the liberation movement, so she was raised in an environment that was acutely aware of the *Buraku* condition and needs. Such awareness is common among the same generation in western Japan. K.K. indicated that she had taken part in a children's liberation gathering since elementary school, and felt that the explanation given about children's liberation gatherings in the book titled *Akebono* (a side reader about *Dowa* education used in Nagano Prefecture) was greatly different from her sense things. She said she absolutely hated *Dowa* education at school:

A: In higher grades in elementary school and in middle school, you had *Dowa* education, didn't you? Did you feel the gaze by children from other districts to the children in the *Dowa* district? Did you feel something?

K.K.: I didn't feel anything special from surrounding children. In my middle school days, our class was reading *Akebono*. While we were reading it, the article about the "children's gathering" appeared. I told them coolly that I went to such a gathering, and so students understood that I took part in the gathering. But then I read *Akebono* and found out that the gathering was the place where discriminated children of *Buraku* got together. It was also written that these children were poor. Then I thought I was a poor child [*laugh*] and I was afraid that friends around me might see me differently after reading the book. I didn't like the class of *Akebono* and I hid in the shadow of my standing book on my desk and waited until the class was over.

A: When did you start to feel happy doing the liberation movement?

K.K.: When I was in 9th grade. . . . My homeroom teacher at that time was very frank and funny and he said, "I don't know about it at all, so let's study together." Then I came to think that it was all right, we should study together.

A: You belonged to the generation in which you got *Dowa* education in a sense completely. How did you take the truth that you came from a *Buraku*?

K.K.: I didn't feel it as a handicap. What shall I say? At the beginning, I didn't feel it was a handicap, but I sometimes felt it was when I became a middle school student. I felt it was like a kind of secret. So I just told the fact to only close friends or a boyfriend, but I didn't want to tell it to even them. It was like a secret. So, I felt it neither as a pride nor a disadvantage. This was my little secret. [*laugh*] However, I began to feel that this was important, as I got to know the facts. The weight or the importance in the way of telling the facts began to change. So, conversely, I hated *Dowa* education at school. But *Dowa* education in children's liberation gathering was greatly useful and understandable. *Dowa* education at school was incomplete, so I didn't want it to be taught at school. I wondered why teachers explained in that way. If *Dowa* education was done only at school and I didn't go to the gathering, I might think it was a disadvantage, even when we talked about *Buraku* in my family. Maybe I would have kept thinking that inside I was a discriminated person and I would have held that idea for a long time. And maybe I would not have taken part in the movement.

That K.K. did not take it negatively that she came from a *Buraku* and did not try to hide it completely resulted from her participation in *Dowa* programs outside of school and from discussions within her family. However, her criticisms of *Dowa* education at school stemmed from the fact that only a certain perspective of *Buraku* issues was being discussed and from the portrayal of *Buraku* children as poor and underprivileged. These sentiments were shared by Y.T., who lived in Nagano Prefecture (she was born around 1980):

I really hated *Dowa* education. I went to the children's liberation gathering from my first grade to middle school. I didn't know the meaning of going to the gathering. Friends in the neighborhood went to the gathering and I thought they enjoyed it. As I went to the gathering, I noticed that I came from the *Buraku*. After that, the *Dowa* education class at school was the worst for me. You found the words *Eta* (extreme filth) or *Hininn* (non-human)—these are the name for those of pariah status in Tokugawa Period—in the class unconcernedly. Since I found that I was the person concerned, I thought I shouldn't tell that I came from the *Buraku*. I thought it was not a good idea that I make it known that I came from *Buraku*. There was a lot of bullying in school. I got an idea that *Buraku* students were surely bullied. I decided to hide the truth because I was so worried it would be found out that I came from *Buraku*. The worst time of *Dowa* education continued after I entered middle school. After a while, when I entered middle school before *Dowa* education class, I was talking with some close friends. Someone said," What is the next class?" "It may be *Dowa* education." "Is it true? Isn't it the most languid class?" "It is tiresome, indeed." My friends asked me for agreement and I couldn't help agreeing with them. If I said to them, "You shouldn't talk like that. You should study '*Dowa* education' seriously," they would notice that I came from *Buraku*. I couldn't stand it, so, I had to say to them, "It might be tiresome, indeed," and I wanted to change the subject as soon as possible. After that the class of *Dowa* education and the fact that I came from *Buraku* became a burden and I became afraid of contacting other people and so, even when I was with friends, I wouldn't show my feelings and I tried to get along well with them. (Takahasi, 2003, pp. 42–43)

CONCLUSION

It has been assumed that school experiences of *Buraku* people were not so different throughout Japan and across different generations. At the same time, most Japanese have assumed that typical *Buraku* people were only those who lived in western Japan. However, my research has demonstrated that school experiences of *Buraku* people are considerably different between western and eastern Japan. In western Japan, most *Buraku* women in the old generation could not finish elementary school or had a poor attendance record because of poverty. Many *Buraku* women in the middle generation could not finish compulsory education or had to abandon going on to high school because of poverty. Most *Buraku* women in the young generation received systematic *Dowa* education, belonged to children's liberation gathering clubs, studied *Buraku* issues in the school curriculum, and developed their *Buraku*min identity as they grew older.

In contrast, the school experiences of *Buraku* women in eastern Japan were quite different from those in western Japan. In the old generation, there was almost no one who could not finish compulsory education because of poverty. But, as students, most of them were discriminated against by children from non-*Buraku* districts. Those in the middle generation had no experience of discrimination at school (except one person in Nagano), but they had never received *Dowa* education at school. Finally, people of the young generation who came from Nagano Prefecture did not have a good impression of *Dowa* education in school.

To sum up, for *Buraku* women in western Japan, school experiences of most of the young generation have dramatically improved as compared with those of the old and middle generations. For *Buraku* women in eastern Japan, on the other hand, school experiences of most in the young generation did not much differ from those of the middle generation—though the experiences of the young generation were not so miserable. The features of the school experiences of *Buraku* women in eastern Japan that differ from those in western Japan were caused by differences in the size of the *Buraku* districts, the situation of each *Buraku*, differences in *Dowa* education, and the history of the *Buraku* liberation movement. Thus, issues of education for *Buraku* people must be treated with attention to regional differences.

REFERENCES

Association of Teachers of *Dowa* Education in Nagano (Ed.). (1986). *Cries of people who have weathered the storms of life learn from the oldest residents of Buraku*. Osaka: Kaiho Publisher.

Buraku Liberation and Human Rights Research Institute (Ed.). (2001). *21 Families of Buraku: Changes and problems of life judging from life history*. Osaka: Kaiho Publisher.

Buraku Liberation Research Institute in Eastern Japan. (2003). Necessity of human network be sent from Chiba. *Create Tomorrow, 52–53* (November 30), 17–28.

Buraku Liberation Research Institute in Nara (Ed.). (1984). *Report from interviews about life, labor, culture. Have lived like this: Education*. Nara: *Buraku* Liberation Research Institute in Nara.

Central Women Headquarters of *Buraku* Liberation League (Ed.). (1993). *Women's flag of the crown of thorns: The pass I have walked*. Osaka: Kaiho Publisher.

Hattori, A. (2004). Interior and grasp of 'discriminated self': From life history of *Buraku* people. *Senshu Sociology, 16* (March 22), 70–82.

Higashi, Y. (Director). (1992). *A river without a bridge* [Hashi no nai kawa] [Motion picture]. Tokyo: Toho Company Ltd. [Previous versions released in 1969 and 1970.]

Kadooka, N. (1999). *Youth in Buraku*. Osaka: Koudan Publisher.

Kaiho Publisher (Ed.). (2003). *Interview—Buraku people: The present situation and from here of 12 people*. Osaka: Kaiho Publisher.

Kanegae, H. (1996). *Social standpoints to 'Dowa' education* (New ed.). Tokyo: Akashi Shoten.

Takahasi, Y. (2003). Facing with discrimination about marriage. *Create Tomorrow, 52–53* (November 30), 42–48.

Women Headquarters of *Buraku* Liberation League in Osaka (Ed.). (1993). *Women who have created their own tomorrow: Get over a wall of discrimination*. Osaka: Kaiho Publisher.

TAEYOUNG KIM

The Education of *Zainichi* Koreans and Their Identity

7

WHO ARE THE *ZAINICHI*? In this chapter I will address the issue of *Zainichi* Koreans and their place within the Japanese educational system and Japanese society at large. The discussion first focuses on the education of *Zainichi* in Japan, with an overview of the history of education of the *Zainichi* and the various educational systems that have been established, which have led to multiple *Zainichi* identities. The present educational situation for *Zainichi* children will then be examined in terms of how the educational experiences of *Zainichi* have shaped their identity through participation in ethnic activities at school, contrasting Japanese schools with Korean schools. Finally, the future role of education for *Zainichi* children will be addressed, with regard to the Japanese school system and the problem of cultural essentialism in *Zainichi* education.

THE MEANING OF *ZAINICHI*

"*Zainichi*" is the term commonly used to refer to Koreans living in Japan. *Zainichi* is represented by the characters "在日" in kanji. The character "在" means "existence," while "日" means "of Japan." Because there was a time when Koreans made up the majority of foreigners living in Japan, the term *Zainichi,* or "existing in Japan," became synonymous with *Zainichi* Koreans. Over the years, even though there have been many other foreigners who have come and gone from Japan, the word *Zainichi* has retained a special meaning referring to the descendants of Koreans who were brought to Japan as a result of Japanese colonial rule of the Korean Peninsula. The unique nuance of this word and how it is used is significant, not only personally but politically.

Up until the early 1980s, the population of *Zainichi* Koreans accounted for 85% of all non-Japanese residents in the country. Some *Zainichi* have been in Japan for 70 years, and it can be said their "existence" in the country has become absolute, or permanent. However, after the mid-1980s, many

TABLE 7.1 Ratio of *Zainichi* Koreans (South Koreans and North Koreans) to Total Alien Registrants

Year	Total alien registrants	Zainichi Koreans	Ratio (%)	Year	Total alien registrants	Zainichi Koreans	Ratio (%)
1978	766,894	659,025	85.9	1993	1,320,748	682,276	51.7
1979	774,505	662,561	85.5	1994	1,354,011	676,793	50.0
1980	782,910	664,536	84.9	1995	1,362,371	666,376	48.9
1981	792,946	667,325	84.2	1996	1,415,136	657,149	46.4
1982	802,477	669,854	83.5	1997	1,482,707	645,373	43.5
1983	817,129	674,581	82.6	1998	1,512,116	638,828	42.2
1984	840,885	687,135	81.7	1999	1,556,113	636,548	40.9
1985	850,612	683,313	80.3	2000	1,686,444	635,269	37.7
1986	867,237	677,959	78.2	2001	1,778,462	632,405	35.6
1987	884,025	676,982	76.6	2002	1,851,758	625,422	33.8
1988	941,005	677,140	72.0	2003	1,915,030	613,791	32.1
1989	984,455	681,838	69.3	2004	1,974,747	607,419	30.8
1990	1,075,317	687,940	64.0	2005	2,011,555	598,687	29.8
1991	1,218,891	693,050	56.9	2006	2,084,919	598,219	28.7
1992	1,281,644	688,144	53.7				

Note. Ratio: Zainichi Koreans/Total alien registrants.
Source. Ministry of Justice, http//www.moj.go.jp.

"newcomer" foreigners came to Japan to live and, in recent years, the proportion of *Zainichi* Koreans has declined to only one third of all non-Japanese residents. In addition, the second-, third-, and fourth-generation *Zainichi* Koreans who were born in Japan have become the majority of *Zainichi* Koreans in present-day Japan. First-generation *Zainichi*, who were born in Korea and came to Japan, comprise only 10% of the total *Zainichi* population; their social position and identity in Japanese society are quite different from those of the *Zainichi* Koreans born in Japan.

The latter half of the 1980s brought many foreign workers to Japan, and the multinationalization of Japanese society continued to accelerate into the 1990s. As shown in Table 7.1, the number of registered aliens in Japan increased from 1.3 million in 1993 to nearly 2 million in 2004, representing 1.5% of the total Japanese population. The *Zainichi* population peaked at 693,050 in 1991 and has decreased every year since, constituting only 30.8% of total registered aliens in Japan in 2004. Although these figures give the impression that the *Zainichi* population is shrinking, the apparent reduction in numbers is the result of about 10,000 *Zainichi* acquiring Japanese citizenship each year. Obtaining Japanese citizenship has the bizarre consequence of masking the existence of ethnic *Zainichi* Korean people within Japanese society (see Table 7.2).

TABLE 7.2 Number of *Zainichi* Koreans Who Acquired Japanese Citizenship

Year	Number	Year	Number	Year	Number	Year	Number
1952	232	1966	3,816	1980	5,987	1994	8,244
1953	1,326	1967	3,391	1981	6,829	1995	10,327
1954	2,435	1968	3,194	1982	6,521	1996	9,898
1955	2,434	1969	1,889	1983	5,532	1997	9,678
1956	2,290	1970	4,646	1984	4,608	1998	9,561
1957	2,737	1971	2,874	1985	5,040	1999	10,059
1958	2,246	1972	4,983	1986	5,110	2000	9,842
1959	2,737	1973	5,769	1987	4,882	2001	10,295
1960	3,763	1974	3,973	1988	4,595	2002	9,188
1961	2,710	1975	6,323	1989	4,759	2003	11,778
1962	3,222	1976	3,951	1990	5,216	2004	11,031
1963	3,558	1977	4,261	1991	5,665	2005	9,689
1964	4,632	1978	5,362	1992	7,244	2006	8,531
1965	3,438	1979	4,701	1993	7,697	2007	8,546
						Total	313,245

Source. Nationality Section of Civil Affairs Bureau, Ministry of Justice, http//www.moj.go.jp.

THE EDUCATION OF *ZAINICHI*

Research on *Zainichi* education must be viewed at both structural and curricular levels. At the structural level, the question is, how have *Zainichi* been treated by the Japanese school system? In other words, how has Japanese society addressed the *Zainichi* population and their education? Confronting this concern is important for *Zainichi* in order to make evident to the broader Japanese society ways in which the situation might be improved. The curricular level pertains to the detailed discourse related to "ethnic education": how ethnicity is reflected in the curriculum and how children's identity is shaped by it. These issues involve the role and representation of *Zainichi* in the curriculum, which in turn affect how *Zainichi* internalize their own place in Japanese society. Because of their importance in influencing children's developing sense of self, these curricular issues require serious consideration within the *Zainichi* community.

Up to this time, research has considered primarily the structural dimension of *Zainichi* education, and curricular issues have gone unaddressed. Historically, ethnicity has remained out of the main curriculum in Japanese schooling, and ethnic populations have been left to develop and implement their own culturally appropriate programs. The role and content of ethnic education has been determined by *Zainichi* leaders, who offered ethnic education in separate Korean schools. It has also been considered inappropriate for anyone from the outside to critique or offer advice to these leaders.

Unfortunately, the relative isolation and lack of open discussion have persisted over the years and remain major obstacles to improving the quality of ethnic education for *Zainichi* children.

HISTORY OF EDUCATION OF *ZAINICHI* AND ESTABLISHMENT OF THEIR IDENTITY

As a means of resistance first to Japanese and then to American control, *Zainichi* formed a discourse to establish and maintain their identity as *Zainichi*. The following discussion reveals a part of this history in chronologically. In 1945, with the defeat of Japan in World War II, Japanese colonial rule of Korea came to an end. At the time, 2 million Koreans lived in Japan as "Japanese" as a result of Korea's status as a Japanese colony from 1910 to 1945. The official nationality of these ethnically Korean people was Japanese, and they were prohibited from using a Korean name, speaking the Korean language, and providing ethnic education. They were faced with the imposed duties of a Japanese name, Japanese language, and a Japanese lifestyle. They were forced to mentally become "Japanese."

After the war, most Koreans organized resources to return to their home country and find employment; however, 600,000 Koreans decided to stay in Japan. In October 1945, The League of Koreans—whose nationalist and socialist ideology had led to their oppression by the Japanese government during the war—acted to assist those who remained. This group held as one of its main missions the establishment of Korean schools that would focus on the retention of Korean culture and language. Starting with only a few language classes, the enthusiasm for Korean education burgeoned and by 1948 there were 541 elementary schools, 9 junior high schools, and 36 schools for young men. The emphasis on Korean ethnic identity with a socialist slant caused fear within the American Occupation leadership. Korean schools were viewed as enemy institutions that were playing a leading role in the development of Korean socialists or nationalists.

At the beginning of the occupation, GHQ (General Headquarters, the offices of the Allied Occupation led by the United States) left the schools alone. However, with the rise of the Cold War, GHQ began to monitor Korean schools and the policy switched from noninterference to oppression. According to Allied Occupation policy, the existence of Korean schools was a menace. In January 1948, the Japanese Ministry of Education, which received instructions from GHQ, sent notification ending approval of Korean schools. On April 10, 1948, a law to close down Korean schools was enacted in Kobe (Hyogo Prefecture), where significant numbers of Koreans lived, producing a significant protest action, called the *Hanshin Kyouiku Tousou* (Hanshin educational struggle). Administration of Korean schools by both nationalists and socialists was the central issue. Following the protest, on April 24, the governor of Hyogo withdrew the law closing the schools. GHQ did not recognize this action and instead declared a state of emergency. Over a thousand Koreans were arrested. On the April 26, a Korean school close-down order was issued in Osaka, and 13,000 Koreans held a protest meeting. The armed forces of GHQ fired on the crowd and a 16-year-old Korean boy was shot dead. Despite intense resistance from the Korean population, armed GHQ and Japanese police pressure kept the schools closed and the protests died down.

For the Koreans remaining in Japan, the reactions of the government and GHQ were incomprehensible. Koreans held the belief that "It is natural for us, Koreans, to have our own school and teach ethnic education to our children because we want to take back our homeland, history and culture." But, instead, *Zainichi* were expected to become like Japanese in language and behavior, having their fundamental human rights taken away. Ironically, the postwar degree of coercion and suppression of ethnic education was more severe than the persecution and hardships endured by the *Zainichi* population during Japanese colonial rule. With the Peace Treaty at San Francisco on April 28, 1952, *Zainichi* Koreans were stripped of their Japanese nationality and treated as foreigners, and thus their children were excluded from the Japanese public educational system. In 1965, with the concluding of the Japan–Korea Treaty, South Korea was positioned as the "only legal government on the Korean peninsula." Japan and South Korea did not recognize the legitimacy of the North Korean government. In December of that year, two notifications were released by the Japanese Education Ministry. One encouraged entrance of *Zainichi* Koreans' children to Japanese schools. However, these schools dealt with Korean children the same as Japanese children, without any attention to Korean ethnic identity. A second notification stated that the Japanese government did not recognize North Korean schools as legitimate schools.

Zainichi, whose mother tongue had been taken from them forcefully, started a movement of resistance. They fervently asserted that their national education was a spiritual home for them, enabling them to hold on to the dignity of their nation and build up national solidarity. In the 1970s, *Zainichi* demands went beyond educational needs to the demand for human rights. By the 1980s, these demands included reforms involving racial discrimination in the workplace, the social security system, and suffrage. *Zainichi* attitudes changed gradually, and their viewpoint shifted from one based in Korea to one based in their new home in Japan. Some *Zainichi* worried about losing their identity, language, and culture through assimilation into Japanese society, and asserted: "It is important to have the ideology of education based on unification of South Korea and North Korea, and national education must be used for character building" (Yang, 1985, p. 159).

By the mid-1980s and 1990s, things began to change as people realized that the majority of *Zainichi* were second- and third-generation individuals who has been born and grew up in Japan. The idea of a "diverse *Zainichi*

TABLE 7.3 Zainichi Koreans: Ratio of Permanent Residents to Alien Registrants

Year	Alien registrants	Permanent residents	Ratio (%)
1999	636,548	517,787	81.3
2000	635,269	507,429	79.9
2001	632,405	495,986	78.4
2002	625,422	485,180	77.6
2003	613,791	471,756	76.9
2004	607,419	461,460	76.0
2005	598,687	447,805	74.8
2006	598,219	438,974	73.4

Note. Ratio: Permanent residents/Alien registrants.

Source. Statistics on alien registrants, Immigration Bureau, Ministry of Justice.

identity" was thrown into the limelight. Table 7.3 shows the ratio of *Zainichi* qualifying as permanent residents relative to all *Zainichi* registered aliens in Japan. Objections to continuing the existing identity scheme began to be raised. These objections created a crisis for ethnic education because many *Zainichi* were afraid that "Each *Zainichi* would be isolated and assimilated into Japanese society, and, as a result, their identity would become vague" (Minzoku-Kyouiku Sokusin Kyokugikai, 1995, p. 10). Thus, those responsible for ethnic education emphasized ethnic identity rather than diversity. A strong statement was often made that "*Zainichi* should see through the discriminatory structure of Japanese society and rise up to win 'liberation for human beings' and should have national awareness and pride" (p. 10). The history of *Zainichi* education can be said to be a history of resistance against Japanese society and the pressure for assimilation. A discourse of "we *Zainichi*" became increasingly emphasized, and the category of *Zainichi* became natural and essential. This discourse promoted a monolithic *Zainichi* identity, focusing on the "restoration of culture," with an emphasis on "national awareness and pride" and "bonds with the Korean homeland" (p. 10).

THE CURRENT STRUCTURE OF *ZAINICHI* EDUCATION

There are three kinds of schools available to *Zainichi* in Japan: Japanese public schools, North Korean schools (built by The League of Koreans in Japan, which has supported North Korea), and South Korean schools (built by *Zainichi* who have supported South Korea). Roughly 90% of *Zainichi* children go to Japanese schools, with the remaining 10% subdivided between the North Korean and South Korean schools. Because the government does not officially

TABLE 7.4 Number of *Zainichi* Koreans Who Are Alien Registrants, by Age, 2006

Age	Number	Age	Number	Age	Number
Over 80	23,382	50–54	48,222	20–24	40,887
75–79	15,312	45–49	48,413	15–19	24,283
70–74	23,047	40–44	48,708	10–14	19,457
65–69	32,704	35–39	54,476	5–9	16,101
60–64	38,490	30–34	54,650	0–4	12,297
55–59	48,110	25–29	49,680		
				Total	598,219

Source. Ministry of Justice, http://www.moj.go.jp/.

track students based on ethnicity, the actual distribution is not available, so these figures have been derived through rough calculation.

Just after World War II in 1945, there was one kind of school for *Zainichi* Koreans: "Schools of Koreans." Then, in 1948, two nations were born on the Korean Peninsula, the North Korea (PDRK) of socialism and communism and the South Korea (ROK) of capitalism and liberalism. The two nations were intensely antagonistic. *Zainichi* Korean society was influenced by these events and became divided between supporters of the south and supporters of the north, producing potent antagonism. Naturally, *Zainichi* Korean schools were also affected, separating into different schools for supporters of the two sides, each school reflecting the contrasting ideologies of the north or the south. This split continues today, with selection of schools reflecting the thinking of parents. When they "come out" as *Zainichi* Koreans, supporters of either North Korea or South Korea choose an ethnic school for their children. Discrimination follows. Thus, most *Zainichi* parents choose to send their children to Japanese schools. This choice is not related to ideological opposition toward the north or the south, but is intended to protect the children from discrimination. In Japan, children are required to attend elementary and middle school. As shown in Table 7.4, in 2006 there were about 60,000 *Zainichi* children from 5 to 19 years of age. Among foreign children who needed to learn Japanese, there were, as of 2006, 861 children whose first language was Korean (Table 7.5). Those children were considered newcomers compared with the other roughly 59,000 *Zainichi* children (of either South Korean or North Korean nationality) attending Japanese schools.

Ethnic Education in Japanese Public Schools

In many Japanese schools, mostly in the western part of Japan, after-school classes are offered for *Zainichi* children to give them an opportunity to learn their national culture. The classes are called "ethnic classes" or "ethnic clubs."

TABLE 7.5 Minority Student Enrollment by First Language

First language	Number enrolled, by year		
	2004	2005	2006
Portuguese	7,033	7,562	8,633
Chinese	4,628	4,460	4,471
Spanish	2,926	3,156	3,279
Filipino	1,799	2,176	2,508
Korean	902	859	861
Vietnamese	718	754	808
English	501	487	466
Other language	1,171	1,238	1,387
Total	19,678	20,693	22,413

Source. Ministry of Education, Culture, Sports, Science and Technology, 2007, http://www.mext.go.jp/b_menu/houdou/17/04/05042001/05042001.htm.

There were approximately 160 such after-school programs in Osaka Prefecture as of March 2003. The educational aim of these ethnic classes is primarily to help *Zainichi* children become aware of what it means to be Korean and to encourage them to take pride and responsibility for being Korean in Japan. This is done by giving students the opportunity to learn the history of their country and think about helping each other while developing themselves. In addition, as members of Japanese society, children who attend these classes acquire an international way of thinking that will allow them to take part in society without discrimination. Leaders of the *Zainichi* are responsible for teaching the classes and developing the curriculum, which focuses on language, geography, history, customs, and national music, as well as traditional musical instruments and dance. In the Korean ethnic clubs of Japanese schools, Korean instructors are employed. Details of the curriculum are organized by the instructor.

A significant problem that arises from these ethnic programs is that the premise of exploring diversity runs contrary to the philosophy of assimilation espoused by the Japanese educational system. The education programs for *Zainichi,* as well as those for other ethnic children, are not considered a major or important component of the Japanese public education system. Ethnic classes are considered one of many extracurricular activities, and payment for the instructors and leaders is not a priority for many self-governing bodies, resulting in very little support. Some self-governing bodies do provide a subsidy, however the sum of money is often very small. Consequently, ethnic classes are in an insecure position, often wholly dependent on resources from the local *Zainichi* community. Although the Japanese education system has begun to stress the importance of cultural diversity, the system does not embrace multiculturalism. It is not attuned to cultural pluralism at all. For example, in the middle school in Moriguchi City, Osaka, where I taught in 1992–1993, children learned about the problem of human rights for *Zainichi* in the same context that they learned of human rights for people in other countries.

North Korean Schools

The role of the Japanese government creates differences in treatment between South Korean and North Korean schools. North Korean schools were built by the ethnic national organization: the League of Koreans in Japan. There are 80 North Korean schools in Japan that provide 3 kindergartens, 67 elementary schools, 38 middle schools, 10 high schools, and 1 college. According to the League of Koreans in Japan, the objective of North Korean schools is:

> In 21st century, we educate our children to become a person who has responsibility for creating a peaceful and affluent society based on compatriot love and ethnicity. We educate children as a promising Korean who has a world view and has knowledge of his/her ethnicity and "intelligence, virtue, healthy body" and can work for the prosperity of his/her motherland and the people and contribute to the development of his/her society and work hard in both Japanese and international society. (Chongryon, n.d.)

The worldview espoused in this mission statement is *Juche*, which adds socialism to Confucian values. *Juche*-ism is the guiding thought of North Korea and serves as its official ideology. The North Korean government claims that Kim Il-Sung founded the philosophy and Kim Jeong-Il developed it.

The underlying educational aim of North Korean schools is heavily influenced by politics in North Korea, though the content and focus have recently changed. In the past, the curriculum of North Korean schools in Japan was the same as that of schools in North Korea. However, a precise duplicate of the North Korean curriculum was not suitable to address the reality of children born and raised in Japan. As generations changed and opportunities and responsibilities became more diverse, second-generation *Zainichi* began to advocate for a curriculum adapted to the needs of Koreans currently living in Japan. Thus, the curriculum for North Korean schools was restructured in 2003 with the following aims:

1. Support an abundant ethnicity and a firm racial consciousness.
2. Study the history of *Zainichi* society and have self-consciousness as protagonists in society.
3. Have the ability and nature to work in Japanese society and the larger international society.

TABLE 7.6 Comparison of Curricula of North Korean Schools and Japanese Schools

Subject	North Korean schools	Japanese schools	Difference
Korean language	21.0		
Japanese	12.8	20.8	−8.0
English	4.3	3.8	+0.5
Social science, geography, history	8.2	7.7	+0.5
Math	14.6	14.3	+0.3
Science	8.2	10.2	−2.0
Music, art	10.7	11.4	−0.7
Physical education, home economics, information	7.5	13.3	−5.8
Others	12.8	18.6	−5.8

Note. Values are percentage of time devoted to the subject. Difference: North Korean schools minus Japanese schools.

Source. http://www.chongryon.com/j/edu/index7.html.

4. Educate children to be able to make a happy and rich society full of vitality.
5. Change the content of education to put ethnicity forward.
6. Schools are to become open places for ethnic children who have potential in the future and whose parents have a variety of thoughts and principles.

These objectives are achieved through a different curricular emphasis in North Korean schools in comparison with Japanese schools (see Table 7.6). Studies in geography and history in the North Korean schools focus more on Korean and less on Japanese subject matter. In social science, students study:

1. The Korean people, with a focus on *Zainichi* ethnic culture
2. The experiences of *Zainichi* first-generation immigrants in Japan and their achievements in building up the *Zainichi* community
3. The rights and life of *Zainichi*
4. South Korean society and the problem of unification between North and South Korea
5. Japanese geography, history, and society

Historically, pictures of Kim Il-Song and Kim Jeong-Il were displayed on the classroom walls, but those have now been removed.

Costs of teachers and teaching materials are provided by the tuition paid by each family. Up until the 1970s, there was also support for educational expenses from North Korea. Because the Japanese government does not recognize foreign schools as formal educational institutions, there is no Japanese government funding. Therefore, the financing of ethnic schools is very unstable and teachers' salaries are often delayed.

One of the major problems for schools that focus on ethnic identity (or that serve a single ethnic group) is that they are not acknowledged by the Japanese government as regular schools. According to Article 83 of the Fundamental Law of Education, foreign schools are treated as belonging to the "miscellaneous" category. This classification applies not only to Korean schools but also to schools aligned with other nations or ethnic groups. Consequently, they receive no government subsidies, resulting in extremely high tuition fees. The cost of attending a North Korean school is roughly seven times the cost of attending a Japanese public school. In addition to the increased cost of tuition, students at North Korean schools are not eligible for the student discount for transportation.

Perhaps even more salient, a student who graduates from a Korean school is not credentialed as being a high school graduate. As a result, students from the North Korean schools must attend a correspondence school or pass a qualification examination before gaining admittance to the Japanese university system. Students attending North Korean schools not only have academic challenges but they also frequently become targets of bullying from Japanese students whenever tensions arise between Japan and North Korea. Female students who wear traditional clothing are often subject to harassment. The difficulties of academic credentialing and cultural harassment have reduced student interest in North Korean schools and, as a result, the number of new students enrolled continues to decline.

South Korean Schools

South Korean schools were established by the South Korean National Body in Japan, which supports South Korea. There are four school groups in Tokyo, Kyoto, and Osaka, consisting of four high schools, three middle schools, three elementary schools, and two kindergartens. The main difference between the South Korean and North Korean schools is that three South Korean schools have been acknowledged as regular schools by the Japanese government: two schools in Osaka authorized as private schools in 1951, and a school in Kyoto admitted as an international school in 2003.

According to the home page of one of the South Korean schools in Osaka (http://www.keonguk.ac.jp/), the goals of South Korean education are:

1. To educate children to have a cosmopolitan nature based on Korean culture—a nature that can interchange with various people instead of closed nationalism
2. To educate children to have an ability to adapt to an international society
3. To develop and enlighten children's nature with a desirable attitude
4. To not care about nationality

The aim of South Korean education is for Korean and Japanese teachers to work together toward world peace and to educate children in their own culture (language, history, geography), resulting in national pride and the ability to contribute to the development of the world and their community. Children go to South Korea for a school trip to see Korean traditional culture and visit historic spots. Students who want to enter college are given help as much as possible for entering either a Korean or a Japanese college.

EDUCATIONAL EXPERIENCES OF *ZAINICHI* AND ESTABLISHMENT OF THEIR IDENTITY

The type of schooling *Zainichi* children receive has profound effects on their developing sense of self-identity. Accounts of the experiences of two young women will illustrate some of the issues *Zainichi* face as they try to find their place in Japanese and Korean society.

Ethnic Activities in Japanese Schools

As the instructor of the ethnic children's association for *Zainichi* children in Takatsuki City, Osaka, from 1996 to 1998, I had the opportunity to observe students' experiences with ethnic education and gain an understanding of how these courses impacted establishment of their identity as *Zainichi*. A ninth-grade girl named Ran (her true name), a third-generation *Zainichi*, participated in the ethnic class. Ran had been born and brought up in a community with a large concentration of *Zainichi* residents. There was an established children's ethnic class in the district, and Ran started to participate when she entered elementary school. Because her parents were working, she stayed with other children until the class ended for the day. She liked the class very much in her elementary school days and became interested in studying everything about South Korea and North Korea. As a third-grader, she started to learn the Korean drum, *changgo*, and made substantial progress. For her, Mondays, Wednesdays, and Saturdays were ethnic class days in the community. Tuesdays were *changgo* days, and on Fridays Ran joined an ethnic class in her school. She spent the entire week in various ethnic activities. Through these activities, Ran became proud of her ethnic background. At that time, she used a Japanese name in school, but became interested in using her Korean name. While still in elementary school she asked her parents if she could use her Korean name at school. Her parents resisted, afraid that she would be bullied by other children at school. So, Ran waited to use her Korean name until she entered middle school, when she changed her name without consulting her parents.

Because she used a Korean name at school, Ran became a symbol for the ethnic class. She was regarded as a "model of promising Korean children," full of pride and self-assertiveness. At the beginning of each academic year,

Ran was asked by her teacher to tell her Japanese classmates about her personal history as a Korean child, as well as how she felt about herself. The teacher thought that Japanese children could understand her better, and felt that sharing her experience with the class would reinforce and validate her ethnic identity as well. However, for Ran, talking about herself increased the likelihood of being bullied, as other students felt she was showing off. She began to feel that these presentations were her duty, part of her obligation as a *Zainichi* child. She became uncomfortable, and the responsibility of being a model student began to weigh heavily on her. The teachers' discourse on "respecting the ethnic identity of Korean children" had the reverse effect of making Ran feel more burdened by her *Zainichi* identity. As a result, in middle school Ran began to feel discriminated against by Japanese students and lost much of the confidence that she felt in elementary school. She often complained during ethnic classes that nobody would take her seriously, and she became enthusiastic about participating in the ethnic class activities to forget about the discrimination she felt in school. As one of her instructors pointed out, she "embodied a character commensurate with group life" and maintained a strong sense of responsibility in associating with group peers. She grasped quickly what the teacher or instructor expected of her and worked seriously to meet the expectation. For her, therefore, the community-based and school-based ethnic classes endorsed self-esteem as a Korean girl, but the bullying and discrimination that she felt from other students at the Japanese school made her *Zainichi* identity feel like a burden as well.

After middle school, when Ran entered high school, she returned to using her Japanese name. For *Zainichi,* using a Korean name and disclosing that they are Koreans in Japanese society is stressful. And it is much harder for children. They have to recognize that they are seen differently by others when they use a Korean name. They must be self-assertive, and they always have the responsibility of being Korean. Ran felt this pressure throughout middle school. Although she decided to use a Japanese name when she entered high school, many of her classmates entered the same high school, so many students knew that she was *Zainichi*. It would be a hasty conclusion to assume that her decision was based on a desire to escape from the heavy pressure of living in Japan as a Korean. Her decision was not so backward. She joined in activities of the *Zainichi* group in high school and talked a great deal with other *Zainichi* students about the difference of environment between middle school and high school, and about the dealing with Japanese students who have little understanding of *Zainichi*. Changing her name from a Korean name to a Japanese name did not mean that she had lost her self-awareness as a *Zainichi*. Rather, it was a survival strategy she employed to help herself live in a discriminatory society.

In addition to the stress associated with changing her name, once Ran entered the ninth grade she felt uneasy because of a coming entrance examination for high school. Only two girls, Ran and another Korean girl in the class, had not attended cram school. The class members were filled with anticipation of preparing for the entrance examination. Ran was unable to keep up with the other students and said, "I don't like the idea that a person's value is decided depending on whether he/she has a good or a bad school record. I think there should be more important things." She gradually became frustrated and started to think about attending cram school. Her instructor said to her, "You don't have to study so hard." Ran replied, "Other students are studying very hard." The competitive nature of the exam and the pressure Ran felt about it continued to increase.

While helping Korean children with their studies is supposed to be an important component of ethnic classes, the ethnic class teachers prefer to focus on ethnicity rather than on helping students develop their academic ability. Grouping around ethnic identity—to unite or share a common idea—is assumed to be more important for Korean children than focusing on academic grouping and competition. Ethnic class teachers often tell students, "You should participate in an ethnic class rather than receive a supplementary lesson." Put simply, the value placed on academic ability in Japanese classes and the values emphasized in ethnic classes are completely different. Ran wanted to meet both the expectations of the ethnic community and those of the academic community. She found herself struggling to do both.

Experiences in North Korean Schools

Sungni (her true name) is a third-generation Korean young woman who is 20 years old. She was born in eastern Japan and went to a North Korean middle school, a Japanese high school, and a Japanese public college. She took time off from college when she was a sophomore and entered a college in Busan, South Korea. This interview was conducted during her time in Korea. Sungni had North Korean nationality until she went to South Korea to study, which required her to change her nationality from North Korean to South Korean. For those procedures, she had to join a South Korean ethnic group, which meant a border transgression for her because she had been living in the world of North Korean people. The educational ideology of North Korea heavily influenced young *Zainichi* North Koreans living in Japan. Even though she thought that there was something wrong about the ideology, Sungni was very fond of her friends and teachers in the North Korean school. She had also had positive experiences in the Japanese schools, but she said the bonds with her peers and teachers in the North Korean school were much stronger and could not be compared with the bonds she had made in the Japanese schools. The North Korean schooling experience was a source of establishing her identity as a North Korean *Zainichi*.

When Sungni went to South Korea to study, she was greatly shocked when told by a native Korean roommate that she was not South Korean but Japanese. This came as such a surprise to her because North Korean *Zainichi* are proud of being Korean; they have studied their language and culture to ensure the connections between themselves and their homeland. The *Zainichi* feel discriminated against in Japan, especially whenever a troubling development comes out North Korea and they are made to feel they are not Japanese but Korean. When her roommate told her that she was not Korean but Japanese, this attacked her constructed identity as a Korean. However, during her stay in South Korea, she was also told by another Korean student that she was a great Korean and was the pride of Korea. This comment served to reinforce her Korean identity and helped her understand that native Koreans saw *Zainichi* from different angles and did not understand the situation for Koreans in Japan.

Soon after she went to South Korea, Sungni was happy to be told that she was the same as a native Korean. But later, when I interviewed her, she began to express ill feelings toward what she had been told. Native Koreans thought *Zainichi* would be pleased to be told they were Korean. Sungni realized that the native Koreans thought involuntarily that *Zainichi* lived ill-fated lives and that native Koreans lived justly. She thought that while these people appeared to be good, they did not want to acknowledge the history or the experiences of *Zainichi*. So, Sungni decided to say to young native Koreans, "I am a Korean but I am different from you."

Sungni now admits that she prefers living in Japan. In the beginning when she went to Korea, she thought she should get used to life in Korea and develop a resolution to live there forever. Gradually, however, she became worried about the difference of values between native Koreans and herself. When interviewed in June 2004, she stated:

> In my memory, there is the world where only *Zainichi* are living. Sometimes I hated to be in its easiness, but I really liked the world; everybody was so friendly and we cried, got angry or were pleased together. I had a lot of such memories. I have 13 classmates and our dream is we will get married and have a baby around the same time and let our child go to the same school together and we, mothers, go to school on a parents' visiting day and talk together a lot. We don't want our school to be closed down. It is certain that the place where I will go back to is Japan or I should say that the place where I will go back is where my friends, my teachers and my parents are living. I really hate that our school is closed down.

Among her classmates, she was one of two students who went to South Korea. Her classmates sent her off with a warm heart. They said to her, "Be sure to study and to get something out of the experience. See how South Korea really is." She felt their love for her.

HOW SHOULD EDUCATION FOR *ZAINICHI* BE CONDUCTED IN THE FUTURE?

Role of the Japanese School System in Zainichi *Education*

The Japanese government does not acknowledge schools for foreign children as regular legal schools, and ethnic education classes are not recognized as important components of the education system for minority students. Japanese society does not accept the idea that education reflecting minority needs is necessary. Thus, it is easy to characterize the Japanese educational system as assimilationist. Japanese education has not reached a stage of cultural pluralism and is far from achieving a multicultural stage. *Zainichi* Koreans have the same responsibilities and duties as Japanese people (paying taxes and so on), and they are given the same general rights as the Japanese. However, if they want services that are relevant to their lives, they are told that is a luxury. The reality that foreigners and immigrants and their children might have different needs than native-born Japanese people is not part of the national discourse. Japan has forced foreigners to tacitly follow a policy of assimilation to receive full benefits from Japan and to secure their own rights. Foreigners are told they should be thankful for the opportunity to live in Japan. This attitude reinforces for foreigners the sense that they need to assimilate the Japanese way of being. However, when the situation is reversed—when Japanese live in a foreign country—can they truly become "countrymen" of that foreign country?

Persons have a right to acquire the necessary information and skills to live in society at large and at the same time to maintain "multicultural citizenship," details of which may vary depending on ethnicity or situation. In Japanese society, rights are apt to be judged in terms of quantity. A right may exist, but what is necessary to exercise that right may be diverse; in Japanese society, the quality of exercise of that right is ignored. This is true of the right to study. There are surely a variety of ways of exercising the right to study depending on ethnicity or situation, in addition to basic academic ability. *Zainichi* have rights to receive mandated information or skills necessary to live in society at large; in addition, they need to acquire special skills as *Zainichi*. Their right to education is multicultural. The Japanese government must implement a system of a tax-supported education for foreign children. This is important not only for the foreign children, but also for the children of the *Nikkei* (Japanese emigrants and their descendants), who have been returning from South America in increasing numbers in recent years.

Cultural Essentialism in Education for Zainichi

Educational research on *Zainichi* has so far focused mainly on the system—the mechanics of kinds of schools available to *Zainichi*, accreditation, and so on. There has been little discussion about the *content* of education or the role of ethnicity. The content of ethnic education has been a sanctuary controlled by the leaders of the *Zainichi*, and it has been taboo to invade this holy ground. Education has always relied on these leaders, which has prevented ethnic education from developing to meet the needs of *Zainichi* in modern society.

Education of *Zainichi* can be said to reflect a history of resistance. It has been forced to stand face to face against the Japanese pressure for assimilation. *Zainichi* have been deprived of their culture under Japanese control and have had negative images implanted in their minds. In that sense, *Zainichi* are in a defective existence racially. Thus, there has been the perception that the *Zainichi* can become a real nation by acquiring the trappings of ethnic culture—through studying the Korean language, playing traditional musical instruments, and eating traditional food—as well as overcoming the sense of cultural deprivation and negative self-awareness. Under such circumstances, ethnic education has been carried out. But this has led to cultural essentialism, creating assumptions of common qualities and needs among all *Zainichi*. Ethnic education of *Zainichi* has failed by ignoring individual diversity within the group because strengthening the identity of *Zainichi as a group* has been regarded as having preeminent importance. Because common historical experiences, memories, and traditions have been greatly emphasized, the practical aspects of living, such as acquiring the necessary means to live in the present society, have not been given sufficient attention. The situation is similar to the "cultural model" or "fictive kinship" discussed by Ogbu (1978).

The dilemma related to cultural essentialism is not only a problem for education of *Zainichi* but also a more universal problem for multicultural education in general. Nakajima highlighted this dilemma by quoting Bullivant (1984):

> When children with an ethnic background select curriculum of their cultural heritage, language, history, custom or other lifestyle, the selection doesn't relate to equality of education or life chances. Equality of education or life chance is influenced by structure, classes, economy, politics and human rights of a culturally complex society and is influenced by control of the ruling group that is near social rewards or economic resources. So, ... it is extremely simple to conclude that teaching cultural heritage leads to excellent self-esteem and good results and it results in getting a better job.... If such multi-cultural programs were extremely emphasized, minority people wouldn't use their energy or interest to learn English, a dominant language, which is necessary for them to live. (Nakajima, 1991, p. 15)

Bullivant further pointed out that it is necessary to redefine the meaning of culture to eliminate this dilemma. According to one definition:

> Culture is essentially a form of a "survival device," which will develop forever based on adaptive changes to enable people to deal with various problems of life in a special environment. Ethnic children should study this kind of culture and not a culture like a fossil. (Nakajima, 1991, p. 16)

Ethnic-focused education for *Zainichi* provides an alternative track for living in Japanese society, but it does not enhance chances for *Zainichi* to enter the mainstream of Japanese society. *Zainichi* can be good players of traditional musical instruments and speak fluently in the Korean language, but such skills might be valued only in their world. Even if the circumstances around *Zainichi* improve, without a stronger and broader educational foundation they will be limited in the amount of information or skills they can apply in building a successful life.

CONCLUSION

Wil Kymlicka (1995) discusses the concept of rights of the group, describing "internal restriction" and "external protection." Internal restriction refers to a situation wherein a certain group's rights can restrict its members' freedom in the name of group solidarity or cultural purity. External protection refers to rights of a minority group that restrict the economic and political powers of mainstream society to prevent that society from infringing upon resources or systems of the minority group. Thinking in terms of this dichotomy is highly suggestive of a productive approach to addressing the problems of *Zainichi* identity politics and exclusion. *Zainichi* Koreans must talk more seriously about internal restriction and external protection and try to balance the two aspects to carry out high-quality education in the future. As a teacher in an ethnic class I have seen the processes in action. In ethnic classes, students who do not agree with the common idea of desirable ethnicity are excluded. This exclusion inside the *Zainichi* community is really no different from the exclusion of *Zainichi* from Japanese society at large. This is a demonstration of the theory of self-contradiction. Various opinions are shut in by shielding themselves behind the exclusion from Japanese society. It is not right. Exclusion inside the world of ethnic education of *Zainichi* must be avoided.

REFERENCES

Bullivant, B. M. (1984). *Pluralism, cultural maintenance and evolution.* Clevedon, Avon, UK: Multilingual Matters.
Chongryon. (n.d.). *Contents of ethnic education.* http://www.chongryon.com/j/edu/index2.html
Kymlicka, W. (1995). *Multicultural citizenship: A liberal theory of minority right.* Oxford, UK: Clarendon Press.
Minzoku-Kyouiku Sokusin Kyokugikai [Ethnic Educational Council] (Ed.). (1995). *Ten years history of Ethnic Educational Council.* Osaka: Minzoku-Kyouiku Sokusin Kyokugikai.
Nakajima, T. (1991). Dispute and problems about multiculturalism. *Nishiyama Gazette, 39.* Kyoto: Nishiyama College Press.
Ogbu, J. (1978). *Minority education and caste: The American system in cross-cultural perspective.* New York: Academic Press.
Yang, Y. (1985). Educational problems of *Zainichi* children. In E. Isomura, Y. Ichibangase, & T. Harada (Eds.), *Lectures on discrimination and human rights: Vol. 4. Ethnic groups.* Tokyo: Yuzankaku.

NAOMI NOIRI

The Education of Minorities in Japan

Voices of Amerasians in Okinawa

THIS CHAPTER provides a general overview of the education of minority children in Japan, with particular attention to the issues facing Amerasians. Since 1990, when changes were made to the Immigration Control and Refugee Act of Japan, the number of *Nikkei* (Japanese emigrants and their descendants), especially those of Brazilian origin, has increased dramatically. Meanwhile, as Kim noted in the Chapter 7, the percentage of Koreans among all foreign residents has fallen from around 82% in 1984 to 29% in 2006. The number of Chinese in Japan has exceeded that of Koreans since 2007. Changes in the national ethnic composition of Japan's minority groups have affected the current educational situation. Using a study of the Amerasians in Okinawa, I will elucidate some of the issues that face children from ethnic minorities in Japan. "Amerasians" in this context refers to a group of Okinawan residents whose fathers are in the U.S. military (or are ex-U.S. military) and whose mothers are Japanese. Throughout the study, Amerasian children talked of abuse, exclusion, and identity. This group will be examined in detail in order to provide insights into the issues that face children from ethnic minorities in Japan. The Amerasian School in Okinawa serves as a useful case study with which to examine problems facing the educational system in Japan (Noiri, 2000, 2001). The final part of the chapter focuses more closely on the education of minority groups in Japan, particularly on how "good" education can be obtained—not only for foreign students but for all students.

ETHNIC MINORITY CHILDREN IN LOCAL SCHOOLS

Local public schools in Japan have faced a rapid increase in a new type of foreign student since 1991. They are referred to as "newcomers." These young people have migrated with their families to Japan from abroad and in most cases do not have Japanese as their first language. As Kim noted in Chapter 7, up through the 1980s, the vast majority of foreign students in schools in Japan were of Korean descent, usually known as *Zainichi* children. Several generations have passed since the colonial period when Japan dominated Korea and, as a result, most Korean children in Japan speak Japanese as their first language. These children, whose families came to Japan during the colonial period and who do not have any difficulties with Japanese, are called "old-timers" in contrast to the more recent "newcomer" migrants. The first wave of newcomer students in the post–World War II era were the children of war-displaced Japanese (*chuugoku kikokusha*), who first began to arrive in the 1970s. *Chuugoku kikokusha* are Japanese children who had been left behind in China during the chaos at the end of the war and were raised by Chinese parents. After the opening of China in the 1970s, some of these (now grown) "children" returned to Japan with their family members. Their children were considered racially Japanese but had a Chinese cultural identity. In addition, starting in the early 1980s, a small number of Southeast Asian refugees began to arrive in Japan and their children started to enroll the public schools. However, because Japan never admitted large numbers of refugees, these students tended to be concentrated in a few schools with special programs for refugee families.

It was not until the 1990s that the scale of newcomer students dramatically increased. The Ministry of Education, Culture, Sports, Science and Technology (MEXT) has published data on the number of foreign students each year since 1991, and the number of these students has increased by nearly fourfold since then (Figure 8.1). By 2004, there were around 20,000 foreign

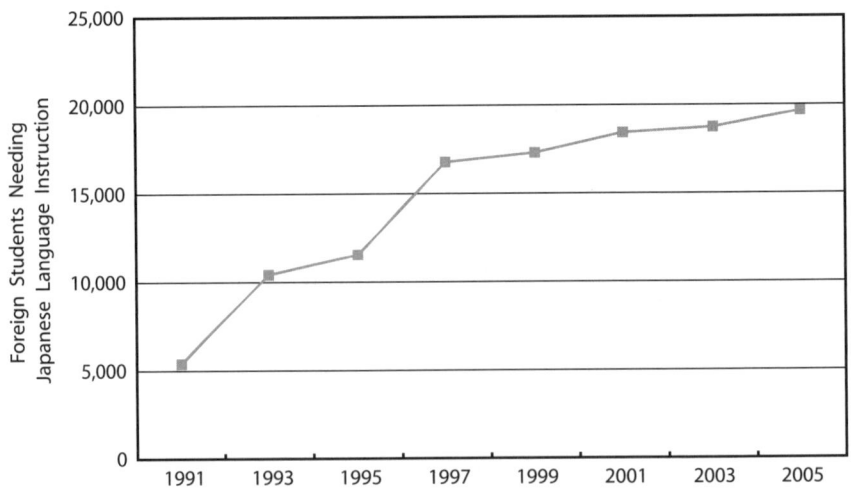

FIGURE 8.1 Number of Foreign Students in Public School Who Need Basic Japanese Language Instruction

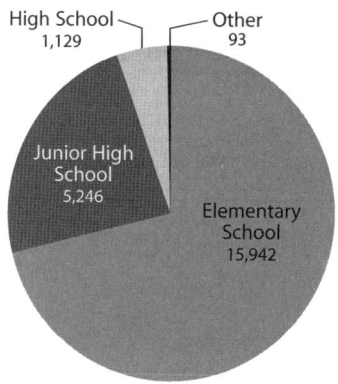

FIGURE 8.2 Number of Foreign Students Who Need Basic Language Instruction, by Level of Schooling, 2006

students in schools who needed instruction in the Japanese language. Most of these students were enrolled in elementary schools, and only a small percentage were in high school (Figure 8.2). This distribution may reflect the difficulties these students face in passing the high school entrance exam or may simply reflect the family demographics of those who chose to return to Japan to work.

The largest group of newcomer students are Portuguese-speaking *Nikkei* (of Japanese descent) from Brazil whose parents moved to Japan for job opportunities (Figure 8.3). However, a significant portion of newcomers also come from Chinese-speaking and Spanish-speaking households. Chinese-speaking children may be children of returnees or children of recent Chinese immigrants seeking economic opportunity in Japan.

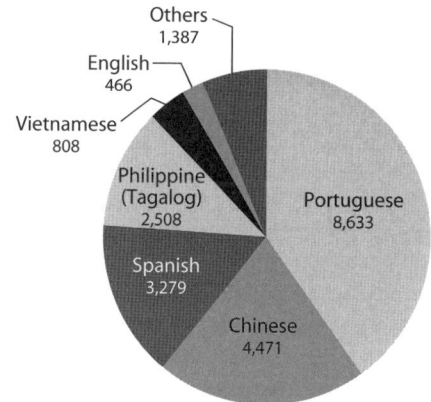

FIGURE 8.3 First Language of the Foreign Students Needing Basic Language Instruction, 2006

Source. Survey research on foreign students needing instruction in Japanese language, 2006, Ministry of Education, Culture, Sports, Science and Technology (*Monbukagakusho*), http://www.mext.go.jp

Newcomer Students but Not New Problems?

When non-Japanese-speaking students began to first show up in significant numbers in the public schools, MEXT dealt with the issue through allocation of special teachers to schools with a certain number of newcomer children. The objective was to facilitate teaching of the Japanese language to the newcomers through conducting language workshops for teachers and other measures (Ota, 2000, p. 6). Ota analyzed the policies from a pedagogical perspective:

> Teaching Japanese is one of the highest priorities for schools and teachers in the education of newcomer students.
> Newcomer students are pulled out of regular classrooms to a so-called Japanese Language Room.
> Teachers in the Japanese Language Room are responsible not only for teaching newcomer students Japanese but also for their adjustment to schools and Japanese students. Emphasis is given to thinking and behaving like other Japanese students.
> Newcomer children have only a limited opportunity to use their native language in schools.
> With the advent of newcomer student populations, schools have tended to also initiate so-called "international education programs" that aim to provide students with a global and international perspective.
> Since all instruction in regular classrooms is in Japanese, it is extremely difficult for newcomer students to understand what is taught in the classrooms. Less than one-half of them go on to high school, compared with nearly 100% of their Japanese peers. (pp. 7–8)

Newcomer students face serious problems, such as a high proportion of underachievement as well as exclusion, racial abuse, loss of native language, low self-esteem, and identity conflict. Ota noted that local public schools have introduced a "treat all equally" approach that proposes treating foreign students as Japanese students. The approach has some positive aspects, including free education and a lunch provided for all students. On the other hand, the negative side of the approach is forced assimilation and inequality as a result of treating everyone equally. When newcomer students achieve a Japanese language level that is sufficient for oral communication, they are moved from the Japanese Language Room to the regular classroom. If the students can behave in the same way as Japanese children, a teacher might think that there is no problem. Most foreign students sit quietly in the classroom, keeping their eyes on a textbook, but they are unable to comprehend much of the material due to their low cognitive level of understanding the Japanese language. Under the "treating equally" approach, specific needs of education for minority students are overlooked in many cases (Ota, 2000, p. 26).

"Treating Equally" Approach and Mainstream of Educational System

Ota (2000) pointed out that the "treating equally" approach has its roots in the treatment of Korean students in public schools. As Kim discussed in Chapter 7, the Japanese government has oppressed Korean ethnic schools. For public schools, on the other hand, the policy MEXT transmitted to prefectural boards of education was that "Korean students should not be treated differently" (Ministry of Education, Japan, 1965). This policy, designed for promoting inclusion of *Zainichi* children in Japanese public schools, was also aimed at keeping them away from Korean ethnic schools. As a form of risk management, the policy was intended to reduce attendance at schools associated with North Korea and thus decrease the influences of communism, a main concern of the Japanese government. Ota noted that the inclusion policy for *Zainichi* children has reflected on the "treating equally" approach for newcomer students since 1990s. The approach encourages ethnic minority children to stay away from segregated ethnic schools, to speak Japanese, and to behave in the same manner as Japanese children in public schools.

I agree with Ota's (2000) viewpoint. However, another aspect of the issue is how the mainstream educational system of Japan has influenced the education of minority students. Public schools in Japan have tended to neglect the diversity and inequality present among children that is reflective of their family and community background. After World War II, the existing Ministry of Education issued a new Fundamental Law of Education (see Chapter 1, by Fujita) that established a new type of education intended to be adequate for a democratic society. The Fundamental Law introduced ideals such as equal opportunity, competition, and self-help. Since then, teachers in local public schools have encouraged all students to believe that they have an equal chance in accessing higher education. Inequality as a result of competition is simply viewed as a result of the hard work or the laziness of each student.

"Treat all equally," then, is an approach for all students, not only for foreign children. Ethnic minority children, however, are one group of students who are seriously disadvantaged in this approach. This is due to their limited Japanese language abilities, as well as their lack of economic, social, and cultural capital. Possessing all of these factors enables mainstream Japanese students to more successfully gain access to higher education. From this point of view, the "treating equally" approach can be categorized as a Japanese version of "color blind" theory in the United States, in which the issues of racism, underachievement, and low self-esteem of minority children are shifted into the discourse of equal opportunity and self-help. Another minority group that is seriously disadvantaged in this approach is special needs children who have a physical or mental handicap. Clearly, ethnic minority students in Japan have their own special difficulties. In terms of enrollment in schools, foreign children who do not have Japanese citizenship are excluded from compulsory education. An educational board in a local community may enroll foreign students into public schools as a voluntary service. Thus, as a system-wide policy, local public schools basically offer education only for Japanese nationals; as a result, foreign students are marginalized. There are, of course, certain Japanese teachers who can make a difference in this situation, and some of their work positively influences each school level. However, this relatively limited influence does not lead to changes in the educational system as a whole. Foreign students learn Japanese language while their Japanese peers learn international studies. Such treatment strikes a balance between the marginal and the mainstream. Foreign students are included and marginalized at the same time. Even though some Japanese teachers have introduced international education to promote mutual understanding between Japanese students and foreign students, ethnic minority children are still marginalized in the educational system.

INTERNATIONAL CHILDREN IN JAPAN

Before considering the issue of the education of Amerasian children, I will briefly summarize the situation of racially mixed children, the so-called international children, in Japan. The term "international children" comes from the Japanese word "*kokusaiji*," which means a child who has a Japanese parent and a foreign parent. More than 20,000 international children were born in Japan in 2004 (Figure 8.4). Thus, these students are larger in number than

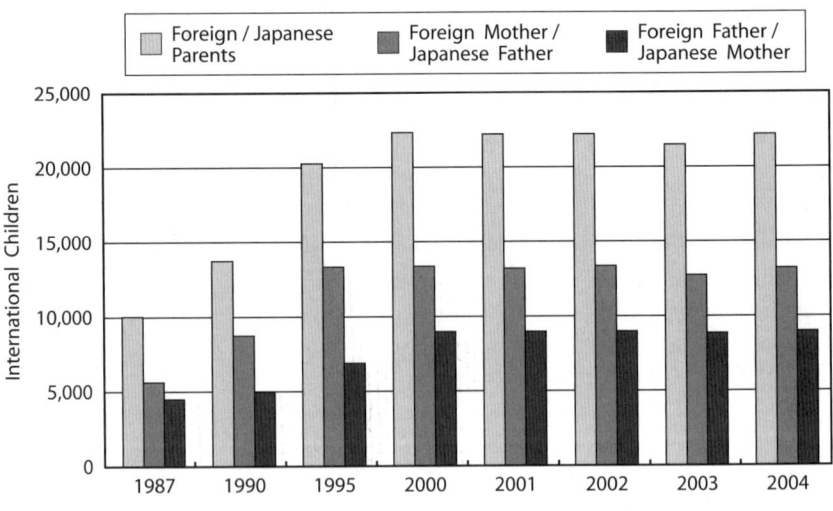

FIGURE 8.4 Parental Background of International Children Born in Japan

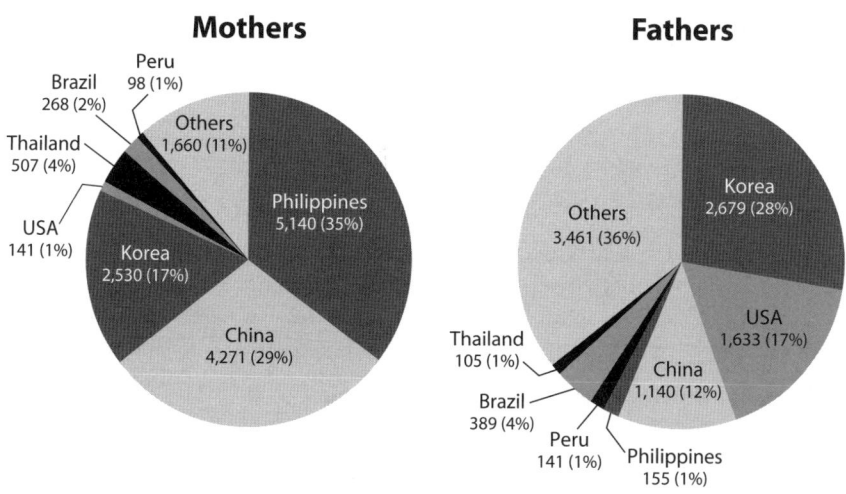

FIGURE 8.5 Nationality of Foreign Mothers and Fathers of International Children Born in 2007

Source. Survey research on the movement of population, 2007, Ministry of Health, Labor and Welfare, http://www.mhlw.go.jp/toukei/index.html

the foreign students who need basic instruction in learning Japanese (refer to Figure 8.1). Both of these groups of children increased in size rapidly during the 1990s. Although the number of international children continues to grow, they are not given much attention by the Japanese educational system. While MEXT has only responded to the increase of non-Japanese-speaking foreign students, I would insist that the increase of international children is a new and challenging trend facing the educational system in Japan, one suggestive of a new dimension of diversity among children in Japanese schools.

In international marriages, the number of couples in which the husband is Japanese and the wife is a foreigner was 35,993 in 2006. Meanwhile, the number of the couples in which the wife is Japanese and the husband is a foreigner was only 8,708 in the same year. As a result of the imbalance, there have always been more children who have a foreign mother and Japanese father than children who have foreign father and Japanese mother (Figure 8.4). In terms of ethnicity of the foreign parents, children who have Filipino mothers comprise the largest group of international children; only a small number of children have Filipino fathers (Figure 8.5). Another imbalance is the significant number of children with American fathers and the very small number of children with American mothers. The pattern of international children is reflective of the trends of international marriage and migration in

Japan, including migration that seeks better opportunities for employment, the large number of women from the Philippines, and the existence of the U.S. military base in Japan.

EDUCATION FOR DOUBLES: VOICES OF AMERASIANS IN OKINAWA

In this section, I will discuss the AmerAsian School in Okinawa (AASO) as a case study of one challenge to the Japanese educational system. The AASO is a nonprofit, grassroots school for Amerasian children whose fathers are American, especially military and ex-military serviceman of U.S. bases, and whose mothers are Japanese. It is one of the few "ethnic" schools in Japan, similar to Brazilian schools and Korean schools. One distinctive characteristic of the AASO is that it is the only ethnic school in Japan designated for racially mixed children.

Amerasians in Okinawa

In Okinawa, a prefecture in the southern part of Japan, the ethnic background of international children is completely different than it is on the main islands. The existence of huge U.S. military bases impacted patterns of international marriage and births of international children. The number of children who have foreign fathers is higher than the number who have foreign mothers (Figure 8.6). About 80% of all foreign fathers are U.S. citizens. A majority

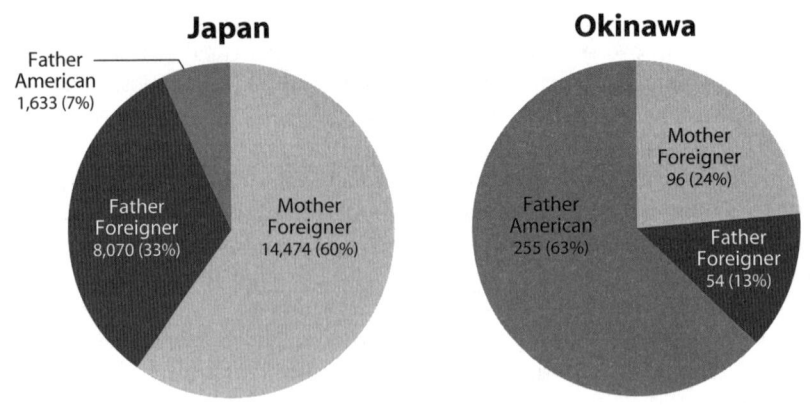

FIGURE 8.6 Parentage of International Children in Japan and Okinawa, 2007

Source. Survey research on the movement of population, 2007, Ministry of Health, Labor and Welfare, http://www.mhlw.go.jp/toukei/index.html

TABLE 8.1 Schooling of Amerasian Children with Dual Citizenship in Okinawa

	Primary school	Secondary school	Total
Public schools	404	55	459
DoDDS and free schools	196	61	257
School unknown	55	6	61
Total	655	122	777

Note. DoDDS, Department of Defense dependents school.

Source. The survey results on schooling of the foreign students and the students with dual citizenship, Department of Education, Okinawa Prefecture, 2000.

of the children are Amerasians and have a direct connection with the U.S. military base. Each year about 250 children are born to American fathers and Japanese mothers in Okinawa.

Schooling of Amerasian Children. A majority of the Amerasian children attend public school in Okinawa (Table 8.1). Terumoto (2003, p. 4) noted that the proportion of Amerasian children of "school unknown" (8.5%)—that is, those who were not attending public schools, private schools, or Department of Defense dependents schools (DoDDS; schools on the U.S. military bases that offer free education for the children of U.S. solders and civilians)—was extremely high compared with the total proportion of "school unknown" in Japan (0.02%).

The establishment of the AASO revealed the existence of a minority in Okinawa that had been facing unequal opportunity for schooling and racial abuse in public school. The AASO was founded by five mothers of Amerasians in 1998. The school offers English–Japanese bilingual education for around 80 students from kindergarten through ninth grade. Over the course of 11 years, fourteen out of eighteen graduates matriculated to public high school in Okinawa, while the other four entered high school in the United States, on a U.S. military base in Okinawa, or in an international school in Okinawa. The name of the school, *AmerAsian,* symbolizes a school policy that respects both American and Asian culture equally.

Before the founding of the AASO, there was only a limited range of places where Amerasian children could learn (Table 8.2). The public schools were not a realistic choice for most Amerasian children, whose primary language was English. Survey results (Table 8.2) showed that most Amerasian students in public schools do not have difficulty speaking and learning in Japanese, suggesting that those children who do have difficulty following Japanese classes would not have a place in the public school (Terumoto, 2001, p. 179).

TABLE 8.2 Proficiency in Japanese of Amerasian Children with Dual Citizenship in Okinawa

	No difficulty in conversation or learning	No difficulty in conversation; difficulty in learning	Difficulty in both conversation and learning	Other	Total
Primary school	353	40	5	6	404
Secondary school	44	9	1	1	55
Total	397	49	6	7	459

Source. The survey results on schooling of the foreign students and the students with dual citizenship, Department of Education, Okinawa Prefecture, 2000.

Abuse and prejudice are other serious obstacles for Amerasians who study in the public schools. The following is a comment of one student of the AASO who had transferred from a public school:

> When I was in the third and fourth grade, we learned about the war. The teachers' explanations went like this: "In Okinawa Americans raped Japanese women. Things like that happened and there are now a lot of cases of an international marriage." So, naturally, my classmates asked me such questions as "Was your mother also raped by an American G.I.?" "Your mother married an American man just for his looks, right?" (Thayer, 2003, p. 53)

Other options for schooling were quite limited. The DoDDS was not an option for Amerasian children whose father had retired from a job on the military base or for those who lived with a single mother. An international school, Okinawa Christian School International (OCSI), had been a popular option for Amerasian children until the school faced an environmental incident in 1997. After that, approximately 80 children left the school because of anxiety about their health (Thayer, 2003, p. 47). The OCSI encountered foul-smelling fumes in a new school building in 1996, when it moved from Urasoe City to Yomitan Village. The site was a place where there had once been an industrial waste disposal facility. Some parents demanded a relocation of the school, but the OCSI decided to stay (*Okinawa Times*, 1997, p. 2). Some of the students' mothers decided to start a new school of their own.

The reason for the AASO's founding was lack of choice to learn elsewhere. Moreover, the mothers were eager to create a place in which the mixed ethnicity of Amerasian children would be treated positively. They noticed that monolingual education in either English or Japanese that aimed at creating "an American" or "a Japanese" was not adequate for Amerasian children. Ms.

Midori Thayer, who is the principal at the AASO noted, "Both American schools and public schools in Japan tend to treat an Amerasian student as a *hafu*: a half-valued person" (Thayer, 2003, p. 48). To overcome the negative stereotype of *hafu*, the AASO introduced the bilingual education that is called "education for 'doubles.'"

The AASO encourages Amerasian children to accept their hybridity positively. The concept of "double" is not based on an essentialism that assumes an Amerasian to be American and Asian by birth. The AASO expects Amerasian children to cultivate multiple identities depending on the child's experience of movement across national borders, family life, and working life. "Double" in education for doubles is the antithesis of *hafu*, a symbol of positive self-esteem with hybridity (Thayer, 2003, p. 49).

Language and Identity in the AASO. Eighty percent of the classes at the AASO are taught in English. The students learn language arts, mathematics, natural science, social science, and athletics in English. Meanwhile, the students learn Japanese, social science, Japanese history and geography, and mathematics in classes that are taught in Japanese. It is obvious that the bilingual education in the AASO emphasizes English much more than Japanese. The background for this approach to bilingual education is that the founding mothers wanted to offer opportunities to the Amerasian children that connected them to their American fathers and U.S. society. Over half of the students live with single mothers outside the U.S. military base. Learning in English at the AASO is a precious chance for them to positively accept their hybrid status. Other students who live with their fathers need to keep and increase their English proficiency in order to communicate with their fathers. English is a communication tool and a symbolic tie for the Amerasian children.

Another purpose of bilingual education is to overcome the prejudice against being *hafu*. In Okinawa, there are two common stereotypes of Amerasians. One is *shima hafu*. The term "*shima*" means "island" in Japanese. In this context, *shima* refers to Okinawa—denoting a person who cannot speak English. These children are typically characterized as "fatherless poor *hafu*" who cannot enter the U.S. base or go to America. The other *hafu* are those who can speak English, enter the base, and go to America (Noiri, 2001, p. 144). Ms. Thayer noted:

> I was keenly aware of the harsh view of Amerasian children and their mothers in Okinawa society. If an Amerasian child goes to a Japanese school and cannot speak in English, the child will be labeled an "Illegitimate Base Child." This is not only painful but also mortifying for a mother. (Thayer, 2003, p. 49)

Meanwhile, the AASO does not expect all students to be perfectly fluent in English and Japanese, because students come from several distinct backgrounds:

1. Children from the DoDDS or OCSI
2. Children who have attended the AASO since kindergarten
3. Children who have moved from the United States
4. Children who have moved from Japanese public schools in Okinawa
5. Others

The students in categories 1, 2, and 3 have studied in English. However, their English proficiency is varied depending on their family life and the experience of living in America. The AASO respects their diversity, offering a flexible curriculum in a small class (Noiri, 2000, p. 233). The AASO is the only place in which Amerasian children can stay together every day. In this context, the AASO provides an ethnic community for Amerasian children. Their experience of learning with Amerasian friends—helping each other and having a sense of belonging—sustains and supports the process of seeking a personal identity.

CONCLUSION

Good Education Not Only for Minorities But for All Children

Highlighting and praising minority cultures within the classroom is useless for students of ethnic minorities if diversity is marginalized in the educational system as a whole. Rather than highlighting the "otherness" of ethnic minority children, it is necessary to specify Japanese school culture. What significant forms of cultural capital are necessary to survive in school and to gain access to higher education? Who has this capital and who does not? Examining Japanese school culture leads one to a critique of the "equal treatment" approach. To reach mutual understanding between minority and majority in the area of education, it is important to analyze the school culture and educational system as a whole. Many Japanese students share the same difficulties as ethnic minority students, such as lack of economic, social, and cultural capital; inequality; assimilation pressure that forces them to act like other students; underachievement; low self-esteem; and exclusion. Good education for ethnic minority students might actually be good for all Japanese students. Each student needs to be supported in various ways, rather than be treated equally, in order to obtain an equal result. As resources are limited, the educational system cannot offer equal results for all students. However, there are some children who do not even have access to the starting line of competition.

Hybridization as a New Dimension of Diversity

The experiences of Amerasians in Okinawa suggest that the Japanese educational system does not respond to the social dynamics of hybridization. "Are you American, or Japanese?" "You should be good at English, because you are a *hafu*." Such labeling occurs not only at a personal level but also at an institutional level. The challenge of the AASO reveals both the myth of "education for Japanese nationals" and the "existence of a pure, distinctive ethnic group." In reality, language and culture are not fixed in each child, but are flexible, continuing to change. However, international education in public schools tends to fix a dividing line between "us" as Japanese and "them" as foreigners. As a result of such a simplistic ethnic dualism, some foreign students are encouraged to represent and appeal to "their own ethnicity" on special occasions, such as international celebrations. Thai Eika pointed out that some educationalists and teachers, who are keen to treat various cultures in the classroom positively, never question the assumption of a "pure, essential ethnic culture" (Thai, 2005, p. 32). It is crucial to examine diversity inside ethnic minority children that includes inequality, conflict, and hybridity. The process requires reflecting on the diversity inside "us," which includes privilege, differences, and the dynamic interaction between minority youth and nonminority peoples.

REFERENCES

Ministry of Education, Japan. (1965). *Treatment on education of South Korean nationals who live in Japan according to the Japan–Korea treatment: An announcement for the head of educational boards in prefectures and the governors of prefectures*. Tokyo: Monbusho.

Noiri, N. (2000). Amerasians in Okinawa. In M. Yamamoto (Ed.), *Bilingual education in Japan* (pp. 213–252). Tokyo: Akashi Shoten.

Noiri, N. (2001). The educational movement of Amerasians. In H. Terumoto (Ed.), *AmerAsian School: Message for co-living relation from Okinawa* (pp. 116–154). Tokyo: Fukinoto Shobo.

Okinawa Prefecture. (2008). *U.S. military and Okinawa*. Web site of Okinawa Prefecture, http://www3.pref.okinawa.jp/site/view/

Okinawa Times. (1997, May 14). No impact on human body. *Okinawa Times*.

Ota, H. (2000). *Newcomer children in Japanese public schools*. Tokyo: Kokusaisyoin.

Terumoto, H. (2001). The movement to establish the rights of Amerasians. *Bulletin of College of Education, 58*, 177–194. Naha, Okinawa: University of the Ryukyus.

Terumoto, H. (2003). Schooling of the Amerasian (International children). In N. Noiri (Ed.), *The educational rights of Amerasians in Okinawa* (pp. 1–9). Research paper of the MEXT Foundation. Tokyo: MEXT.

Thai, E. (2006). "Multicultural co-living relation" and "Japanese": Re-thinking of "culture" and "co-living." *Intercultural/Transcultural Education, 22*, 27–41.

Thayer, M. (2003). The goal of the AmerAsian School. In N. Noiri (Ed.), *The educational rights of Amerasians in Okinawa* (pp. 82–113). Research paper of the MEXT Foundation. Tokyo: MEXT.

PART III

Reflections on Forces Affecting the Future of Japanese Education

GEORGE A. DeVOS

Challenges to Japanese Education

Concluding Thoughts

9

THIS VOLUME brings together the research of several outstanding Japanese specialists, who examine the Japanese educational system past and present. Professors Gordon and LeTendre were able not only to assemble them for a most productive conference but also to elicit from them their research findings, which, collectively assembled, give us a very vivid picture of what is being attempted and what is working or not working in Japanese education today. No society now exists in isolation. Societies today are aware of how education is conducted globally and are influenced by the strategies attempted elsewhere. The clarity of perception and the topics addressed by the contributors to this volume emphasize how Japanese governmental specialists and others are seeking self-consciously, with their present approaches to education, to better distribute knowledge among all youth. What is being done in Japan has been influenced by what is observed to be done elsewhere. All modern societies are complex in nature. Each has its own particular history of developing ethnic and minority membership. All educational systems offer means for changing the social status of some of the members of a society. By implementing systems of deliberate learning, they enhance the relative status of particular social groups by distributing the knowledge afforded more equally than has been true in the past.

EDUCATIONAL POLICY AND DIVERSITY

The work presented in Gordon and LeTendre's symposium represented a very important combination of educational policy at the highest levels along with attention to minority issues in Japan. Japan is facing a reality forced upon it by its own policies of immigration. The basic problem is to develop educational policy that recognizes the diversity within Japan. Until recently, Japanese authorities have chosen to ignore the needs of Korean, Okinawan, and other resident foreign communities. Schools developed by Korean communities, largely identified with North Korea, have not been given equal status, and their graduates have not been given access to higher education equal to that of graduates of Japanese schools. For 30 years, the "Special Measures" gave *Burakumin* communities the opportunity to receive extra funding for school buildings, housing, health facilities, roads, and other physical improvements. These opportunities were granted in response to pressure from *Burakumin* activists and other human rights organizations. However, many *Burakumin* were never affected by these measures, for various reasons: their community refused to participate, they were denied recognition, or they did not live in an officially recognized *Buraku* community. Now that the Special Measures have been discontinued, whatever advantages were made available to *Burakumin* have ended. During the Special Measures, teachers were able to give special attention to *Burakumin* students and special funding was available. However, from a psychological point of view, the benefits accruing from recognition as *Burakumin* had to be balanced with the continuing stigma of such identity. The efforts of the political movement to achieve a new identity for *Burakumin* essentially failed. Some *Burakumin* children were able to fashion a new positive identity, but most either had to pass as non-*Burakumin* (and hope that their identity would be forgotten and ignored) or had to cope with the continuing negative affects of their *Burakumin* identity.

JAPANESENESS

The issue of what it is to be "Japanese" is crucial. The definition of who is Japanese is essentially racial; Koreans, even those who have been in Japan for generations, cannot qualify. The indigenous Ainu, not to mention other Asians, exist in special but essentially foreign categories as the Japanese identity is narrowly constructed. While clearly a part of the Japanese race, the *Burakumin* have been the unmentionable group due to ancient but still potent notions of pollution. The idea of pollution rests within a racial understanding that full status is denied to those who perform necessary but ritually unclean and often undesirable jobs. The unofficial Japanese discourse about Japaneseness ignores the *Burakumin*. One of the core issues in Japanese identity is language. It is very, very difficult for a Japanese person to admit or recognize or even hear the Japanese language used by someone not recognizably Japanese. The introduction of immigrants from formerly Japanese communities in South America has confused the definition of Japanese even further. The clearly racial definition that opened immigration to include these people of Japanese ancestry has been sorely tested by their non-Japanese cultural patterns and their lack of Japanese language. This phenomenon emerged earlier in the case of Japanese Americans, who when visiting Japan were expected to speak proper Japanese and when unable to do so were considered to be somehow outside the definition of true Japanese.

The Amerasian population that has resulted from the American military occupation of Okinawa and other parts of Japan introduces yet another variation that challenges the definition of Japanese identity. While the Ainu and the Okinawans and even the Korean soap opera stars can be treated as exotic products of Japanese society, they remain outside the identity of Japanese. They are entertainment and museum exhibits to view, and they live in places that are interesting to visit, but at a deep psychological level they remain outsiders. While it is possible in Japanese society to think of someone as being socialized for success and achievement, it is also true that one cannot become Japanese through socialization. Japaneseness must be inherited.

STATUS INEQUALITY AND EDUCATION

In the past, gender and ethnic differences defined those worthy of advanced knowledge unequally. What can be observed now is to what extent, and how, Japanese educational institutions are dealing with forms of status inequality inherited from the past. The Japanese today are self-consciously attempting to overcome the status inequities of their premodern past. These inequalities relate not only to recognized or nonrecognized minority groups but also to gender. In most current societies, people no longer think about preserving concepts of relative purity and pollution. But in the past, many selectively determined educational opportunities were based on the relative purity considered operative for women or men, as well as for specific occupational segments of the population. Generally, society no longer considers the relative purity of women as affecting their education, but in the religious sphere, in some faiths at least, some concepts of relative purity still tacitly govern eligibility for special training in leadership. The priesthood can still be limited to males, and women can be forbidden to touch sacred objects. In Japan, as elsewhere, there were taboos that isolated women during their menstrual periods and also governed what they could learn at school.

In my own work in Japan, I dealt with concepts of purity and pollution as they still implicitly governed special hereditary occupations related to what is considered social "caste." Caste inequality was not only directed inwardly toward the *Burakumin* and their special occupational groups, but also outwardly toward non-Japanese populations, especially their ethnic neighbors who were considered to be inherently inferior. The concept of relative intellectual inferiority was heavily influential in the organization of Japan's educational system in the past. Although the lower castes were declared officially "human" in 1872, the outcastes, now called *Burakumin,* continued to live in special ghettoes and their relatively poor performance in school was expected. In official policy, at least, there have been attempts to rectify the effects of such minority status, but as in the United States and elsewhere, presumed differences about the intellectual potential of specific groups still covertly remain. It is now politically incorrect to voice such beliefs about differences, but they remain a subcurrent in Japan as they do in the United States, and they still govern social attitudes.

The IQ test, which has been much maligned in the United States and Japan, represents an earlier attempt to understand individual differences in academic achievement. The measure of unequal ability provided a basis for some form of differentiated teaching. When the IQ test was still being given in Japan, it was shown that Japanese children did better on the performance aspects of the test compared with American children. But because the IQ test is language-biased, American and European children did better than Japanese children on the verbal components. However, since the 1960s, the American emphasis on equal rights has overshadowed any benefits to be gained by measuring intelligence. Similarly, Japan has adopted this stance. In Japan, the ideology of equal ability and unequal effort has continued to be dominant. The consequence for *Burakumin* and Korean communities was that their lifestyles were blamed for the lack of school success. Parents were accused of being unwilling or unable to provide the appropriate guidance that would lead their children to put forth the effort required to achieve success. This belief reinforced the poor self-respect within such communities and thus reinforced the disadvantage faced by their children.

In Tokyo's Arakawa Ward, which I studied in the 1960s, there was a lack of identity as a *Buraku* community even though that ward had been the site of the execution grounds for the Tokugawa Regime and was still a location of many leather workers (executioner and tanner being two of the traditional occupations of *Burakumin*). There remain important differences between the Osaka area and the Tokyo area in terms of how *Burakumin* are recognized. While it is true that *Burakumin* individuals can attempt to pass as non-*Burakumin*, they must still deal with the psychological burden of their identity. Because place of residence is one of the most obvious indicators of *Burakumin* heritage, individuals may attempt to pass as non-*Burakumin* by changing their address two or three times but still, internally, they must suffer the stigma of their identity.

DELINQUENCY AND IDENTITY

The intellectual community in education, as in other fields, is now a global one and the Japanese now employ concepts of minority status as do Americans. Nonetheless, I well remember the denial of any knowledge of the outcaste *Burakumin* minority I encountered among ordinary Japanese in the 1960s. I first approached the topic as a way to understand the relatively high delinquency rate and poor school performance of some districts in the cities of Osaka and Kobe. Only after I demonstrated my definite knowledge of the existence of *Burakumin* and Koreans in some districts would certain individuals be forthcoming with information about *Burakumin*. The fact that there were Koreans who for several generations had lived in Japan but were not Japanese citizens was readily acknowledged, but the existence of *Burakumin* was a topic that was treated with the same aura of delicacy as was given to any discussion of homosexuality in the past in the United States.

The statistics on delinquency in the cities of Osaka and Kobe indicated a delinquency rate of five times the ordinary in *Buraku* sections of the city and up to seven times the ordinary rate in areas inhabited by Koreans. Generally, I found that the delinquency rate for schools was the obverse of the rate of relative good school performance. It must be noted that the citizenship status of many Koreans continues to be an issue. Many cannot envision their ethnic identity without maintaining their loyalty to a Korean political entity. In the 1960s, Korean Japanese were often accused of criminal acts. Korean Japanese were expected to change their name to a suitably Japanese one in order to be accepted. The continuing split of North and South Korea creates factions among those of Korean ethnicity in Japan. They demonstrate their continuing loyalty by embracing different educational institutions.

FAMILY AND PEER GROUP INVOLVEMENT IN EDUCATION

Mothers who discredit their husbands and the fathers of their children are a main factor in driving young boys to have low self-respect and to make choices that result in delinquency. In the Korean and *Burakumin* communities that I studied, these patterns were prevalent. The teachers in the schools were well aware of such attitudes on the part of mothers. The families of outcastes and Koreans were far less stable than other families. Fathers were often unemployed, and some deserted their families. There were many cases of alcoholism. The mothers, in many instances, were directly antagonistic toward their wayward or inadequate husbands. It was interesting to note when comparing the interviews of parents with a delinquent child and those without from the same city area that the mothers of nondelinquent children expressed more positive feelings about their husbands than did those with a delinquent child.

The stigma attached to these communities within the larger Japanese society contributed to the lack of hope and self-respect needed to make the effort required by Japanese schooling. Patterns of hopelessness persisted in these communities, creating individual patterns that made it more difficult to achieve in work or school, and more difficult to create the family conditions that were needed in order to achieve success. Intervention or involvement with the families of students who become delinquent or do poorly in school is not usually considered to be within the purview of the educational system.

In my own contacts with education in the United States, I have observed a diminution in the use of auxiliary psychological and social service personnel, as cost-cutting measures have become more important in state school systems. It is too readily presumed that improvement of poor school performance can be ameliorated only by changing teaching methods or the professional activities of teachers.

In some school situations, the peer group must be more directly considered a major factor in determining how any individual child within the system is operating. Yet, in some studies of school performance, the peer group is ignored as a continuing major determinant of classroom behavior of many pupils. In my own school observations in Japan among majority Japanese, I noticed that peer group participation could operate to induce the compliance and obedience of some students. I was initially alerted to phenomenon of peer group as conformity enhancer by work with the school records of American-born Japanese *Nisei* in the state of California during the pre–World War II period. These students were acutely self-consciously aware of their school performance compared with the school majority. *Nisei* were considered ideal students by their teachers. They received better grades and more often became valedictorians or specially recognized class performers than did majority pupils. On average, during the 1930s, the Japanese in the United States had 2 years more schooling than did their same-age peers. Peer group attitudes of *Nisei* reflected the intense family pressure experienced at home.

In my research in Japan, I found that mothers would readily assume responsibility for any poor performance on the part of a child. A mother would quickly feel guilt for poor performance, as well as sense the positive performance of a child as evidence of her good mothering. Regardless of the husbands' relative adequacy, mothers of nondelinquent children were more protective about their husbands than were those with a delinquent child, who were more overtly critical, even disparaging. Children were aware of how their behavior could reflect on their mother. They would frequently express guilt in stories elicited by the Thematic Apperception Test, which I administered to a large population of Japanese during my field research. Their spontaneous stories amply demonstrated this readiness for children to feel guilt about their school performance creating possible injury to a self-sacrificing mother.

SOCIAL REGULATION AND EDUCATION

Considered anthropologically, educational processes must be put into a larger context of social interaction and development. As children grow up, they are being regulated as well as educated. This regulation does not only take place in school. It is part of a total regulation system, which involves parents and other adults, as well as official social regulators called police. It has been my contention that the delinquent acts of students must be studied as an integral part of the overall educational performance of a school system. The police are involved with the school system. To perform their regulatory functions, teachers need to come into better and continuous communication with both police personnel and parents. The verb "police" means to help regulate or keep in order. Only if order fails does one punish. In some areas of Tokyo, the local police come into personal contact with all the people of their district, including the teachers in the local schools. The teachers' relationship with the police is obviously regulatory, not punitive. If a teacher is having potential difficulty with a student, a police officer can be called in informally before anything happens.

While studying delinquency cross-culturally in Europe and Japan, I have observed differences in the use of police and parents in cases of difficulties with particular students. In Genoa, in northern Italy, I saw how police would be informally brought in by teachers to intimidate some students or to break up gangs as soon as they began to form. The police, who were often from the southern part of the country, would be informally brought in to deal with parents who were also migrants from the south. In American schools, it would not be amiss to periodically bring in police officers to give students positive contact with police officials. The teacher would in this way develop personal relationships in an anticipatory manner, not only ex post facto. In Japan there has long been a cooperative relationship among parents, teachers, and the police. All of these were involved in the decisions affecting children's lives. The cooperation between the police, teachers, and parents allowed for day-to-day regulation of children's behavior and thus the prevention of delinquency. If the police are seen only as dealing with troubles and crises, then there is a lack of routine regulation that can help prevent problems. In the United States, the police have not been able to serve this function. There have been too few studies of how to involve parents or practice therapeutic intervention through them. And there has been no recent study I know of that examines how the police could positively perform an auxiliary educational function within a school system.

AUTHORITY AND RESPECT

In Japan, adulthood is defined as being truly Japanese. The idea of adulthood as somehow separate from Japaneseness is not normal. Adulthood is accepting the normality of control from those in authority. There is very little sense of democratic process. A child is taught to accept control by those in authority, along with the promise that he or she will be able to exercise control upon achieving adulthood. From earliest childhood it is known that one must join networks in order to have any influence over one's own life. The idea is to find a spot within such networks and use that association to gain one's advantage. Respect for those with authority is assumed; respect is not earned. Those in authority include parents, teachers, government officials, and business management. However, it is generally accepted that true power rests within informal networks among those in authority and not necessarily within those individuals holding formal leadership positions. Those in formal leadership are accorded respect, though they may or may not actually hold sway with the informal networks. School principals hold formal positions of power, but rarely if ever are they able to exercise authority. Authority actually rests within informal networks of older teachers, including perhaps the vice principal. These informal networks often can be traced to old school ties.

EDUCATION AS A SOCIAL SCIENCE

The work in this volume is a reflection of how education as a field of study is one of the basic eight social sciences and deserves recognition as such. Political science and economics are quickly recognized; so too are sociology and anthropology. History and geography are not as quickly seen as social sciences, but more questions arise in the minds of some when psychology or education are considered as scientific disciplines. The present work amply demonstrates the social science nature of the field of education. The study of education is not simply about deliberate inculcation of methods of practice used in a society to pass on knowledge generationally to the young. It makes its own theoretical contributions to the study of any particular society and the institutions set up to impart knowledge to different members of any social group. One learns about how a society seeks deliberatively to perpetuate itself and advance itself through what is passed on by education, not only through its youth but also through mature adults in some instances. Any social scientist as a deliberate observer must, in some respects, become an anthropologist, remaining detached and viewing behavior from the outside. And as an observer, one must also be a practicing psychologist to better understand the psychological processes at work in an educational system that is changing the mental processes and self-identities of those being observed.

HARUMI BEFU

Societal and Cultural Context of Educational Issues

10

THE CHAPTERS in this volume abundantly demonstrate the complexity of the current educational situation in Japan. I will examine this complexity first as it relates to the majority ethnic Japanese and second in relation to minorities, whether they are ethnic Japanese or foreign.

ETHNIC JAPANESE

For the education of the majority Japanese, one of the most pressing issues is the consequence of the widening gap between the haves and the have-nots. A recent newspaper article (*Asahi Shinbun*, 2008) reported a positive correlation between the educational attainment of parents and the amount of investment in their children's education, giving a distinct educational advantage to children of well-educated (and by implication, on the whole, wealthier) parents. As the income gap between the rich and the poor increases, one might even say that a virtual caste system is developing in Japan, where transgenerationally, the poor will continue to receive poor education and consequently remain poor and the rich will be able to sustain their wealth level through better education.

This educational bifurcation is directly reflected in the employment world, where graduates of elite universities manage to obtain permanent employment positions with job security, good wages, social services, and pensions, while in recent years graduates of nonelite universities and high school graduates can get only temporary jobs—without any of these benefits. These poorly educated workers are recruited into the ranks of the *freeta* (short-term workers), *parto* (part-time workers), and *haken* (temporary workers dispatched from employment firms) and are known as the "working poor." These individuals are forced to work at or near the minimum wage without job security, and they cannot rise above the lowest rung of the socioeconomic ladder because of the poor wages.

The widening gap between the educationally privileged and the educationally unfortunate is reflected in the status of Japanese educational achievement in international comparisons. Educational achievement takes a pyramidal shape, the top achievers being few, and the majority being near or at the bottom of the pyramid. This educational pyramid is supported by the similarly pyramidal socioeconomic structure, where at the bottom, low achievers achieve less and less because of their parents' ever-decreasing income and other resources allocatable to their children's education. This downward trend in the scores for low achievers consequently drives down Japan's mean achievement scores in international comparisons.

How should Japan cope with this problem? A variety of policy proposals have been made and some have even been implemented, such as smaller class size, resumption of Saturday classes (which was dropped several years ago, as Fujita noted in Chapter 1), increasing educational budgets at the national and local levels, creating "laning" of students according to their achievement levels, and raising teacher qualifications. Whether these measures can reverse the worsening trend of Japan's educational achievement on the international scene is anyone's guess. Educational achievement of a nation is a complex phenomenon, not easily analyzable through a few factors such as those enumerated above—factors that can be consciously manipulated through legislation. While not negating the importance of these "policy" factors, additional variables that are not so easily changeable—such as the increasing number of two-income families, single-parent homes, and domestic violence, as well as changing perceptions and expectations regarding parents' educational responsibility to their children—should also be closely examined as elements affecting academic performance of students.

EDUCATIONAL PROBLEMS OF MINORITIES

The educational bifurcation discussed in the preceding section relates to the minority issue inasmuch as minorities are mostly on the have-not side of the bifurcation. Education of minorities may be analyzed along two major axes: the minority axis and the sociopolitical axis.

The minority axis consists of the different minorities within Japan (Goodman, 2008), some of whom are classified as "normal" ethnic Japanese, the most notable being the *Burakumin* (Nabeshima and Kanegae, in Chapters 5 and 6; Samuel, 2008). At the opposite end of this axis in terms of how similar or dissimilar they are to the majority Japanese are illegal, "overstay" aliens, mostly from South and Southeast Asia (Onishi, 2008). In between are the Ainu (Sjöberg, 2008), the Okinawans, and returnee children of corporate businessmen sent on overseas assignments, followed by those commonly known as *Chugoku zanryu koji,* who returned from China mostly in the 1980s and 1990s after being left behind in the confusion of the war with the Soviet Union. This axis also includes the old-timer and newcomer Koreans (Kim, in

Chapter 7), the Chinese, the Latin American *Nikkei* (Ishi, 2008), legal as well as illegal Southeast Asians (notably Filipina wives of Japanese men; Suzuki, 2008), and finally refugees.

Each of these groups has its own unique background of entering Japan and its own relation with Japan, and thus needs to be analyzed separately. For example, old-timer Koreans are individuals who were either in Japan at the end of World War II or are their descendants. Those who were in Japan at the time had Japanese citizenship by virtue of the fact that Korea was a Japanese colony. But they were stripped of their citizenship when Japan signed the peace treaty in 1952. Because of their large numbers, nearing a million in 1952, and their concentration in a few locations in Japan, such as Osaka (Kashani, 2006), Koreans established their own ethnic schools, often using Korean as the language of instruction. These schools, however, were not recognized as legitimate educational institutions by the Japanese government, and at various times in history were forcibly closed by the Japanese authorities (Tanaka, 2006). The division of the Korean peninsula into North and South split the old-timer Korean population in Japan into pro-North and pro-South political groups, with a deep cleavage between them. All of these events have had considerable impact on the education of Koreans in Japan. For example, there are North Korea–oriented Korean schools and South Korea–oriented Korean schools, with understandably profound ideological differences in their curricula.

This is a far cry from the situation for virtually all the minorities from South and Southeast Asia, most of whom are overstayers. Their history of migration is recent, and their numbers are too small to afford their own schools. Their children are thus forced to attend, if they attend school at all, regular Japanese schools. Thus, educational issues Koreans face and issues the South/Southeast Asians face are necessarily radically different. In short, these minority groups are each differentially impacted in the educational process in Japan as far as various social and political issues are concerned.

The sociopolitical axis, as related to the educational process, includes human rights, civil rights, citizenship, equity/equality, multiethnicity, multicultural education, and finally school/classroom disorder (absenteeism and bullying). In the following discussion I will consider how the two axes—minority group and sociopolitical issues—intersect with one another. It is not possible to analyze each of the minority groups with respect to each of the major issues enumerated here. However, it will suffice to sample some of the major concatenations of the group axis and issues axis to illustrate this approach.

In terms of civil rights, first of all, foreign children do not have the same rights to receive education as Japanese citizens. For the latter, parents have the legal obligation to send children to school and school has the legal duty to educate them. In this respect, the Ainu and Okinawan minorities are in the same category as the majority Japanese. But for foreign minorities, the government assumes no such obligation, and parents have no legal obligation to educate their children. Because of this difference, while schools are serious about educating Japanese children, foreign students tend to be neglected. Foreign students are much more likely to be absent for this reason—and also because they do not feel comfortable in a school setting that is culturally foreign to them, they do not understand class instructions given in Japanese and are therefore bored in school, and they often have no friends in class or, worse, are bullied by Japanese students. Completing high school among them is a noteworthy accomplishment rather something that is simply assumed, as is the case for the majority Japanese. Attending college, moreover, is a highly exceptional feat among foreign students.

As for human rights, verbal and sometimes physical abuse, which is common in Japanese schools, takes on different dimensions when directed toward foreign students. Children who came from China with their parents or grandparents (*Chugoku zanryu koji*) after those individuals were left behind at the end of the war are called "Chinese," the subtext being "You don't belong here. Go back to China." Indeed, outwardly, they look Chinese in terms of bodily comportment, gesture, and notably language. But they are unmistakably Japanese in their identity, which was the very reason why they came (back) to Japan. Similarly, those of Japanese descent from Latin America are often called "*gaijin*" (foreigners), and Amerasians in Okinawa, with Japanese mothers and American soldier fathers, are called "*hafu*" (half; subtext: "You are an incomplete Japanese") or "American" (subtext: "You are less than Japanese" or "You don't belong here; you should leave") by classmates. To shield their children from such abuses, parents of Amerasian children established the AmerAsian School in Okinawa (Noiri, in Chapter 8; Murphy-Shigematsu, 2002).

At the basis of the bullying of foreign children by Japanese children, and in fact at the basis of the Japanese exclusion of foreigners, is what I call the *habitus of homogeneity*—an ethnocentric disposition to exclude anyone other than ethnic Japanese. Obversely, the Japanese people, children included, tend to assume that if one looks Japanese, one should be able to behave, speak, and think Japanese. The *Nikkei* children from Latin America are often asked by Japanese schoolmates why they cannot speak Japanese. Their inability is assumed to be due to low intelligence, rather than insufficient enculturation, resulting in these native Japanese children looking down on the Latin Japanese children (Seiyaa & Higa, 2007). Thus, foreign language speakers are not only forced to speak Japanese but are made to feel inferior for their inability to speak Japanese well and for speaking a foreign language in a culture in which ethnic Japaneseness holds the only legitimate—and moreover hegemonic—status.

As mentioned earlier, for old-timer Korean children the issue is totally different. They were born and raised in Japan, and thus have no problem with the Japanese language. The issue for them is rather one of citizenship and civil rights. The Korean schools are not certified by the Ministry of Education as normal educational institutions, and thus are ineligible for government subsidies and other privileges. For example, until recently, graduates of Korean high schools were not eligible to take entrance examinations for public colleges.

Fundamental to this way of treating foreigners is the basic tenet in Japanese judisprudence that the Japanese people, called "*kokumin*" in the Japanese constitution, are on a different legal footing from non-*kokumin* (NIRA Citizenship Research Group, 2001, p. 152). That is, *kokumin* deserve certain basic citizenship rights to education, which others do not. Such inequity may be regarded as a violation of human rights, because Japan is a signatory to the 1959 United Nations Declaration of the Rights of the Child, which guarantees education to every child without distinction as to national origin.

Even more problematic is the situation for the children of the overstay (illegal) foreign workers. These children's education is at the whim of the Immigration Authority, which may remove such a child from school without prior notice to the parents or the school.

Zero-Sum Game

There is a dilemma in the process of minority assimilation and acculturation. On the one hand, total assimilation and acculturation assumes the minority child totally embracing Japanese culture. At the opposite theoretical extreme, a child totally retains his or her native culture. Most observers of minority children in Japan, as well as ordinary Japanese, accept this zero-sum game model, wherein to the extent a child become acculturated, he (or she) loses his (or her) original culture. Thus, total biculturalism and bilingualism is a theoretical impossibility. What makes this zero-sum game model a self-fulfilling prophecy is the fact that the dominant culture of Japan is imperialistically homogeneous. It is intolerant of other cultures, pressuring minorities to accept the dominant culture and abandon their own.

Positive-Sum Game

Against this zero-sum game perspective, we may consider a more comprehensive, positive-sum game model, in which while embracing Japanese culture, the child may simultaneously retain his original culture totally, or lose it totally. This theoretical model allows the child to be totally bicultural and bilingual, freely moving in and out of the two cultures. But it also admits cases where a child loses his original culture in varying degrees as he becomes assimilated into Japanese culture, as well as cases where a child rejects the host culture in varying degrees and retains his original culture. In short, this model subsumes the zero-sum game model as a special case. In fact, there are many instances of the positive-sum game model in action in Japan, where a child retains, for example, Portuguese and at the same time develops fluency in Japanese. Unfortunately, these cases are ignored or are considered exceptions.

The importance of the positive-sum game outlook is obvious. For Japan to develop into a multicultural society, it is essential that Japanese adopt the positive-sum model, such that gaining Japanese culture is not seen as necessarily sacrificing the child's native culture. One way in which this may be accomplished is through what Sekiguchi (2003, p. 143) calls the "cross-cultural model," where within the child's ethnic community and at home, the child retains and practices his original culture, and while outside these realms, the child assimilates the host culture. Civil rights are also at issue here. The question of civil rights enters as foreign parents of school age children do not have the voting right to participate in the political process at the national level and in most local elections. Thus, these parents cannot be party to decision-making regarding their children's education.

CONCLUSION

Future directions of education in Japan must take account of the complex issues surrounding the widening gap in educational opportunity between the rich and the poor, as well as the challenges of educating minority children. Minorities in Japan, especially foreign children, are inevitably going to increase in numbers, as will their countries of origin (Willis & Murphy-Shigematsu, 2008). The issues and problems of minority children discussed here are an integral part of the wider issues and problems facing their parents. As Watado (2002, p. 38) notes, for multiculturalism to take root in Japan, its basic values such as freedom, justice, and human rights must be not only incorporated into policy and institution but also internalized as mental habit (in short, what Bourdieu, 1979, calls "habitus"). This requires nothing less than replacing the conventional *habitus of homogeneity* with a *habitus of heterogeneity*.

Through legitimation of multicultural citizenship, foreign children would acquire the right to retain their culture and language with pride while participating in the social and political processes of the host country. On the one hand, a degree of assimilation and acculturation of children would allow foreign children to adjust to the Japanese school setting, learn Japanese, and keep up with the curriculum. On the other hand, multiculturalism would allow them to retain their foreign culture and take pride in it. Japan needs to develop an environment that can foster such multiculturalism. For this to happen, Japan needs to abandon its zero-sum game model of acculturation and embrace a positive-sum game model.

REFERENCES

Asahi Shinbun. (2008, July 27). International edition.
Bourdieu, P. (1979). *La distinction: Critique sociale du jugement*. Paris: Editions de Minuit.
Goodman, R. (2008). Afterword: Marginals, minorities, majorities and migrants—Studying the Japanese borderlands in contemporary Japan. In Willis & Murphy-Shigematsu, *Transcultural Japan* (pp. 325–333).
Ishi, A. (2008). Between privilege and prejudice: Japanese-Brazilian migrants in 'the land of yen and the ancestors.' In Willis & Murphy-Shigematsu, *Transcultural Japan* (pp. 113–134).
Kashani, S. (2006). Colonial migration to the 'Manchester of the Orient': The origins of the Korean community in Osaka, Japan, 1920–1945. In S. I. Lee, S. Murphy-Shigematsu, & H. Befu (Eds.), *Japan's diversity dilemmas: Ethnicity, citizenship, and education* (pp. 168–189). New York, Lincoln, and Shanghai: Universe.
Murphy-Shigematsu, S. (2002). *Amerajian no kodomo tachi: Shirarezaru mainoritei mondai*. Tokyo: Shuueisha.
NIRA Citizenship Research Group. (2001). *Tabunka shakai no sentaku: 'Citizenship' no shiten kara*. Tokyo. Nihon Keizai Hyoronsha.
Onishi, A. (2008). 'Becoming a better Muslim': Identity narratives of Muslim foreign workers in Japan. In Willis & Murphy-Shigematsu, *Transcultural Japan* (pp. 217–236).
Samuel, Y. (2008). The marvelous in the real: Images of *Burakumin* in Nakagami Kenji's Kumano saga. In Willis & Murphy-Shigematsu, *Transcultural Japan* (pp. 181–196).
Seiyaa, M., & Higa, M. (2007). Dai-ni waakushoppu. Okinawa ni okeru kokusai kekkon kosodate to kyooiku. In Y. Andoo, N. Suzuki, & N. Noiri (Eds.), *Okinawa shakai to Nikkeijin gaikokujin Amerajian*. Tokyo: Kubapuro.
Sekiguchi, T. (2003). *Zainichi Nikkei Burajiru-jin no kodomotachi—I-bunka-kan ni sodatsu kodomo no aidentiti keisei*. Tokyo. Akashi Shoten.
Sjöberg, K. (2008). Positioning oneself in the Japanese nation state: the Hokkaido Ainu case. In Willis & Murphy-Shigematsu, *Transcultural Japan* (pp. 197–216).
Suzuki, N. (2008). Between two shores: Transnational projects and Filipina wives in/from Japan. In Willis & Murphy-Shigematsu, *Transcultural Japan* (pp. 65–85).
Tanaka, H. (2006). Emerging political and legal challenges of ethnic schools in Japan. In S. I. Lee, S. Murphy-Shigematsu, & H. Befu (Eds.), *Japan's diversity dilemmas: Ethnicity, citizenship, and education* (pp. 150–167). New York, Lincoln, and Shanghai: Universe.
Watado, I. (2002). Hirogaru mariachi karuchuraru na shakai kuukan to tabunka shugi no kadai. In I. Watado & C. Awamura (Eds.), *Tabunka kyooiku wo hiraku—Marichikaruchuraru na Nihon no genjitsu no nakade* (pp. 18–44). Tokyo: Akashi Shoten.
Willis, D. B., & Murphy-Shigematsu, S. (Eds.). (2008). *Transcultural Japan: At the borderlands of race, gender, and identity*. London and New York: Routledge.
Willis, D. B., & Murphy-Shigematsu, S. (2008). Transcultural Japan: Metamorphosis in the cultural borderlands and beyond. In Willis & Murphy-Shigematsu, *Transcultural Japan* (pp. 3–44).

JUNE A. GORDON AND GERALD LeTENDRE

A New Policy Context for Schooling in Japan

11

SINCE THE ALLIED OCCUPATION, Japanese public schooling has been the object of significant political debate within Japan. For most of this time, the government has portrayed its policies as blending traditional schooling with imported reforms and has emphasized the school's role in national aspirations for prosperity and international recognition. National policymakers, often working in close cooperation with business interests, have emphasized the fact that Japanese schools have shown amazing success in preparing their (male) students for productive lives as industrial and scientific craftsmen and as conscientious and hard-working bureaucrats and managers. Voices of dissent have always been present in Japan (Lincicome, 1995), and scholars have again and again challenged the government's depiction of education (Horio, 1988). It was Japan's own media that widely promoted the use of the term "examination hell" (*shiken jigoku*) and relentlessly focused on problems such as bullying (*ijime*) and school violence (*konai boryoku*). While these themes were often picked up by Western critics and used in U.S. educational debates (LeTendre, 1999) in rather desultory fashion, Japan's internal educational debates and issues were rarely covered in depth by the English-speaking media.

For example, outside of a few experts, it is not widely known that Japan's female students have fared less well than their male counterparts, as traditional roles for adult women have been slow to change even as young women have shown educational success (Brinton, 1988, 2001). And while Japanese scholars have long been aware that the success of Japanese schooling has largely bypassed both students from low-income Japanese families and those defined as "minority" or "foreign" by Japan's narrow terms of citizenship and full participation in Japanese culture, few non-Japanese scholars have written of such phenomena (Gordon, 2005b, 2008; Okano & Tsuchiya, 1999)

During the conversations at the 2006 symposium that initiated this book, Japanese scholars spoke openly of the charged political and social environment they faced as researchers. Dr. Fujita noted that there was a significant shift in the early 1990s in how politicians treated education and educational reforms. He cited the ways in which politicians had begun to use education as a way to attract votes as well as how educational reforms had become part of a larger "package" of neoliberal market reforms. Fujita and others also noted that the traditional basis of group education—the construction of a strong sense of a homeroom class in elementary education—had been weakened by parental pressures for more individual attention. Both Japanese teachers and educational researchers have found themselves responding to multiple and diverse groups holding specific educational agendas. Armed with political and educational savvy, these groups are often highly vocal in their criticism of the educational system and teachers. The situation appears linked to the larger social unrest and dissatisfaction that has swept through Japan as the old economic order has dramatically changed. Looking ahead, we see several long-term changes that will continue to influence Japan's educational debates and attempts at policymaking as identified in the chapters of this book.

THE END OF "LIFE IN MIDDLE-CLASS JAPAN"

The contributions by Fujita and Kariya (Chapters 1 and 2) both identify factors that have worked to erode the image of a homogeneous, "middle-class" Japan, an image that has served Japan well for much of the post–World War II period. Up until the collapse of the bubble economy in the 1990s, few Japanese publically expressed dissatisfaction with their economic status (Kajimoto, 2006). Postwar reconstruction and economic growth brought dramatic improvement for almost all Japanese. As noted by Nabeshima (in Chapter 5), for nearly three decades Japanese society as a whole experienced a steady increase in its standard of living, which served to obscure economic, linguistic, and cultural differences. This long economic upturn, combined with promotion of an ideology that taught people to value what they have and to sacrifice for what they do not, created a powerful sense of identity and motivation for many Japanese. An ideology of merit-based educational attainment, promoted by the government, fostered a widespread acceptance of the hierarchical nature of the school system and of society itself (DeVos, 1973; LeTendre & Rohlen, 1998).

The economic crisis of the 1990s and 2000s weakened this ideology and caused many Japanese to question whether they indeed had any chance fulfill the mythical dream of movement up the educational ladder, access to a prestigious university, and final attainment of secure, lifetime employment (Ishida, 2001). As the Japanese economy is now contracting even more in the face of the global recession, the belief system that sustained the educational system, and individual motivation to excel in school, continue to unravel (Kariya, 2006). On top of the economic malaise, several other demographic changes are also destabilizing patterns of educational attainment and labor market transition: a decrease in the number of school age children, an increase in private schooling, a decoupling of the school/work transition in the noncollege tracks, a shortage of job offers to high school graduates, a shift toward later marriage combined with living at home into one's thirties, an increase in immigrant children attending Japanese schools, and the termination of benefits and programs for descendants of Japan's historically disenfranchised group, the *Burakumin*.

These changes suggest that educational debates will become even more politicized, as various interest groups struggle to maintain their economic status. Education will remain the main conduit of social mobility but will be continually challenged to demonstrate its efficacy and fairness. Popular phrases such as "*kachigumi*" or "*makegumi*," meaning "winner" or "loser" (Kondô, 2005), or recently, "*karyu shakai*" (Miura, 2005), meaning "lower-class society," suggest the Japanese will be increasingly aware of class differences, and that educational debates will increasingly focus on the relationship between education attainment and employment.

As a result of diminished confidence in schools and teachers, along with diminished expectations for educational returns, Japan will continue to see the rise of new categories of education-related problems, such as *freeta* (unattached temporary workers), *ochikobore* (students who fall behind academically), *kogyarumama* (teen mothers), and *tōkōkyohi* (school refusers). As seen in this volume, Japanese scholars are neither uniform in which aspects of education or society they scrutinize, nor in how they interpret education and social data. They are subject to the same problems faced by their counterparts around the world—any study can be quickly manipulated in the general media. What authors in this volume share is a concern that Japanese society must simultaneously deal with "old" issues of social inequality and marginalization that remain unresolved while dealing with "new" issues now arising from changing demographic and economic trends and increasing scrutiny of the educational system from both within and without Japan.

EDUCATION UNDER GLOBAL SCRUTINY

It is not uncommon to hear people blame educational reforms for creating the lowered academic achievement among youth (Bjork, 2008). Such simplistic responses to complicated sets of issues are not unique to Japan. As Fujita noted in his symposium presentation, all nations are facing a more "glocalized" environment in which the political battles over education are no longer defined locally but rather on a global stage as scrutiny of social, economic, and educational policies increases. For example, changes in history textbooks have created full-blown diplomatic issues with important neighbors such as China and South Korea. Global policymaking bodies and international associations (such as the Office of Economic Cooperation and Development, OECD) will continue to exert normative pressures on Japan and other nations to bring their educational practices into line with those of other nations. Increasingly, it is clear that global concepts like "individuality" or "rights of the child" have had a profound impact on Japanese society and policy. Both media and citizens' action groups work to bring international issues "into" Japan, forcing the government to respond with specific policies, and bringing debates about marginalized groups into the global spotlight.

While nurturing its historic ties to the glories of imperial China, Japan has a definite problem with the economic and political challenge presented by its neighbor. As China is predicted to displace Japan as the world's second largest economy within a few years, tensions between the two nations are not likely to decrease. Chinese politicians are likely to push for more equitable treatment of Chinese residents in Japan, whether they are university students struggling to obtain housing or newly arrived families facing discrimination in schooling and the workplace. Japan will increasingly be called upon by China and other East Asian nations to offer genuinely equal opportunity to its Asian newcomers as well as to individuals from Korean and *Burakumin* backgrounds. The historic role school has played, as described in Kanegae's contribution (Chapter 6), will likely become more, not less salient, as groups seek recognition of the ways in which schooling as limited their ability to attain middle-class status in Japan.

REFORM, CHOICE, AND PRIVATE SCHOOLS

Ongoing school reform is part of the global dialog that has affected and will continue to affect Japan. Dissatisfaction with the school system seems inevitable as the pendulum swings to respond to the various demands by competing sets of parents and policymakers. Both Tsukada and Sakai (Chapters 3 and 4) have detailed the highly stratified nature of the Japanese secondary system and the complex decisions that students face. The private schools that began to proliferate during the 1980s, particularly at the high school level, claimed to offer parents an alternative path (Benjamin & James, 1989), though usually to private universities (Ono, 2001), for students who either could not or would not keep up with the exam-oriented grind offered in public schools. These private schools expanded in the late 1990s in spite of the economic recession and the decrease in student enrollment. Private schooling claimed to offer both a competitive edge for students entering universities as well as a curriculum and environment that catered to the individual needs of students. While more expensive than public schools, the range of private schools is great, making some still affordable to the shrinking middle class. These institutions benefited from the flight of parents who feared that curricular reforms (Kariya & Rosenbaum, 1999) would place their children at a disadvantage, but in reality many of these private institutions have diluted their admission standards as well as their curriculum to make themselves more attractive to young people and their parents looking for some avenue that might lead to additional years in school.

Private schools are one policy "solution" to creating diverse pathways into higher education. The importance of college attendance will not decrease, but rather will shift to create new sets of "winners" and "losers" in the educational attainment game. Interestingly, it is in higher education where we see the most devastating repercussions in terms of privatization, due in large part to the fact that most of Japanese higher education is in the hands of the private sector. The widely discussed "2007 problem" refers to the year in which the slots available for students entering higher education equaled the number of applicants, meaning that any student interested in attending a college or university can now find an opening somewhere in the system, if he or she can afford it. This has led to a wave of reforms in the traditional exam-based entrance system. In many cases, students are now able to enter a university by submitting essays, letters of recommendation, and interviews, instead of, or in addition to, taking the traditional exam.

The government has also exacerbated the pace of change (Goodman, 2005). In 2004, the 87 national universities were told that they would no longer be under the protection of the Ministry of Education and were granted independent corporate status. With this supposed independence came several mandates, including among them:

1. Stripping of university faculty and staff of their status as civil servants
2. Strengthening of the office of the university president
3. Participation of nonacademics in the selection of university administration
4. Open competition for funding
5. Accountability and evaluation by outside third parties

While the target of government reforms was national universities and the purpose, it was argued, was to instill in the public's mind the idea that not even these elite institutions were exempt from structural changes, all institutions of higher learning have felt the effects. Within the market-driven context of privatization and fiscal constraint, mergers between institutions have become commonplace, as is presumed collaboration with industry and business under the guise of making education more practical. The combination of a smaller demographic base of students and the reform of higher education offers the potential for increased alternative routes to enter higher education and a reduction of inequality. So far, there has been little evidence of this. Changes in the admission policies give the appearance that the strict use of exam scores as a measure of one's intelligence has less significance and that some traditionally marginalized youth may be admitted as a result. But, there is concern that this more subjective form of admission could lead to even greater barriers for students who do not fit or who have special needs, while dramatically raising public critique of the recommendations teachers provide.

PUBLIC SCHOOL TEACHERS: CAUGHT IN THE MIDDLE

Running through almost every chapter in the book is the central question of what role teachers will play. The breakdown of the myth of middle-class Japan now allows a multitude of education-related issues to rise to prominence on the national political scene. For example, the decrease in numbers of births, combined with an increase in the education of parents, has led many middle-class families to indulge their children not only materialistically but emotionally. This has led to a crisis, some argue, of permissiveness where children are allowed, if not encouraged, to pursue their dreams, often dreams that their parents were not able to attain for themselves. Yet, parents' increased education has paradoxically created a much more unstable and vulnerable position for teachers, placing them under more scrutiny while providing them with less support (Gordon, 2005a).

The variety of educational reforms mentioned throughout the book are attempts to supposedly provide young people with a greater range of learning opportunities. The problems of implementation, however, have been significant, due in no small part to teachers' lack of familiarity with the changes of new curricula and vaguely stated goals (Bjork, 2008). The mandated educational reforms as analyzed by Fujita (2000) create a scenario of chaos and unpredictability in many Japanese classrooms unlike anything in the postwar era (Asada, 2005). Most teachers, who now are nearing retirement age, find themselves caught between responding to these reforms or adhering to a method of practice that appears to cater to parents' desire for retention of scripted exam prep coursework. This is especially true in junior high schools and academic high schools (Kudomi, 1999).

Yet Japanese teacher training appears inadequate to prepare incoming teachers to deal with the new issues and conditions. Paradoxically, most teachers who are now near retirement were exposed in varying degrees to *Dowa Kyoiku* (see Nabeshima's and Kanegae's Chapters 5 and 6), a curriculum focused on the social needs of marginalized youth, in particular the historically outcaste *Burakumin*, including those who lived in low-income areas. Many of these educators have been at the forefront of the human rights movement for generations. With the end of the Special Measures legislation, which provided a form of affirmative action for *Burakumin* students, and a shift away from issues of cultural discrimination and toward a focus on socioeconomic isolation, some teachers have been left wondering how to use their training to inform the next generation of educators. Teachers who entered the classroom during the 1970s and 1980s complain that new teachers are out of touch with the antidiscrimination, social justice agenda under which they were trained (Gordon, 2008).

The question, then, is, who will provide the leadership to address issues of social integration, social justice, and the preparation of students to live and work in a globalized economy? If the cultural role of the teacher becomes one of subject specialist, will Japan see a model of teaching that resembles the widely rejected *shihan gakkou* teacher model—the pedantic, "drill and kill" style of teaching common in the 1950s? Dramatic reforms in funding, outlined by Kariya in Chapter 2, may require extensive reorganization of local practices of teacher hiring and training. There is a widespread perception in Japan that teachers no longer can motivate youth with the expectation that hard work will pay off in the marketplace after moving through the appropriate channels of the educational system. Some claim that the decline in respect for teachers is related to the disconnect between educational preparation and occupational opportunities for young people. Others say that it has more to do with the lack of professionalism in the teaching force. Still others say that major changes are needed in the way teaching is conceived in communities, particularly those under duress. Increased competition in the labor market and fewer jobs with security have created a situation where young people are opting out of traditional avenues and into more flexible and, some might say, creative work. There are positive aspects to these changes. Lifetime employment, now a thing of the past, could be viewed as oppressive as much as liberating. However, this will mean that teachers will have to teach and advise students in ways that allow for a myriad of life paths. The old model of one education for all is being eroded from multiple sources, and teachers will continue to be on the front line of social change as new views of education and society arise.

A MULTICULTURAL JAPAN?

The Japanese sense of self has shifted. As the authors in this volume demonstrate, Japanese scholars themselves frame some of the most serious challenges facing Japanese education as a question of how the Japanese as world citizens (aware of their responsibilities as a leading industrialized nation and as a partner in responding to global concerns that affect all) should respond to social and educational issues. This is a dramatic sea change, but it does not appear to be one that is monolithic. Japan still faces significant challenges in eradicating notions of essentialism and purity that have superficially bound together those who view themselves as "Japanese." It will need to embrace the diversity that has existed for centuries in this island nation and own up to the historical legacy resulting from the stigmatization of "the Other" as those who "do not fit." For a country that has denied class and ethnic distinctions for so long, how will Japan respond in the next decade to its need for an educated labor force as the birth rate remains low or falls even further? How will a fractured and compromised higher education system regroup and redefine itself in the face of students' malaise and parents' movement out of the public education system? No longer the dominant economic force, will

Japan hide in the shadow of China as a quaint recluse, clinging to traditions and concepts of purity out of sync with the modern world, or will it emerge as a facilitator in the new world order?

Schools have always been the locus of socialization and indoctrination, and they will continue to serve this master for years to come. Teachers are on the forefront of the process. Responding to these challenges is in many ways their greatest task. As human capital formation becomes more complicated and its results more crucial for individual life-chance determination, "equality" in education increases in significance. In particular, if inequality in education expands at the early stages in schooling, people's feeling of "fairness" in a meritocratic educational competition erodes. Providing "best practices" for all students in a "high skills" global society requires better learning environments and more skilled teachers. It also requires equal distribution of resources. Unfortunately, this is not the direction Japan is moving. Rather, there is a transition toward greater decentralization, a shift that will not only expand inequality in educational finances among different regions, but will also deprive people of a sense of fairness in educational competition. If the nationally subsidized system is abolished in the name of decentralization, each local government may be given more discretion to decide how to pay for compulsory education. But, unless other administrative decentralization follows, the centralized control over national curricula or other regulations may be left intact. At worst, financial discretion will increase the "freedom" of local government to implement budget cuts in compulsory education. The Japanese myth of egalitarian education and society is on the edge of vanishing at the gate of a neoliberal "learning capitalist society" (Kariya, 2006).

Changes in government policies, while problematic for Japanese from all walks of life, are devastating for those who exist on the margins of society. The children of these families grow up with little expectation that they will carry on to higher education, and yet they are subject to the same educational system that has trained its teachers to be blind to differences and to resist identification of individual needs. But today's Japan is not as it was 20 years ago. At the end of the educational conveyor belt there is neither the guarantee of a corporate job nor the prestige gained from one's alma mater to open doors. For those who figure this out early, the choice is to opt out of the system and attempt to cash in on what cultural and social capital is already available to them. For those without these resources, or the knowledge of how to play the game, the betrayal of no gain from persevering with education might have significant consequences. Given the labor demands, the increase in immigration, the degree of interracial marriage (especially of foreign women to rural Japanese men), and the disaffection of the youth, who are frustrated in their search for employment, stability, and family life, Japanese society could be in for ever greater challenges.

REFERENCES

Asada, S. (2005). Confessions of troubled elementary school teachers. *Japan Echo, 32*(2), 35–37.

Benjamin, G., & James, E. (1989). Public and private schools and educational opportunity in Japan. In J. J. Shields, Jr. (Ed.), *Japanese schooling: Patterns of socialization, equality, and political control* (pp. 152–162). University Park: Pennsylvania State University Press.

Bjork, C. (2008). *Local implementation of Japan's integrated studies reform: A preliminary analysis of efforts to decentralize the curriculum.* Paper at the annual meeting of the Comparative and International Society, New York.

Brinton, M. (1988). The social-institutional bases of gender stratification: Japan as an illustrative case. *American Journal of Sociology, 94*(2), 300–334.

Brinton, M. (2001). *Women's working lives in East Asia.* Stanford, CA: Stanford University Press.

DeVos, G. (1973). *Socialization for achievement.* Berkeley: University of California Press.

Fujita, H. (2000). Education reform and education politics in Japan. *The American Sociologist, 31*(3), 42–57.

Goodman, R. (2005). W(h)ither the Japanese university? An introduction to the 2004 higher education reforms. In J. S. Eades, R. Goodman, & Y. Hada (Eds.), *The 'big bang' in Japanese higher education* (pp. 1–31). Melbourne: Trans Pacific Press.

Gordon, J. A. (2005a). The crumbling pedestal: Changing images of Japanese teachers. *Journal of Teacher Education, 56*(5), 459–470.

Gordon, J. A. (2005b). Inequities in Japanese urban schools. *The Urban Review, 37*(1), 49–62.

Gordon, J. A. (2008). *Japan's outcaste youth: Education for liberation.* Colorado Springs, CO: Paradigm Publishers.

Horio, T. (1988). *Educational thought and ideology in modern Japan.* Tokyo: University of Tokyo Press.

Ishida, H. (2001). Industrialization, class structure, and social mobility in postwar Japan. *The British Journal of Sociology, 52*(4), 579–604.

Kajimoto, T. (2006, January 4). A vanishing middle class? Income disparities rising in Japan. *The Japan Times.*

Kariya, T. (2006). *The ending of diploma society and where to go next? The answer is going towards a "learning capitalist" society.* Paper presented at the "Ending the Postwar?" conference, University of Sheffield, Sheffield, UK.

Kariya, T., & Rosenbaum, J. E. (1999). Bright flight: Unintended consequences of detracking policy in Japan. *American Journal of Education, 107*(3), 210–230.

Kondō, M. (2005). Japan's new misfits. *Japan Echo, 32*(1), 7–8.

Kudomi, Y. (1999). Teachers facing the confusion and conflicts in today's Japan. *Hitotsubashi Journal of Social Studies, 31*(2), 69–83.

LeTendre, G. (Ed.). (1999). *Competitor or ally: Japan's role in American educational debates.* New York: Falmer.

LeTendre, G., & Rohlen, T. (1998). Merit or family background? Problems in research policy initiatives in Japan. *Educational Evaluation and Policy Analysis, 20*(4), 285–297.

Lincicome, M. (1995). *Principles, praxis, and the politics of educational reform in Meiji Japan.* Honolulu: University of Hawai'i Press.

Miura, A. (2005). *Karyu sha-kai [Underclass society].* Tokyo: Kobunsha Shoten.

Okano, K., & Tsuchiya, M. (1999). *Education in contemporary Japan: Inequality and diversity.* Cambridge, UK: Cambridge University Press.

Ono, H. (2001). Who goes to college? Features of institutional tracking in Japanese higher education. *American Journal of Education, 109*(2), 161–195.

About the Contributors

June A. Gordon is a Professor of Education at the University of California at Santa Cruz. She received a Ph.D. in Educational Leadership and Policy Studies from the University of Washington and a B.A. in East Asian Studies from Stanford University. She has served as Visiting Research Professor in the Graduate Faculty of Education of the University of Tokyo and received a Japan Foundation Research Fellowship for the study of "Newcomers in Japan: Schooling and Identity Negotiation." Her publications include *Japan's Outcaste Youth: Education for Liberation*; "Schooling in Japan of *Burakumin*: Shifts in Policy and Local Practice," in *Race, Ethnicity and Education*; "The Crumbling Pedestal: Changing Images of Japanese Teachers," in the *Journal of Teacher Education*; and "Inequities in Japanese Urban Schools," in *The Urban Review*.

Hidenori Fujita is a Professor at International Christian University (ICU) in Tokyo. He received a Ph.D. from Stanford University in 1978. Before moving to ICU, he had been a Professor at the University of Tokyo for 17 years and Dean of the School of Education there from 2000 to 2003. He is member of the Science Council of Japan. He was president of the Japanese Association of Educational Sociology from 2000 to 2003, member of National Commission on Education Reform in 2000, senior program officer of the Japan Society for the Promotion of Science from 2004 to 2007, and a member of the Central Council for Education in 2005. His major publications include *Child, School and Society: Irony of an Affluent Society*; *Education Reform*; *Culture and Society: Distinction, Structuration and Reproduction*; *Sociology of Education*; *Civic Society and Education*; *Family and Gender*; *Reappraisal of Compulsory Education*; *Whither Education Reform: Differentiated Society or Kyosei Society?*; and *For Whom Is "Education Rebuilding"?*

Takehiko Kariya is a Professor in Sociology of Japanese Society in the Department of Sociology and Nissan Institute of Japanese Studies, University of Oxford. He received a Ph.D. in Sociology from Northwestern University and a B.A. and an M.A. from the University of Tokyo. His research includes comparative sociology, sociology of education, and social change in postwar Japan. His recent publications include *Increasingly Stratified Japan and the Educational Crisis* and "Japan at the Meritocracy Frontier: From Here, Where?" (co-authored with Ronald Dore), in *The Rise and Rise of Meritocracy*, edited by Geoff Dench.

Gerald LeTendre is Professor-in-Charge of the Education Policy Studies Department of the Pennsylvania State University. He received a B.A. in Sociology from Harvard University, based on research among Tibetan refugees, and then taught for 3 years in the Japanese public school system. He received an M.A. in Sociology and a Ph.D. in Education from Stanford University, with a Japan Foundation Fellowship for his dissertation, a Johann Jacobs Young Scholar Award, and a National Academy of Education/Spencer Post-doctoral Fellowship. His publications include *Learning to Be Adolescent: Growing Up in U.S. and Japanese Middle Schools*; the editing of *Competitor or Ally?*; the co-editing of *Teaching and Learning in Japan*; and *Intense Years* (co-authored with R. Fukuzawa).

Harumi Befu is Professor Emeritus of Anthropology at Stanford University, where he served from 1965 to 1995. He received a Ph.D. in Anthropology from the University of Wisconsin. He served as Professor of Anthropology and Director of the Institute for Cultural and Human Research at Kyoto Bunkyo University in Japan until 2000. His major works include *Japanese Civilization in the Modern World* and *Japan: An Anthropological Introduction*. Among his recent publications are *Hegemony of Homogeneity: An Anthropological Analysis of Nihonjinron* and the co-editing of *Globalizing Japan: Ethnography of the Japanese Presence in Asia, Europe, and America*.

George A. DeVos is Professor Emeritus at the University of California, Berkeley, where he was a Professor of Anthropology from 1965 to 1991. He received a B.A. in Sociology, an M.A. in Anthropology, and a Ph.D. in Psychology from the University of Chicago. Among his many publications are *Japan's Invisible Race: Caste in Culture and Personality*; *Socialization for Achievement: Essays on the Cultural Psychology of the Japanese*; and *Heritage of Endurance: Family Patterns and Delinquency Formation in Urban Japan* (all with Hiroshi Wagatsuma); *Symbolic Analysis Cross-Culturally: The Rorschach Test* (with L. Bryce Boyer); *Status Inequality: The Self in Culture* (with Marcelo Suarez-Orozco); and *Social Cohesion and Alienation: Minorities in the United States and Japan*.

Haruhiko Kanegae is a Professor in the Department of Humanities, School of Letters, at Senshu University. He received an M.A. in Pedagogy from Tokyo University. His areas of research are sociology of education and sociology for human liberation. His publications include *Why the Sexual Harassments Are*

Big Problems?; *Social Viewpoints for Dowa Education*; and *Foreign Workers' Human Rights and Communities.*

Taeyoung Kim is a Professor of Sociology at Toyo University. He received a Ph.D. in Human Sciences from Osaka University. His area of research is primarily the identity and education of ethnic minorities in Japan, including *Zainichi* Koreans. His publications include *Beyond Identity Politics—Identity of Koreans in Japan* and "Change of *Zainichi Chousenjin*," in *International Sociology* (new version), edited by Takamichi Kajita.

Yoshiro Nabeshima served as an Associate Professor in the Osaka City University Research Center for Human Rights (formerly, *Dowa Mondai* Research Institute), the first academic body in Japan devoted to research on *Buraku* issues. He retired in 2007. He received an M.A. from the Osaka University School of Human Science. He participated in after-school activities for *Burakumin* children as a student activist in 1982, which led him to study Educational Sociology. His publications include *The Hidden Inequality Between Social Classes*, which focuses on academic achievements among children from different family backgrounds, as well as unique features of *Burakumin* children's achievement.

Naomi Noiri is an Associate Professor of Sociology at the University of the Ryukyus. She received an M.A. in Sociology from Ritsumeikan University. Her research includes the education of minority children in Japan and the diaspora identity of Okinawans. Her publications include "Two Worlds: The Amerasian and the Okinawan," in *Social Process in Hawaii*, edited by Joyce N. Chinen.

Akira Sakai is a Professor at Otsuma Women's University. He received a B.A. and a Ph.D. from the University of Tokyo. His research includes the sociology of education and clinical studies of schooling. Publications include *Clinical Sociology of Education on Supporting Students' Advancement to University: An Action Research in a Commercial High School* and *Learning to Teach in Two Cultures: Japan and the United States* (co-authored with N. Ken Shimahara).

Mamoru Tsukada is a Professor in Sociology and American Studies, School of Cross-Cultural Studies, at Sugiyama Jogakuen University. He received an M.A. and a Ph.D. in Sociology from the University of Hawai'i at Mānoa, as well as a B.A. and an M.A. in American Studies from Hiroshima University. His research includes sociology of education and comparative sociology, as well as life history studies. His publications include *Yobiko Life: A Study of the Legimation Process of Social Stratification in Japan*; *The Entrance Exam System and Teachers' Life Course*; and *The Contemporary American Society through a Study of Teachers' Life Histories*.

Index

SUBJECTS

Note. Information presented in figures or tables is indicated by *f* or *t*.

AASO. *See* AmerAsian School in Okinawa (AASO)
Abe, Shinzo, 1, 13, 37
ability grouping, 48, 56
absenteeism, 81–82
academic achievement
  in newly established high schools, 78
  in urban-liberal elite schools, 72–73
  in U.S. vs. Japan, 55–56
accountability, 55
accreditation, of foreign schools, 157
achievement
  of *Burakumin*, 122–123, 124*t*, 125
  gender and, 196
  in newly established high schools, 78
  in urban-liberal elite schools, 72–73
  in U.S. vs. Japan, 55–56
admission
  competitiveness in, 68–69
  exams, 69–70, 74–76
  open, 57
ages, of teachers, 60, 61*f*
agriculture study track, 90*t*
aid, for schooling, 32–33, 33*f*, 34*f*
Akebono (*Dowa* education reader), 143–144
alien registrants, 148*t*, 152*t*
Allied Occupation, 1, 20, 89, 150–151
allocation, resource
  budgets and, 57
  changes in, 61–63, 62*t*, 63*f*
  competition and, 57
  compulsory education and, 57–58
  equality and, 56
  Japanese government in, 55

local shift in, 60
opportunity and, 57
per capita, 58
progressive distribution in, 57
student demographics and, 61
in United States, 55
All Romance (journal), 116–117
Amerasians
  definition of, 165
  in Okinawa, 172–173, 172*f*
AmerAsian School in Okinawa (AASO), 172–176
anti-union conditions, 77
approaches, objectivist vs. constructivist, 27–30, 27*t*, 29*t*
Asada, Zennosuke, 117
Asaka *Buraku*, 113–117
Association of High School Scholarship Students, 140–141
attendance, 21, 81–82, 90*t*
Australia, scores in, 25*t*
authority, 187–188

background, family, 80–81
behavior problems, 22, 23*f*, 79–80, 83
boards of education, 20
bonding social capital, 46
bottom high schools, 80–82
Brazilian Japanese, 165, 167, 167*f*
bridging social capital, 46
bullying, of *Buraku* women students, 136
Buraku
  Asaka, 113–117
  in case study, 113–117

208

Buraku (continued)
community improvements, 118
community services shift in, 120–121
corruption amidst, 119–120
definition of, 109
female students from
  bullying of, 135–136
  derogatory term for, 135–136
  Dowa education and, 143–145
  in Eastern Japan, 134–135, 141–142
  in Fukuoka, 134
  as ignorant of status, 141–142
  in Kochi Prefecture, 140
  middle generation school experiences, 138–142
  in Nagano Prefecture, 135, 141
  in Nara Prefecture, 134
  older generation school experiences of, 134–138
  in Osaka, 134, 139
  poverty among, 135, 138–139
  recalled educational experiences of, 132–133
  teacher discrimination toward, 139
  teacher home visits and, 139
  teachers ignoring, 137–138
  in Tokushima Prefecture, 139
  in Western Japan, 140–141
  in Western Japan vs. Eastern, 134–135, 145–146
  younger generation school experiences, 142–145
in history, 114
housing projects in, 118
Liberation League, 111, 112, 117, 120
organization in, 111
origin of term, 131
undesirable facilities near, 116
Burakumin, 9
All Romance incident and, 116–117
Asada and, 117
in Asaka *Buraku*, 113–117
businesses of, 114
definition of, 109
Dowa Council report and, 112–113
Dowa districts and, 113
Dowa Measures and, 111–123
education of, 121–126
future of, 127–128
history of, 110–111
jealousy toward, 119–120
Liberation League, 118–119
Matsumoto and, 111
in Meiji government, 114–115
mobilization of, 118–119
negotiations by, 118–119
other Japanese vs., 110
political organization of, 111
population of, 110, 131
as race, 131
representative bodies of, 118–119
research on, 109
in social stratification, 39
soldiers, 111
student entrance rates among, 122, 123*f*

Canada, scores in, 25*t*
capital
  human, 54–55
  social, 17, 45–46
career choice factors, 98–104
career support programs, 94–95, 95*t*
caste system, 110, 183–184
CCE. *See* Central Council of Education (CCE)
CEFP. *See* Council on Economic and Fiscal Policy (CEFP)
Central Council of Education (CCE), 36–37
Central Harmony Organization, 111
centralized education, 59
certificates, in vocational schools, 82
Chicago School, 44
China, 199
Chinese, as first language, 154*t*
Chinese Japanese, 165, 166, 192
choice, school, 19, 24
Chourinbo (derogatory term for *Buraku*), 135–136
civic symbiosis, 45*t*
civil rights, 191–192
classical liberals, 12
Class Size and School Staff Standards Act, 58, 60
class sizes, 13
co-existence (*kyosei*), 42–46
Cold War, 150–151
Coleman Report, 55
collectivism, 12
"combined pollution," 80–81
commerce study track, 90*t*
commercial high schools
  in academic hierarchy, 87
  career choice factors and, 98–104
  employers and, 88
  employment after, 91–92, 92–94
  job recruitment and, 92
  Nozomi, 91–92, 92*f*
  overview of, 88–98
  postgraduation career support programs with, 94–95, 95*t*

commercial high schools (*continued*)
  student narratives from, 92–94
  student postgraduation outlooks in, 95–98
  transformation of, 89–98
Communism, 67–68
Community Improvement Special Measure Act, 112
competition
  in admissions, 68–69
  fair, 57
comprehensive learning time (*sogo tekina gakushuu no jikan*), 13, 26
compulsory education, 20, 57–58, 59
constructivist approach, 27–30, 27*t*, 29*t*
control, government, 59
control orientation, 70–71, 71*f*, 78–80
control-oriented education, 76–77
conviviality, 43–44
corporal punishment, 79
costs, personnel, 62*t*, 63*f*, 64*f*
Council on Economic and Fiscal Policy (CEFP), 36
crime, 23*f*
cultural diversity, 154–155
cultural essentialism, 162–164
cultural pluralism, 155
curriculum, in objectivism vs. constructivism, 29*t*
Czech Republic, scores in, 25*t*

day laborers, 40
degree consciousness, 39
delinquency, 184–185
"democratic" school management, 73–74
demographic changes, 197–198
Department of Defense dependents schools (DoDDS), 173, 173*t*, 174
detention homes, 41*f*
DeVos, George, 109
differences, of educational system, 12–13
differentiated society (*kakusa-shakai*), 32–33
disadvantaged students, 13, 80–81
discipline, 79
discrimination, 11, 39–42, 56. *See also* Burakumin; Zainichi
disorder problems, 22
disparity
  economic, 32–33, 34*f*
  taboo against discussion of, 56
diversity, 154–155, 177, 181–182
DoDDS. *See* Department of Defense dependents schools (DoDDS)
domination
  by Ministry of Education, 59
  of teachers in elite schools, 72

Dotaishin-toushin, 112–113
Dowa Council report, 112–113
Dowa districts, 112–113. *See also* Buraku
Dowa education, 121–122, 139–140
Dowa Measures, 111–123
Dowa Measures Special Law, 112
Dowa Mondai
  definition of, 39, 109
Dowa projects, 112
Dowa Serving Society, 111
dropouts, 21, 81, 91

economic disparity, 32–33, 34*f*
economic recession, 1990s, 87
Edo Period, 39
Educate America Act, 19
Education Act (U.K.), 19
educational exclusion, 39–42
educational policy, 181–182
Educational Reform Committee, 13
education consciousness, 39
education level
  discrimination and, 40
  employment and, 40, 42
  incarceration and, 41*f*
education system
  differences of, 12–13
  recent changes in, 13
  similarities of, 11
effectiveness, 27–30, 27*t*, 29*t*
efficiency, 47, 47*f*
egalitarianism, 55–56, 58
Emancipation Order, 110, 114–115
embracive symbiosis, 45*t*
employability, 11
employers, commercial high schools and, 88
employment
  after commercial high school, 92–94
  after high school, 90*t*, 91
  commercial high schools and, 91–92
  education level and, 40, 42
  gap, 189
  non-regular, 40
  student narratives about, 92–94
English, as first language, 154*t*
entrance examinations, 69–70, 74–76
entrance exam orientation, 70–71, 71*f*, 76–78
equal opportunity, 57, 59
equal treatment, foreign students and, 168–170
essentialism, cultural, 162–164
Estonia, scores in, 25*t*
ethnic activities, in Japanese schools, 158–160

ethnic education, 149–150, 153–155
evaluation
  in objectivism vs. constructivism, 29t
  outcome-based, 17
exclusion, 39–42, 192
exclusive social capital, 46
expectation, boys and, 100–103
expenditures, public education, 55, 61–63, 62t, 63f. *See also* resource allocation

fair competition, 57
family(ies)
  background, 80–81
  career choice and, 98–99
  involvement of, 185–186
  wealthy, 33–36, 35f
feudalism, 110, 183–184
Filipino, as first language, 154t
financial aid, 32–33, 33f, 34f
Finland, scores in, 25t, 31t
first languages, 154t
fishery study track, 90t
five day school week, 31
FLE. *See* Fundamental Law of Education (FLE)
freedom orientation, 70–71, 71f, 80–82
free education, 57
Fukuda, Yasuo, 1, 13
Fukuoka, 134
Fundamental Law of Education (FLE), 157, 169
  in history of reform, 1
  initiation of reform to, 36–37
  survey on, 37

G-8 nations, 9
Gakkougun system, 68–69
gap
  in educational privilege, 189–190
  socioeconomic, 189
gender
  achievement and, 196
  career plans and, 99–104
  identity, 100–101
  religion and, 183
globalization, human capital and, 54–55
global scrutiny, 198–199
go-getter girls, 100
Government Order of Education, 18
graduation rate, 21
grouping, ability, 48, 56
guilt, 186

Hatoyama, Yukio, 19
Hattori, Asako, 132

high schools
  in Allied Occupation, 89
  attendance rates, 90t
  bottom, 80–82
  Burakumin in, 122–126, 124t
  commercial
    in academic hierarchy, 87
    career choice factors and, 98–104
    employers and, 88
    employment after, 91–92, 92–94
    job recruitment and, 92
    Nozomi, 91–92, 92f
    overview of, 88–98
    postgraduation career support programs with, 94–95, 95t
    student narratives from, 92–94
    student postgraduation outlooks in, 95–98
    transformation of, 89–98
  diversity of, 70–71
  employment after, 90t, 91
  entrance exams for, 69–70
  ethnic activities in, 158–160
  history of, 89–91, 90t
  newly established (*Shinsetsukou*), 68, 76–78, 76–80
  night, 83
  nonurban traditional, 74–76
  specialization in, 90t
  types of, 70–71, 71f, 88–89
  urban-liberal elite, 72–74
  vocational, 82–83, 88, 89
high-skills societies, 54
home economics study track, 90t
home visits, 139
homicide, 23f, 24, 41f
Hong Kong, scores in, 25t
human capital, 54–55
human rights, 11
Human Rights Education and Enlightenment Promotion Act, 119
Hungary, scores in, 25t
hybridization, 177

identity
  delinquency and, 184–185
  gender, 100–101
  Japanese, 182–183
  Zainichi, 150–152, 158–161
IMF. *See* International Monetary Fund (IMF)
immigrants, 191
Immigration Control and Refugee Act, 165
incarceration, 41f
inclusive symbiosis, 45t

income disparity, 32–33, 34f, 40
individualism, 12–13
individualization (*koseika-kojinka*), 12–13
industry study track, 90t
inequality. *See also* Buraku; Zainichi
　in Japan, 58–59
　status, 183–184
　taboo against discussion of, 56
International Monetary Fund (IMF), 4
international students, 170–172, 170f, 171f
invisible pedagogy, 29, 29t, 30
involvement, family, 185–186
IQ test, 184
Italy, 187

Japanese, as second language, 166f, 167f
Japanese Americans, 182, 186
Japaneseness, 182–183
Japan-Korea Treaty, 151
Japan's Invisible Race (DeVos & Wagatsuma), 7, 109, 112, 127
job recruitment, 92
Juche-ism, 155. *See also* North Korean schools, for Zainichi

kakusa-shakai (differentiated society), 32–33
knowledge-based economies, 54
Kochi Prefecture, 58, 119, 140
Koizumi, Junichiro, 59
Korea, 152, 153
　North. *See* North Korea
Korean, as first language, 154t
Korean Japanese, 9
　in Allied Occupation, 150–151
　assimilation of, 150, 152
　changing attitudes toward, 151–152
　citizenship of, 148, 149t
　closure of Korean schools, 150–151
　Cold War and, 150–151
　cultural essentialism and, 162–164
　current educational structure with, 152–158
　educational experiences of, 158–161
　education of, 149–164
　ethnic education and, 149–150, 153–155
　first generation, 148
　as foreigners, 151
　future of education of, 162–164
　generations of, 148
　history of education of, 150–152
　identity establishment among, 150–152, 158–161
　Japanese school system's role with, 162
　North Korean schools for, 155–157, 156t, 160–161

　other alien registrants vs., 148t, 152t
　population of, 147–148, 153t
　in social stratification, 39
　South Korean schools, 157–158
　as term, 147
Korean school closures, 150–151
koseika-kojinka (individualization), 12–13
Kumon method, 29
kyosei (peaceful co-existence), 42–46
Kyoto, 117

labor market disparity, 40
Latin Japanese, 192
LDP. *See* Liberal Democratic Party (LDP)
League of Koreans, 150, 152, 155
"league tables," 1, 13
learning style, in objectivism vs. constructivism, 29t
Levelers (*Suiheisha*), 111
Liberal Democratic Party (LDP), 37
Liechtenstein, scores in, 25t
life guidance orientation, 70–71, 71f, 78–80, 80–82
Lithuania, scores in, 25t
local tax-collection authority, 60

Macao, scores in, 25t
mado-guchi (reception windows), 118–119
maladjusted students, 83
market-oriented symbiosis, 45t
matriculation, post-secondary, 21
Matsumoto, Jiichiro, 111
Meiji Restoration period, 18
Meiji revolution, 110
merit-based pay, 17
MEXT. *See* Ministry of Education (MEXT)
migration, 191
Ministry of Education (MEXT), 13, 20, 59
minorities. *See* Amerasians; Burakumin; "newcomers"; Zainichi
mobility, social, 87
moral shift, to privatization, 36–39
multiculturalism, 155, 202–203
murder, 23f, 24, 41f

Nagano Prefecture, 135, 141
Nakasone, Yasuhiro, 19
Nara Prefecture, 134
Nariaki, Junichiro, 37
National Commission on Educational Reform, 36–37
National Commission on Excellence in Education (U.S.), 19
National Committee of *Dowa* Education Research, 121

Index 213

National Council on Educational Reform (NCER), 17, 19
National Survey of Social Stratification and Social Mobility, 126–127
national testing, 19, 26–27, 27t
Nation at Risk, A (National Commission on Excellence in Education), 19, 21
NCER. *See* National Council on Educational Reform (NCER)
neoliberals, 12
Netherlands, scores in, 25t
network, social, 45–46
"newcomers," 165–168
newly established high schools (*Shinsetsukou*), 68, 76–80
New Zealand, scores in, 25t
night schools, 83
Nikkei (Japanese emigrants and their descendants), 162, 165, 167, 191, 192
Nisei (American-born Japanese), 186
Nishida, Yoshimasa, 125
No Child Left Behind Act, 19
Non-Profit Organization Act, 119, 120
non-regular employment, 40
nonurban traditional high schools, 74–76
North Korea, 152, 153
North Korean schools, for *Zainichi*, 155–157, 156t, 160–161
Nozomi Commercial High School, 91–92, 92f
nursing study track, 90t

OBE. *See* outcome-based education (OBE)
objectivist approach, 27–30, 27t, 29t
OCSI. *See* Okinawa Christian School International (OCSI)
OECD. *See* Office of Economic Cooperation and Development (OECD)
Office of Economic Cooperation and Development (OECD), 9
Okinawa, 172–176
Okinawa Christian School International (OCSI), 174
open admission, 57
opportunity, equal, 57, 59
order, social, 42–43
organization, social, 46–48
Osaka, 134, 139
Osaka City University, 109
Otsuma Women's University, 87
outcome-based education (OBE), 19
outcome-based evaluation, 17

pay, merit-based, 17
peaceful co-existence (*kyosei*), 42–46
Peace Treaty at San Francisco, 151
pedagogy, invisible vs. visible, 29, 29t
peer group involvement, 185–186
per capita funding, 57, 58
performance
 financial aid and, 34f
 reform and, 30–32, 31t
personnel costs, 62t, 63f, 64f
perspectives, teacher, 83–86
philosophy, instructional, in objectivism vs. constructivism, 29t
phobia, school, 22
physical discipline, 79
PISA. *See* Programme for International Student Assessment (PISA)
pluralism, 155
police, 187
policy, diversity and, 181–182
politics, of teachers, 84
pollution, combined, 80–81
Portuguese, as first language, 154t
positive-sum game model, 193–194
post-secondary matriculation, 21
poverty, 13, 80–81
preparation classes, private, 73
pre-war vocational schools, 89
private preparation classes (*yobiko*), 73
private schools, 33–36, 35f, 38–39, 199–200
privatization, 36–39
problem students, 83
Programme for International Student Assessment (PISA), 21, 24–27, 25t, 31t
progressive distribution, 57
progressive educationalists, 12
public education expenditures, 55, 61–63, 62t, 63f. *See also* resource allocation
punishment, corporal, 79

rankings, 38–39
Reagan, Ronald, 19
"reception windows" (*mado-guchi*), 118–119
recession, 1990s, 87
recruitment, job, 92
reform
 Gakkougun system, 68–69
 performance and, 30–32, 31t
 survey on, 37
 third wave of, 18–19
refused students, 83
registrants, alien, 148t, 152t
regulation, social, 186–187
relaxed education (*yutori kyoiku*), 1, 13, 19
religion, gender and, 183
resource allocation
 budgets and, 57
 changes in, 61–63, 62t, 63f

resource allocation (*continued*)
  competition and, 57
  compulsory education and, 57–58
  equality and, 56
  Japanese government in, 55
  local shift of, 60
  opportunity and, 57
  per-capita, 58
  progressive distribution in, 57
  student demographics and, 61
  in United States, 55
respect, 187–188
retention rate, 21
retirement, of teachers, 60
"rich flight," 33–36, 35*f*
River Without a Bridge, A (film), 140
robbery, 23*f*, 24, 41*f*
role, of teachers, 201–202
Russia, scores in, 25*t*

Saitama prefecture, 58
school choice, 19, 24
School Education Law, 38
school management, democratic, 73–74
school phobia, 22
schools
  in Allied Occupation, 89
  attendance rates, 90*t*
  bottom, 80–82
  Burakumin in, 122–126, 124*t*
  commercial
    in academic hierarchy, 87
    career choice factors and, 98–104
    employers and, 88
    employment after, 91–92, 92–94
    job recruitment and, 92
    Nozomi, 91–92, 92*f*
    overview of, 88–98
    postgraduation career support programs with, 94–95, 95*t*
    student narratives from, 92–94
    student postgraduation outlooks in, 95–98
    transformation of, 89–98
  diversity of, 70–71
  employment after, 90*t*, 91
  entrance exams for, 69–70
  ethnic activities in, 158–160
  history of, 89–91, 90*t*
  newly established (*Shinsetsukou*), 68, 76–78
  night, 83
  nonurban traditional, 74–76
  specialization in, 90*t*
  types of, 70–71, 71*f*, 88–89

  urban-liberal elite, 72–74
  vocational, 82–83, 88, 89
school vouchers, 1
school week, 5 day, 31
science, social, 188
scolding, 79–80
scrutiny, global, 198–199
secondary schools
  in Allied Occupation, 89
  attendance rates, 90*t*
  bottom, 80–82
  Burakumin in, 122–126, 124*t*
  commercial
    in academic hierarchy, 87
    career choice factors and, 98–104
    employers and, 88
    employment after, 91–92, 92–94
    job recruitment and, 92
    Nozomi, 91–92, 92*f*
    overview of, 88–98
    postgraduation career support programs with, 94–95, 95*t*
    student narratives from, 92–94
    student postgraduation outlooks in, 95–98
    transformation of, 89–98
  diversity of, 70–71
  employment after, 90*t*, 91
  entrance exams for, 69–70
  ethnic activities in, 158–160
  history of, 89–91, 90*t*
  newly established (*Shinsetsukou*), 68, 76–78
  night, 83
  nonurban traditional, 74–76
  specialization in, 90*t*
  types of, 70–71, 71*f*, 88–89
  urban-liberal elite, 72–74
  vocational, 82–83, 88, 89
security, 42–43
segmented symbiosis, 45*t*
segregated symbiosis, 45*t*
self, individualization and, 12
self-realization, 47*f*, 48
Shinsetsukou (newly established high schools), 68, 76–80
similarities, in Japanese education system, 11
Singapore, scores in, 25*t*
sizes, class, 13
Slovenia, scores in, 25*t*
social capital, 17, 45–46
social class, career choice and, 98–99
social exclusion, 39–42
Socialism, 68
socialization, 59

Index 215

social mobility, 87
social order, 42–43
social organization, 46–48
social regulation, 186–187
social science, 188
social stratification, 39
society, differentiated, 32–33
socioeconomic disparity, 32–33, 34f, 189
sogo tekina gakushuu no jikan (comprehensive learning time), 13, 26
South Korea, 152, 153
South Korean schools, for *Zainichi*, 157–158
Spanish, as first language, 154t
specialization, by subject track, 90t
standardization, 12
State Subsidies Law for Compulsory Education, 58
status inequality, 183–184
stratification, social, 39
students
  in bottom high schools, 80–81
  Buraku female
    bullying of, 135–136
    derogatory term for, 135–136
    Dowa education and, 143–145
    in Eastern Japan, 134–135, 141–142
    in Fukuoka, 134
    as ignorant of status, 141–142
    in Kochi Prefecture, 140
    middle generation school experiences, 138–142
    in Nagano Prefecture, 135, 141
    in Nara Prefecture, 134
    older generation school experiences of, 134–138
    in Osaka, 134, 139
    poverty among, 135, 138–139
    recalled educational experiences of, 132–133
    teacher discrimination toward, 139
    teacher home visits and, 139
    teachers ignoring, 137–138
    in Tokushima Prefecture, 139
    in Western Japan, 140–141
    in Western Japan vs. Eastern, 134–135, 145–146
    younger generation school experiences, 142–145
  in commercial high schools, 92–94, 95–98
  demographics of, resource allocation and, 61
  disadvantaged, 13
  international, 170–172, 170f, 171f
  newcomer, 165–168
  in newly established high schools, 78
  non-Japanese speaking, 165–168, 166f, 167f
  in nonurban traditional high schools, 74–75
  in Okinawa, 172–176
  problem, 83
  refused, 83
  in urban-liberal elite schools, 72–73
  wealthy, 33–36, 35f
study tracks, 90t
style, learning, in objectivism vs. constructivism, 29t
Suiheisha (Levelers), 111
survey, on reform, 37
Switzerland, scores in, 25t
symbiosis, 44–46, 45t

tables, league, 1, 13
Taiwan, scores in, 25t
tax-collecting authority, shift in, 60
Teacher Certificate Law, 37
teachers
  administration-oriented, 84–85
  ages of, 60, 61f
  in bottom high schools, 81–82
  control over, 17, 38
  costs of, 62t, 63f, 64f
  discrimination by, 139
  home visits by, 139
  ignoring female *Buraku* students, 137–138
  perspectives of, 83–86
  politics of, 84
  retirement of, 60
  role of, 201–202
  training of, 21
  unions, 67–68, 77, 84–85
  in urban-liberal elite schools, 72
technology schools, 82–83
testing
  entrance, 69–70, 74–76
  IQ, 184
  national, 19, 26–27, 27t
Thatcher, Margaret, 19
Thematic Apperception Test, 186
Third International Math-Science Study (TIMSS), 9, 24–27, 25t
third wave of reform, 18–19
TIMSS. *See* Third International Math-Science Study (TIMSS)
Togo High School
  establishment of, 68
  Gakkougun system and, 69
Tokugawa Regime, 39
Tokushima Prefecture, 139

training, teacher, 21
truancy, 81–82
trust, 45–46
turning points, gender and, 100
tutoring, 38–39
Type A test, 26–27, 27t
Type B test, 26–27, 27t

UNESCO, 4, 9
UNICEF, 4
unions, teacher, 67–68, 77, 84–85
United Kingdom, reform in, 19
United States
  education expenditures in, 55
  reform in, under Reagan, 19
  TIMSS scores in, 25t
university preparation classes, 73
urban-liberal elite high schools, 72–74

Vietnamese, as first language, 154t
violence, 22, 23f, 24, 41f
visible pedagogy, 29, 29t
vocational schools, 82–83, 88, 89
vouchers, 1

Wagatsuma, Hiroshi, 109
wealthy students, 33–36, 35f
week, 5 day, 31
"welfare states," 54
Western individualism, 12–13
women, *Buraku*
  bullying of, 135–136
  derogatory term for, 135–136
  Dowa education and, 143–145
  in Eastern Japan, 134–135, 141–142
  in Fukuoka, 134
  as ignorant of status, 141–142
  in Kochi Prefecture, 140
  middle generation school experiences, 138–142
  in Nagano Prefecture, 135, 141
  in Nara Prefecture, 134
  older generation school experiences of, 134–138
  in Osaka, 134, 139
  poverty among, 135, 138–139
  recalled educational experiences of, 132–133
  teacher discrimination toward, 139
  teacher home visits and, 139
  teachers ignoring, 137–138
  in Tokushima Prefecture, 139
  in Western Japan, 140–141
  in Western Japan vs. Eastern, 134–135, 145–146
  younger generation school experiences, 142–145
World Bank, 4

yobiko (private preparation classes), 73
yutori kyoiku (relaxed education), 1, 13, 19

Zainichi, 9
  in Allied Occupation, 150–151
  assimilation of, 150, 152
  changing attitudes toward, 151–152
  citizenship of, 148, 149t
  closure of Korean schools, 150–151
  Cold War and, 150–151
  cultural essentialism and, 162–164
  current educational structure with, 152–158
  educational experiences of, 158–161
  education of, 149–164
  in equal treatment approach, 169
  ethnic education and, 149–150, 153–155
  first generation, 148
  as foreigners, 151
  future of education of, 162–164
  generations of, 148
  history of education of, 150–152
  identity establishment among, 150–152, 158–161
  Japanese school system's role with, 162
  North Korean schools for, 155–157, 156t, 160–161
  other alien registrants vs., 148t, 152t
  population of, 147–148, 153t
  in social stratification, 39
  South Korean schools, 157–158
  as term, 147
zero-sum game model, 193

Index 217

CITED AUTHORS

Akita, K., 21
Asada, S., 201
Asahi Shimbun, 37
Asahi Shinbun, 189
Asaka no Rekishi wo Tsukuru Kai, 114
Association of Teachers of *Dowa* Education in Nagano, 135

Ball, S., 19
Barber, M., 9
Beck, U., 99
Behrens, W. W., III, 43
Bell, D., 42
Benjamin, G., 199
Berger, P., 93
Berliner, D., 4
Bernstein, B., 28, 29, 30
Berreman, G. D., 110
Biddle, B., 4
Bjork, C., 198, 201
Bliss, J. R., 126
Boli, J., 3
Bourdieu, P., 28, 194
Brinton, M., 196
Brown, P., 19, 35, 65
Bullivant, B. M., 163
Buraku Kaiho Asaka Chiku Sogo Keikaku Jikko Iinkai, 113–114, 115, 116
Buraku Liberation and Human Rights Research Institute, 134, 138, 139, 142, 143
Buraku Liberation Research Institute in Eastern Japan, 143
Buraku Liberation Research Institute in Nara, 134, 135, 138
Buraku Mondai Kenkyu Sho, 111
Burgess, E. W., 44

Cabinet Office, Government of Japan, 40
Carson, R., 43
Central Women Headquarters of *Buraku* Liberation League, 134, 138, 139

Chabbott, C., 3, 4
Chiba, S., 43, 95, 99
Chongryon, 155
Chubb, J. E., 19
Chunichi Newspapers, 70
Clune, W. H., 19
Coleman, J. S., 44–45, 55
Cookson, P. W., 19
Cummings, W. K., 55

Denzin, N. K., 99
Department for Education, UK, 19
Department of Education and Science, UK, 22
d'Ercole, M. M., 32
DeVos, G., 7, 109, 110, 127, 197
Douglass, M., 3

Edmonds, R. R., 126
Elmore, R. F., 19
Esping-Andersen, G., 54

Finkelstein, B., 17
Firestone, W. A., 126
Flude, M., 19
Foljanty-Jost, G., 17
Föster, M., 32
Frederiksen, J. R., 126
Fujita, H., 18, 19, 20, 21, 22, 24, 32, 33, 35, 36, 37, 43, 44, 46, 47, 48, 201
Fujita, K., 109
Fuller, B., 19

Gallie, D., 54
Gan, S., 33
Giddens, A., 54
Goodman, R., 5, 190, 200
Gordon, J. A., 196, 201
Green, A., 65

Halpin, D., 19
Hamano, R., 95
Hammer, M., 19
Hanushek, E. A., 55
Hara, J., 32, 126
Hatakenaka, S., 5
Hattori, A., 140
Hemerijk, A., 54

Hiebert, J., 2
Higa, M., 192
Hirosaki, J., 95, 99
Horio, T., 196

Ikeda, H., 125
Illich, I., 43
Inoue, K., 110, 111
Ishi, A., 191
Ishida, H., 58, 197
Ishikawa, J., 103, 104

James, E., 199
Jones, G., 99

Kadooka, N., 142
Kaiho Publisher, 142
Kajimoto, T., 197
Kanegae, H., 135
Kariya, T., 32, 56, 58, 65, 99, 197, 199, 203
Kashani, S., 191
Kawashima, N., 43
Kazama, A., 91, 92
Kita, K., 113
Kiyonaga, K., 22
Kochi Shi Fukushi Bukai, 122
Kondô, M., 198
Kudomi, Y., 201
Kurokawa, M., 109, 111
Kymlicka, W., 164
Kyoikujihou [*Educational current news*], 68, 69

Latour, B., 4
Lauder, H., 19, 65
Lawrence, R., 22
LeTendre, G., 4, 196, 197
Lewis, C., 21
Lincicome, M., 196
Luckmann, T., 93

Mahara, T., 110, 115
Maughan, B., 126
McKenzie, R. D., 44
Meadows, D. H., 43
Meadows, D. L., 43
Meyer, J., 3
Ministry of Education, Japan, 169

Ministry of Health, Labor and Welfare, 40
Ministry of Public Management, 110
Minzoku-Kyouiku Sokusin Kyokugikai, 152
Miura, A., 198
Moe, T. M., 19
Morita, Y., 22
Mortimore, P., 126
Mourshed, M., 9
Murakami, Y., 43
Murphy-Shigematsu, S., 192, 194
Myers, J., 54

Nabeshima, Y., 109, 122, 124, 125, 126
Nakajima, T., 163
Nara Ken Dowa Mondai Kenkyusyo, 122
National Commission on Excellence in Education, 19, 42
Nihon Keizai Shinbun [The *Nikkei* newspaper], 37
NIRA Citizenship Research Group, 193
Nishida, Y., 125
Noguchi, M., 109, 118
Noiri, N., 165, 175, 176

OECD (Organisation for Economic Co-operation and Development), 30
OECD Examiners, 21, 39
Ogbu, J. U., 110, 123, 125, 163
Okano, K., 5, 196
Okinawa Times, 174
Onishi, A., 190

Ono, H., 199
Ota, H., 168, 169
Ouston, J., 126

Park, R. E., 44
Passeron, J.-C., 28
Popkewitz, T., 3
Power, S., 19
Putnam, R. D., 45, 46

Ramirez, F. O., 3
Randers, J., 43
Research and Training Institute, Ministry of Justice, 24
Resnick, J., 3
Richards, C. E., 126
Roberts, G., 3
Rohlen, T., 197
Rosenbaum, J. E., 199
Rutter, M. J., 126
Ryoke, Y., 110

Saito, R., 99
Sakai, A., 17, 21, 95, 99
Sammons, P., 126
Samuel, Y., 190
Sato, M., 21
Sato, T., 32, 58
Seiyaa, M., 192
Seiyama, K., 32, 126
Sekiguchi, T., 194
Shields, J. J., Jr., 17
Shimahara, N. K., 17, 21
Shimizu, K., 125
Shimomura, H., 99
Shindo, N., 110
Shirahase, S., 32
Sjöberg, K., 190
Steiner-Khamsi, G., 3
Stevenson, H. W., 2, 21, 28

Stigler, J. W., 2, 21, 28
Sugihara, H., 93
Suzuki, N., 191

Tachibanaki, T., 32
Takahasi, Y., 145
Takayama, K., 4
Tanaka, H., 191
Teraki, N., 118
Terumoto, H., 173
Thai, E., 177
Thayer, M., 174, 175
Thomas, S., 126
Tomie, H., 89
Tsuchiya, M., 5, 196
Tsukada, M., 67
Tyack, D. B., 18, 19

Ueda, T., 118
Uesugi, S., 109, 110, 111, 114, 115

Vogel, E. F., 42

Wada, K., 111, 115
Wagatsuma, H., 7, 109, 110
Wallace, C., 99
Watado, I., 194
Whitty, G., 19
Willis, D. B., 194
Willis, P. E., 99
Witte, J. F., 19
Women Headquarters of *Buraku* Liberation League in Osaka, 135, 139, 140–141
Wong, S.-Y., 22

Yamamoto, Y., 114, 115, 116
Yang, Y., 151
Yoshinami, T., 111, 115